The West and the Rest

ABOUT THE AUTHOR

Ian Ross spent forty years working in the tobacco and petroleum industries overseas, where the need to understand other cultures and politics became indispensable to his role. Educated at Cambridge and much later at Henley, he has an MA in Economics and an MSc in Coaching and Behavioural Change. He and his wife have three children, now adults, and four grandchildren. He still loves travelling.

The West and the Rest
Reflections on our Different Ways of Thinking

by

Ian Ross

ENVELOPEBOOKS

Published 2025 in Great Britain and the USA by EnvelopeBooks
12 Wellfield Avenue, London N10 2EA
116 West 73rd Street, New York, NY 10023
www.envelopebooks.co.uk

A New Premises venture in association with Booklaunch

© Ian Ross
Ian Ross asserts the right to be identified as the Author of the Work in accordance with the Copyright, Designs and Patents Act 1988

Stephen Games asserts the right to be identified as the Editor of the Work in accordance with the Copyright, Designs and Patents Act 1988

Cover design by Stephen Games | Booklaunch

All rights reserved. No part of this book may be reproduced, stored or transmitted in any form or by any means, electronic or mechanical, including photocopying, recording or by any information storage-and-retrieval system, without the written permission of the publisher, nor be otherwise circulated in any form of binding or cover other than that in which it is published and without a similar condition being imposed on the subsequent purchaser.

A CIP catalogue record for this title is available from the British Library and the Library of Congress Cataloging-in-Publication Data

Edited and designed by Booklaunch
EnvelopeBooks 22
ISBN 9781915023537

For Kathy

'All storytelling is building on
tradition and what has been before'
Jo Nesbo

In memoriam
Dr Tarek Swelim

SPECIAL EDITION

A collectable edition of this book is available from
www.postcardbooks.org

CONTENT

Preface 3

Introduction 5

Part 1: East Asia 9
Chapter 1   Japan: 1974 to 2001 11
Chapter 2   Laos: 1975 to 2016 22
Chapter 3   Vietnam: 1988 to 2018 50
Chapter 4   Cambodia: 2016 71
Chapter 5   Myanmar: 1989 to 2018 82
Chapter 6   Singapore: 1987 to 2009 97
Chapter 7   The Political Systems of East Asia 108

Part 2: Africa 111
Chapter 8   Nigeria: 1965 to 1999 113
Chapter 9   French West Africa: 2010 to 2013 125
   Burkina Fasso 127
   Guinea 129
   Côte d'Ivoire 131
   Senegal 132
   Summary 133
Chapter 10 Ethiopia and Eritrea: 1994 to 1995 136
Chapter 11 Mozambique: 2012 143
Chapter 12 The Political Systems of Africa 148

Part 3: Latin America 157
Chapter 13 Haves and Have-Nots 159
Chapter 14 Nicaragua: 1977 to 1979 160
Chapter 15 Chile: 1979 to 2008 176
Chapter 16 The Roundabout 191

Part 4: The Soviet Union and its Aftermath	195
Chapter 17 Russia: 1993 to 1998	197
Chapter 18 Ex-Soviet States—Russia: 2003 to 2008	230
Chapter 19 The Imperium	242
The legacy of the USSR in fifteen new states	242
Eastern Europe 2003 to 2008	243
Ukraine 2003 to 2010	248
Belarus: 2007	254
Chapter 20 Central Asia	257
The legacy of the Soviet Imperium, Part 2	257
Kyrgyzstan: 2004 to 2008	261
Azerbaijan: 2004 to 2008	265
Chapter 21 The Caucasus	271
Surrounded states	271
Georgia: 2022	272
Armenia 2022	275
The Politics of the Caucasus	278
Part 5: The Middle East	281
Chapter 22 Arabia and the Arabs: 1991 to 2016	283
The Arab States	284
Saudi Arabia	288
Oman	290
The Political Systems of the Arabs	294
Chapter 23 Other Islamic States	296
Jordan: 2010 to 2015	296
Lebanon: 1993 to 2013	303
Egypt 2010 to 2012	306
The Political Systems of Islamic States	309
Conclusion	313
Chapter 24 Wrapping Up	315
Bibliography	327
Acknowledgements	333
Index	334

PREFACE

My first trip overseas was to spend school summer holidays in Indonesia where my father worked. The Shell compound in Balikpapan, Borneo had been tamed into a semblance of an English suburb but was surrounded by an extraordinary theme park of the unexplored. I found something wondrous and mighty strange. Every sense was experiencing something new. It smelled, tasted, looked and felt like something entirely unexpected but exciting, well beyond what I had previously been able to comprehend. It spurred in me a lifelong obsession with new and strange places. In time, wonder developed into enquiry: why were these lands and cultures so different? Certainly they did not conform to the anglocentric view of what 'decent' societies were supposed to be in the early 1960s.

Professional historians use primary research to develop their ideas. This was impossible in my case because the scope was too wide and because, until recently, I was occupied in other fields. Instead, I have relied on what I saw as my primary sources. I appreciate that these only reflect the period of my experiences and might be outdated or even wrong (though the same caveat could apply equally to primary research.) The result is inevitably an amalgam of personal observation and reading.

If that seems too arbitrary, what I saw was nonetheless fundamental in shaping my view of the world. Anyone working overseas must engage with the societies they encounter, or risk intellectual isolation. Listening rather than lecturing, observing rather than sightseeing, means setting aside inbuilt prejudices about whichever society one is being hosted by, and that is a necessary precondition to understanding, though it is a lesson that took me many years to learn.

All the places I describe I have worked in and many I have

lived in. I have come across societies and governments that seemed to me occasionally threatening, sometimes baffling and often apparently stuck with nowhere to go.

This story is also about my disentangling a morass of impressions, some safe, some faulty, to arrive in the end at where I stand today. In the course of doing so, I shifted beliefs, attitudes and behaviours. An old dog can learn new tricks.

One note: I am not all-knowing nor do I have infinite access to data. Unless otherwise stated, the statistics I quote come from Wikipedia.

INTRODUCTION

The twenty-first century has not turned out to be the peaceful uplands predicted by Francis Fukuyama, who wrote in 1989 that the collapse of Communism was 'the end of history'.[1] Subsequent attempts by the West to export Fukuyama's concept by force or persuasion have failed, most spectacularly in places that have had no previous experience of it. The West has also been unable to reach any ongoing consensus on how to deal with the Rest.

Democracy was in the ascendancy, at least in the West, from 1945 to the early years of the twenty-first century, because it was inclusive. It came to a shuddering halt with the financial crisis of 2008–9, after which cash ceased to be an investment and the welfare net was holed by government austerity. Those who got richer had the surplus funds to invest in other assets such as property. Insipid growth rates widened the gap between rich and poor, leading to the collapse of the implicit social contract between all citizens.

The impact of this can be seen in all Western democracies, with a polarisation of opinion between what we think of as left and right, the former focusing on the inequalities of the domestic political system and the latter on external forces as the cause of their malaise. This is fertile ground for iconoclastic rhetoric: simple solutions to complex problems. In consequence, even Western governments have become less liberal, more controlling, and increasingly driven by the wish to placate their fractious electorates. Foreigners are now an easy target to blame for internal malaise; in a multi-polar world, debate has degenerated into stereotyping.

There is an upside in that the US now recognises that,

---

[1] Francis Fukuyama, 'The End of History', *The National Interest*, No. 16 (Summer 1989).

after its failures in Iraq, Afghanistan, Syria and Libya, foreign policy can no longer be reduced to the formula, 'better dead than red'. It now must deal more equally with China as a global power, and with significant regional players such as Russia, Türkiye, India and Saudi Arabia, as well as reviewing its expectations within the parameters of what is acceptable to the EU, its closest ideological ally. Interdependency is a product of globalisation. Balancing divergent international interests complicates diplomacy and requires democratic governments to carry their voters wth them. I have had to gain a better understanding of the countries I have had contact with; I have written this book in the hope that readers will come with me on that journey.

So far so rational, but to understand other cultures, another lens is required. There are two elements to this: how we react as individuals, and how we react as groups. Neuroscientists and psychologists demonstrate that human beings are driven by subconscious experience, not rational thought. The Cartesian model of 'I think, therefore I am' needs to be turned on its head. We bring our beliefs, attitudes and values unwittingly into every encounter and these are formed by our life experience. The nations and cultures I describe have very different histories from our own, and understanding where they come from is critical in pulling the wool from our eyes. To paraphrase C.S. Lewis, the way you interpret what you see depends on where you are standing.

We are also tribal by nature; cooperation with others lies at the root of civilisation. Here, Wilfred Bion's work on 'groups without purpose', of which societies are an example, provides insights into communal behaviour.[2] Bion identified group response to rising levels of threat, starting with Basic Assump-

---

[2] Wilfred Bion, *Experiences in Groups and Other Papers*, Tavistock Publications, UK (1961).

tion A, where there is none, rising to B, where a threat is perceived but has not yet happened, to C, when the threat is real and imminent. My paraphrase of the three states is *calm*, *agitated* and *desperate* and I suggest that the West was in Mode A from the collapse of Communism until the financial crisis of 2008–2009, since when we have since moved into Mode B. President Volodymyr Zelenskyy has provided one example of the leadership required to reverse this process in Ukraine. I use Bion's formula when it seems appropriate to the narrative.

Bion's work also highlights that some of those who regard themselves as nations, such as the Kurds and Uighurs, are not states, and conversely that some states are not nations, as is true for most of sub-Saharan Africa. Underlying this is another factor: neighbours are not necessarily friends. As the late Toni Morrison has said, we tend to treat those whom we do not know as threats.[3]

As a naïve history undergraduate in the early 1970s, I believed that the disastrous history of the first half of the twentieth century was explained by the belligerent intent of nation states and that internationalism was the solution. My travels soon disabused me of this notion as, although there is much that unites or could unite humanity, there remains the unquestioned primacy of 'the nation' that provides the framework for international diplomacy. The United Nations is not called the United Nations for nothing, and any group that cannot be designated as such cannot properly participate.

I have travelled to many places that few of my compatriots can even find on a map. In all of them I have found something different, and curiosity has driven me to find out why that is so. Learning to listen and accept differences has been a

---

[3] Toni Morrison: Nobel Laureate for Literature. Her writings on the experience of being black in a white-dominated society have greatly influenced the way I think.

rewarding journey. Your enemy is somebody whom you do not know. Wherever possible, I have tried to befriend.

PART 1
EAST ASIA

CHAPTER 1
Japan: 1974 to 2001
'Inc.'

Before taking up my father's invitation in 1974 to join him and my stepmother in Japan, where he had been appointed general manager of a Shell subsidiary, I knew nothing of Japan. I knew little of him, also, having seen him only infrequently since he and my mother had divorced some years earlier, and had developed a premature belief in my own independence from my time at boarding school and university.

My father was a lifelong Cartesian, uncomfortable with conversation that veered into the personal, and preferring intellectual arguments about politics and economics, which he always won—with me at least.

His invitation to stay with him and his new wife came as surprise. I had no interest in their lives, and industrialised Japan was far from top of my list of places I wanted to visit. But having just graduated from Cambridge, and with no idea of what career I wanted to move into, a stint in Japan would at least be better than the dead-end jobs that had kept me afloat until then. What I had not expected was the Rolls-Royce and chauffeur that picked me up from Haneda airport nor the house with a garden big enough for cocktail parties, but I adapted quickly and the life of privilege in Japan became a formative experience, especially in a society that seemed in many ways the obverse of Western values.

Japan introduced me to the sybaritic lifestyle enjoyed by my father's business and social circle. I was insured to drive my stepmother's Japanese sports car and met their friends, Western and Japanese and often intermarried, who seemed to inhabit a world analogous with that of the glitterati of Eden Roc, St Tropez and St Moritz, where David Niven and Sophia Loren were star turns. My father's friends partied a lot and said *desho* (the equivalent of the Australian habit of ending every statement on a rising note to reaffirm agreement) to mark their proficiency as Japanese residents. It was a self-conscious elite, belonging to neither Western nor Japanese culture specifically.

The cultural fog made it difficult for me to understand anything about the country I was living in, and the outside world did not help. Low-rise, featureless concrete structures made everywhere look the same. It was grey, as most of the time was the weather—and the people, as I felt back then. To get to the nearest metro station, Shibuya, I would walk down tiny lanes that criss-crossed residential areas, where all gates were closed and passing strangers looked away, then on to the main drag where a heaving human mass moved at uniform speed towards its destination, like the workers in the film *Metropolis*. Their pace made it impossible to move any faster. I later calculated that my journey to work took exactly twenty minutes—never more, never less.

On the Yamamote loop, one of Tokyo's busiest commuter railway lines, everybody retreated into their private world. Guards treated them like cattle, pushing them into carriages to fill every available space. Once inside, passengers behaved as if alone and unobserved. Men read manga comics, with stories about sado-masochistic sex between doe-eyed women, whose excitement was depicted by images of dripping oysters (depictions of genitalia being forbidden), and men with impossible physiques, whose eyes indicated little less than the desire to dominate—pornography, in other words, but on full public display. Women travellers ignored them.

It took me a long time to recognise that these were survival mechanisms in a highly ordered hierarchical system. At the head office of Mitsui, the doorman (always a man) bows low when the president arrives. The president bows back, not so low, acknowledging that his ability to continue in his role depends to some small extent on the loyalty and service of his employees. In contrast to the West, Japan is a collectivist society where social cohesion and group experience count for more than the will of the individual and personal initiative. This is a nation in which big decisions are made by various combinations of wise heads, giving the nation state an essentially paternalistic, rather than democratic, character.

The stifling hierarchy of obedience and deference requires safety valves, however, but these are available. Once granted a place at university—a fearsomely competitive exercise that involved and still involves going to a second crammer school from the age of five—the Japanese young are free to do whatever they want. During my residency, the preferred rebellion was to be an Elvis impersonator. Yoyogi Park, at the bottom of Omote Sandō, had at least 200 of them gyrating their hips and striking poses every weekend. Others chose to display the mannerisms of the hippy movement, driving around with long hair, bandanas and rock-star garb in tiny trucks that could navigate residential lanes, while shouting incomprehensible slogans (to me at least) through megaphones. Some did their shouting outside big railway stations and wore bandanas that also had slogans written on them. I learned that they were the ultra-nationalists. Nobody took much notice of any of them.

I am talking here only of men. Women were barely visible. A woman was expected to marry a man whom their parents thought appropriate, produce heirs and look after the purse strings. Whereas in the West we talk about a glass ceiling for women professionals, in Japan there was not even a ladder. In the 1990s a colleague visiting the local subsidiary asked the HR director, while looking over rows and rows of neatly aligned desks, 'How many employees do you have?' he asked. 'Two-hundred and twenty.' 'But there must be more than that in this room.' 'I speak only of men.'

This subordinate role had not always been in place. Before the incumbency of General Douglas MacArthur as Japan's US military governor after the Second World War, women had been in charge of running a complex semi-feudal social hierarchy and enjoyed a higher status. When MacArthur abolished the old *daimyo* system, the women were left with a legacy of simply looking after the family purse strings. The consequence, probably unintentional, was that women became *de facto* second-class citizens. Japan still has the lowest proportion of women in top management positions and fewer representatives in parliament than any other country in the democratic world.

As far as marriage is concerned, the Western norm is a love match. It had little application in Japan. Once, in the Akasaka Hilton, I saw a bride dressed exquisitely in a traditional wedding kimono, with tears streaming down her face, on her way to a wedding she was required to consummate.

I attracted the attention of Japanese women who wanted to be treated better than they would be by Japanese men. These were miserable encounters for both of us, because I found that their personalities had been extinguished; they had been trained from birth to assume that what men wanted in a woman was submission, simpering, giggling and modesty. This cultural chasm was as difficult for Westerners to navigate as it was for these women to find a husband who would respect them. The sentimental comforter of Hello Kitty could have come from nowhere else.

As I became if not comfortable then at least accepting of the differences, and as my circle of friends and acquaintances expanded, I began to win admittance to the private worlds that the Japanese inhabit. These were the opposite of the rigid hierarchy and conformity of visible society. Hiroshi, one of my students when I was teaching English in Tokyo, invited me out on a Friday night to his favourite bar, where he had his own bottle of Suntory whisky. I was introduced to everybody, all men, few of whom spoke any English.

Hiroshi ended up as the translator and I was bombarded with questions, most of them about sex. 'Is it true that *gaijin* are hung like horses?' Refusing the request to demonstrate, I told them that the same question was asked where I came from about the size of black penises. Much sucking of teeth. 'This is terrible. I want *gaijin* woman; they like sex, yes? Japanese women just put up with it. But probably, I not be able to satisfy them. Maybe you not either! Maybe they all want black men.' The bar collapsed in laughter.

'Your country no good. All strikes, nobody works. In Japan we all working. It is good. I have car and apartment. And wife —no good in bed, but two sons. Very clever, working hard, good peoples. Maybe one day I become president of company. Then I get *gaijin* mistress, she love me because I am rich and not so worried about small prick.' The laughter got louder. And so it went on. Despite, or perhaps because of, the misogynist theme, I felt like an honorary Japanese.

John Snow was the first openly gay man I ever met. A lead dancer in the London Ballet Company, he had been seconded to Tokyo to train the national ballet. We met for a drink in a popular bar in Roppongi; my choice, but not to his liking. He suggested we go to Shinjuku: 'You might find it interesting.' I followed him to what looked like an uninspiring bar, full, as usual, with Japanese salary men in their grey suits. Perched at the bar we ordered drinks.

Before they arrived I noticed a hand on my thigh. I looked across at the owner of the hand. He smiled. Behind the bar was a mirror. I noticed that my eyebrow was uneven. I smoothed it out. The only option was to feign indifference and appear to be absorbed elsewhere. At that moment I realised what it was like to be a woman and subjected to unwanted attention.

We extricated ourselves and moved on to a fight club inhabited by body builders and their hangers-on, some half-flexing their muscles, the others simpering in admiration at their masculinity. Then on again to another club where a naked couple had cabbage leaves cupped between their palms and made strange noises with them. Some of the clientele were in various states of *déshabillé* and entwined around each other. This seemed to be about some unfathomable artistic statement rather than anything sexual, but how was I to know? Finally to a gay disco, where John gave up. Although I had failed to respond to his overtures, we parted on good terms.

That unexpected experience triggered the thought that Japan was a truly integrated society. The Japanese—men, at least—could find ways of living as they wanted, whatever their preferences. All tastes were catered for. It was liberal in the sense that personal behaviour was unregulated, unless it threatened the communal good.

My Western colleagues and I were temporarily allowed into the Japanese tent because we had knowledge and skills that they wanted to learn from. We had value and so they trusted us, unlike those who had arrived here without connections and who therefore had to deal with a bureaucracy that was both complex and hostile to aliens.

The word 'tent' implies a boundary. The only Japanese who were supposedly outside the tent were the *burakumin*, an underclass, like the untouchables in India, that carried out disreputable tasks that higher-ranking Japanese considered below their status, but this was a legacy of the feudal *Daimyo* system and was becoming irrelevant. It was only the local English-language media that made a fuss about it.

A much harder boundary applied to Japan's much closer foreign neighbours. At a typical margherita party for expatriates, I met a strikingly beautiful women whom I assumed was Japanese. She was in fact Korean, the daughter of forced-labour immigrants, and was employed in a lowly position in a foreign company. I suspect that she had been invited to the party, in spite of her low status, only because of her beauty and availability, and had accepted the invitation only in the hope of meeting and marrying a foreigner, which she would have regarded as her only way out of her social entrapment.

Although Tokyo was alien territory to me, it was not unwelcoming. Some 126 million Japanese wanted to learn English, which meant that I could not stand on a street corner for more than a minute without being accosted by a stranger who would first enquire if I spoke English and then suggest that we go for a coffee (pronounced '*cogh-ee*') together. There was something endearingly innocent about this request. It would take an enquirer some courage to approach a *gaijin*, but the desire to learn was stronger than the habitual avoidance of strangers. Time and effort had been spent in studying English in school; the problem was that as it was rarely spoken, the art of spontaneous conversation in English was a step too far. The inevitable result was mutual and frustrating incomprehension and, for the enquirer, embarrassing loss of face.

As I began to understand the complexity of the Japanese language, I learned why conversation in English was so difficult for the many who wanted it. Although Japanese is not a tonal language like Chinese, and its basic grammatical structure is not so very different from our own, it has multiplicities of linguistic variations that do not map precisely onto our speech variants. There are, for example, about a hundred ways of saying 'I/me/my', depending on context, and this represents a fundamental contrast in the perceptions that underlie language. In addition, the reason that I never heard the word '*ié*' ('no') spoken is that the possibility of denial was culturally taboo. Instead, a sharp intake of breath through clenched teeth would indicate that an unattractive proposition had been made that was too difficult to accept.

Conversely, the word for yes—'*hai!*'—is ubiquitous but does not signal agreement. It might imply no more than 'I understand what you said.' An example of this incomprehension occurred when I was in Tokyo. A delegation from British Leyland, having met the senior management of Toyota, issued a press release to the effect that the two corporations had agreed a joint venture. Toyota then had to issue its own statement refuting the claim, to the embarrassment of both parties. They understood that BL wanted a joint venture but had certainly not agreed to one.

A common story concerned those *gaijin* who thought they had learned the language by virtue of having a Japanese girlfriend. Inevitably they spoke using feminine constructions, a source of much (politely disguised) hilarity to their hosts. This was the first time I had heard the phrase 'the horizontal dictionary', but it was never said with malice.

In Japanese, even more than in English, it is the way in which something is said that determines its reception. In my case, I never got further than stock guidebook phrases, but I did learn to listen very carefully to what Japanese people said to me in English. In later life I developed a close working relationship, even friendship, with a senior executive from Honda. Amid the fog of incomprehension and frustration between our two companies, we were able to establish a level-headed alliance based on mutual respect.

Noam Chomsky, the revered professor of linguistics, has argued that language has a formative influence on the society to which it belongs. Which came first—language or culture—is a bit chicken-or-egg, but there can be no doubt that spoken Japanese reflects an obsession with inclusion, hierarchy and the conventions of social structure.

There is another dimension which is largely invisible to visitors: the ability to look inwards from a macro world that in the 16 per cent of the country that is not mountainous is almost universally ugly. When I am sitting quietly in one of the ancient gardens of Kyoto, the world beyond the walls becomes irrelevant. The eye and then the mind concentrate solely on what is in front of them—raked gravel, a few stones and some moss. The mind tries to establish the rules behind it all but then gives up: it is enough that the simplicity and the carers' obvious attention to detail provide a sensation of harmony that changes one's mood and perspective. This micro-focus is yet another safety valve for the conformity and physical ugliness that surround the Japanese.

Their art and literature follow the same aesthetic: subtle, contemplative and precise. Tanizaki's 1933 essay *In Praise of Shadows* expresses this perfectly.[1] I remain a fan of serious work in both fields, though not of Japan's commercialised sentimentality.

Most visitors, when I was in Japan, wanted to understand how the country had become the world's third largest economy, with full and secure employment, and a standard of living unparalleled in the rest of Asia. All this without natural resources, and from total devastation and penury thirty years earlier.

It had little to do with free-market principles. The key agent was MITI (Ministry of International Trade and Industry), Japan's most important government department, whose policy was little different from the pre-war model of favouring *zaibatsu* mega-companies—conglomerates, essentially.

The rules of the game were *dirigiste*. Toshiba, for example, was in trouble at the time. In the West, bankers would have hiked interest rates and creditors would have sought early repayment of debt. In Japan the opposite happened; this was not competition but the equivalent of a gentleman's club. It was nevertheless an outstanding achievement. Social cohes-

---

[1] Junchiro Tanizaki, *In Praise of Shadows*, Vintage Books (2001).

ion, respect for hierarchy and a culture of collective responsibility facilitated this but there was something else about a pragmatism of learning from failure. Japan believed it had lost the war because of inferior technology rather than lack of fighting spirit. If it was going to succeed in peacetime, therefore, it was its technology that it needed to address.

Consumer goods were an uncontroversial alternative to armaments and it developed them by copying the latest and most advanced consumer products of the West and making them more user-friendly. I doubt whether any other nation could have achieved this, because it relied on a genuinely hybrid idea of what it meant to be Japanese—a strong sense of national character combined with the determination to be successful again by emulating foreigners. By accident or design, Japan had a highly competent civil service aligned to the same ambition.

All of this was presented as both Western and democratic because, on the face of it, it ticked all the boxes: Japan had free elections, a free press and an independent judiciary. But Japan's model is collective rather than an individualistic, something that the West now finds close to impossible to reproduce.

With only a brief interregnum, the Liberal Democratic Party has ruled Japan from the first elections until today. It is neither liberal nor democratic but an agglomeration of factions that, in typical Japanese fashion, keep their disputes inside the tent. It is occasionally rocked by corruption scandals but never enough to threaten its political dominance, buttressed as it is by a constituency system that favours rural wards and lavish investments therein, and where older voters —the bedrock of their support—are in the majority. The ageing profile of the population is also an advantage. If the party has any policy at all, it is that of maintaining social cohesion.

That said, all has not gone so well for Japan over the last

thirty years and its star has dimmed, following the asset bubble collapse of the 1990s. Economic growth has been negligible and much of the scaffolding, such as lifetime employment, has been taken down. I went back to Japan in the first years of the twenty-first century and found the people quieter, less confident, more resigned. Whether the shackles of misogyny had been loosened I cannot say, but it remained a self-contained society which embraced everybody who was Japanese, even down to the *Yakuza* gangs who extorted money for protection and who ran the prostitution and drug trade—but within the boundaries defined by the tent. Japan still has the lowest crime rate of any developed economy.

Liberal democracy, however, applied only to the title of the ruling party. Japan works on entirely different principles. Its culture tolerates everything, 'There is no shortage in Japan of ways in which a person can be many things at once.'[2] It has its winners and losers, the latter primarily women and foreigners. As these groups become more vocal, I have no doubt that they will also be assimilated into the most cohesive, inclusive and paternalistic society I have yet encountered. 'Lost in translation' is a cliché of the West's inability to understand how Japan works. That is becase this is not truly a Western liberal democracy but 'Japan Incorporated'.

---

[2] Christopher Harding, *Japan Story: In Search of a Nation: 1850 to the Present*, Allen Lane (2018).

CHAPTER 2
Laos: 1975 to 2016
Other People's War

With no satisfactory career in prospect, I decided to return home from Japan but broke my journey by stopping off in Bangkok. I also had no satisfactory love life at the time and ephemeral love was available at a modest price but that was not what I was looking for.

After wandering around in Thailand and Malaysia, and shortly after the fall of Saigon and Phnom Penh in 1975, I went to Laos on a tourist visa. The Second Indochina War had been a source of fascination to me since the early Sixties and the opportunity to visit the last accessible state was not to be missed. It was an exhausting process, using overnight buses to get the visa in Chiang Mai (the only consulate still issuing them) and then back to Bangkok, before taking the train to Nong Khai on the border. I ended up with a group of Western travellers whose motives for going there were rather different.

The Thai border police were contemptuous: why would anybody in their right mind want to go to Laos unless they had to? But we had the visas and they had to let us go.

On a fragile *pirogue* we crossed the Mekong, in full spate at the end of the rainy season, and trudged up an informal path towards a small rectangular building stained with mould. Inside was a customs officer, wearing the uniform of the Royalist régime—khaki, trim and with a peaked cap—and a kid of no more than thirteen, in jungle fatigues and a mob cap with a carbine slung upside down over his shoulder. The man asked in French for my passport and began to examine it. The kid gestured for me to put my bag on the table. He then upended it and spilled all my belongings out before rummaging around. Finally he stopped and made it clear that it was my job, not his, to re-pack. He finally asked for the passport, which he read upside down until he came to the photograph. Then he thrust it angrily back to the customs officer. I was free to go.

It was raining again. At the top of the *levée* was a tarmac road that had seen better days. At first sight the place was deserted but then a Toyota saloon pulled out from under the deep gloom of a strangler fig tree. This was the taxi service. The driver took us into town at no more than 20 kms an hour, though there was no traffic. It felt abandoned; there was nobody on the streets and nearly all the shops were shuttered and bolted. Everything was untended. It was a gloomy arrival at a Sixties concrete hotel on Samsenthai, the main street.

The lift was out of order and appeared to have been that way for years. The rooms were boxlike with minimal and shoddy furniture. The walls were streaked with mould and when I opened the fridge, which was both disconnected and empty, a family of cockroaches scuttled away to hide in the gaps between the floor and the walls. I went downstairs to join my travelling companions.

Night had fallen and a few streetlights provided the illumination we needed to explore. We found a square set out in French fashion, with a colonnaded walkway on three sides and the Alliance Française, an ochre building of impressive permanence and colonial design, making up a fourth side to form a quadrangle.

One of the shops was brightly lit—a restaurant. There was space, so we stayed. All the customers were travellers and they were an eclectic crew. A group of Australians, led by a spooky man who spoke in incomprehensible rhymes, called themselves 'The Alphabet People'. There was also a black American, who thought I was a journalist and tried to sell me some outlandish stories (which I later found out not to be so ridiculous) in such a tangled fashion that it was difficult to work out what he was talking about. When he asked for money for these 'scoops,' I explained that he had got my profession wrong.

I had a headache and another Australian said he was a doctor and had just the thing I needed. He gave me a sliver of paper and told me to sniff the contents. The headache went, as did the sense of anxiety that I had felt throughout the journey.

Back in the hotel, I felt I was losing consciousness in a warm and delicious soup and became convinced that if I fell asleep I would die. I suppose I had known in the first place that I had been given heroin but while I had never been reluctant to try mind-altering substances, this was something different. It was about letting everything go, especially your willpower, for the sake of some transient peace.

At the Talat Sao, the morning market in the centre of town had stock that included branded Double-O heroin, guaranteed 98 per cent pure and produced by the remnants of the Chinese Nationalist army in the Golden Triangle and several of the royalist Lao generals.[1] It was widely rumoured that the Pepsi-Cola bottling plant, situated across fields halfway between Vientiane and Thaddeua, was simply a cover for refining opium into heroin, because there was no Pepsi available. Or maybe the plant had just shut down.

Across from the hotel was the Constellation, the fabled haunt of foreign correspondents, run by a French-Chinese owner. Not trusting the security of the hotel, I left my bag there for safekeeping. On my return I was told by the *patron* that the black GI junkie had tried to claim it, on the basis of yet another implausible story. Handing it back to me with a smile, he offered me a cup of coffee, served by his gorgeous daughter. That incident would not have been worth mentioning had I not done some background research on Laos. Most

---

[1] A.W. McCoy, *The Politics of Heroin in South East Asia*, Harper and Row (1973).

of it was useless, because it was written from a Western perspective. The exception was the modestly titled *A History of Laos* written by Martin Stuart-Cox.[2] He was kind enough to edit an earlier draft of this chapter. He also happens to be married to the other daughter of the Constellation owners.

At the suggestion of some young Lao men, we moved to a recently abandoned house close to the Mekong, formerly inhabited by USAID workers. The Americans had left a couple of weeks before, abandoning Six Click City (as the area was called) overnight. I found out many years later that their departure had been expedited by a Pathet Lao demonstration, demanding the Americans' expulsion from Laos. The access road had had its telegraph poles removed and become a runway, or so they said. The compound became the home of Kaysone Phomvihane, the first Communist president, and remained off limits for years.

When they eventually pulled out, the Americans could take with them only what they could carry and the abandoned house felt full of their ghosts. It was like a curtain coming down on the final act, a tragedy that I did not understand or feel comfortable with. I made my excuses and left, going back the way I had come, thinking that at least I had done it and that now was the time to go home and get a sensible job.

Back in Bangkok I phoned my father's friend, Bob Reid, who was general manager of Shell Thailand and who later became CEO of British Rail. He had kindly offered to look after my suitcase during my travels around Southeast Asia. I did not want to trouble him, so I simply asked for directions to his house so I could pick up the case but he insisted that I come in for a drink, an offer I could not refuse.

Our meeting did not turn out as expected. Ten days later, instead of flying back to London, I found myself on a Royal

---

[2] Martin Stuart-Fox, *A History of Laos*, CUP (1997).

Air Lao flight back to Vientiane. I was now an employee of Shell Thailand, on a short-term contract. In the absence of anyone else being willing to go there, Bob had taken the risk of sending me. Considering my recent transient lifestyle, the risk was a large one.

Royal Air Lao did not inspire much confidence. The DC4 was one of the last left flying and made extraordinary noises on firing up, taxiing to the runway and in flight. But it got there, landing at Wattay airport in the dying rays of the day. On the apron it was not the most ancient of flying machinery: there were also DC3 Dakotas, Vickers Viscounts and even a Boeing 303, the less successful competitor to the DC3. An ancient Frenchman, on contract to the UN High Commission for Refugees (UNHCR) to do rice drops, was the only living pilot qualified to fly this plane. He was also an alcoholic. He flew off to Xhieng Khouang in the Plain of Jars one day and did not return. Things like this were neither unexpected nor did they excite much interest. No search party was ever organised.

I was met at the airport by James Davidson, the man I was due to replace. His typical expatriate villa of undistinguished but standard colonial design was next door to the office, itself an elongated bungalow. We got on well and by the time he delivered me to the Lang Xang Hotel that night, most of the staff had gone to bed. I developed an affection for this shabby place, which made only a very half-hearted attempt to offer any real comfort. The head porter was so old and decrepit that I felt I had to carry my bags for him. He spoke no Western language so our relationship was based on smiles and gestures.

I enjoyed my work. All the staff seemed genuinely pleased to see me, and I them. It was a small operation. The American firms Esso, Mobil and Texaco had all left and I suppose that my arrival signalled that Shell was not about to abandon Laos as well, and that gave them a sense of reassurance.

Shell was by then the monopoly supplier of the country's

oil products, all imported from Thailand through Nong Khai. We also administered two aid deals: one for the Soviet Union, supplying crude to the Netherlands in return for refined product delivered to Laos, and the other for the Chinese, who exchanged diesel deliveries into tanks in Hong Kong for what we sold into Laos. The country was essentially landlocked: there were no usable roads from Vietnam or China, the border with Burma was in the hands of warlords and Cambodia was already controlled by the Khmer Rouge. Shell was indispensable, at least for the time being.

Soon after my arrival, there was a 'celebration' of liberation for all three countries of Indochina. But the delegation of patriotic folk singers and dancers from Cambodia was in sombre mood and avoided contact with their regional comrades. The applause for their performance was subdued, too. I thought this might be something to do with Soviet-Chinese rivalry. Neither I, nor any other foreigner at the time, realised that the killing fields had begun.

As purely commercial operators, we kept our thoughts to ourselves. And so we became friends of a sort with the Soviet commercial attaché. He insisted on weekly meetings, followed by lunch. When it was his turn to host, he provided vodka; when it was ours, we brought Scotch. As the junior partner, I was not required to reciprocate every toast he made, which was a mercy. James had developed an almost pathological aversion to these meetings but I liked our Russian colleague. I think he enjoyed being in the company of people who would not report him to the KGB and, once lubricated, would castigate virtually everything about his home country in a never-ending series of jokes. The only time he shut up was when his wife appeared; she was the spitting image of Tamara Press, the world champion shot-putter. Perhaps the social obligations were onerous, particularly for James, but the deal worked perfectly.

The commercial environment became more difficult, however, as the weeks passed. Our first crisis took place when the superintendent of aviation fled to Thailand. A replacement was quickly brought in from England. Unfortunately, and not uncommonly at that time, he had never been abroad before. He lasted three days, resigning after being invited to have lunch with his Lao crew. He took severe exception to being asked to eat sticky rice, and the various grubs that accompanied it, with his fingers.

In his absence I became the aviation superintendent for a while. I was given an instruction manual and a pass that allowed me to go anywhere on the airfield. The event of the week was when the Air France 707 arrived. With a crisp white short-sleeved shirt, neatly pressed Bangkok tailor's navy trousers and all-important badge clipped on my breast pocket, I felt I looked the part. I chatted to the flight crew and took pride in demonstrating to the pilot that I had followed the manual.

I was relieved of this responsibility when another qualified aviation supervisor arrived a few weeks later. David stayed longer than me—and that is a story I will come to later. But I kept the pass and would often visit the airport when the Air France flight arrived. It was nearly always empty on arrival but full upon departure.

Back in the office we would witness this exodus of *vieux colons*. Distributors from all over the country would turn up one by one with whatever assets they had left and pleaded for compensation. We ended up with a yard full of ancient petrol tankers and a large assortment of cars. Exporting these would have required seven permits each and we had no conceivable use for them. It was an act of charity to buy them for nominal sums. I ended up taking home a different car every night.

I watched the nervous queues of French passport-holders at the airport with their Lao wives and assorted children. They were leaving behind a life of relative privilege for an unknown future, their belongings in too many suitcases and not enough money to pay for excess baggage. Then they moved forlornly across the tarmac and up into the plane, looking one last time at the country that had been their home. With the roar of jet engines, they were gone. Another week, and the same would happen again.

Business life was interrupted with the nationalisation of the Banque de l'Indochine, the only bank in town. All accounts were frozen. Laos had become a cash economy. The official exchange rate was 815 kip to the dollar. The unofficial rate had climbed to 35,000. The largest Lao note was 5,000 kip (about 14 US cents) and now all transactions had to be settled in cash. Dealers turned up with sacks full of bank notes. Counting money became a seven-day-a-week occupation for all staff. Unexpectedly they enjoyed this: it brought everyone together. The Lao sense of the ridiculous prevailed: we were wasting our time counting notes that were close to valueless but we had no alternative. When I started to separate out old notes as souvenirs, everyone joined in the search. The notes we found are still on the wall of my study. In the end I had to settle my account with my own kip—less than $5. We had to arrange for a military convoy to take the rest to the bank.

Out on the street there was chaos as queues built up at the filling stations. This was the only time I heard heated argument between buyers and sellers; fuel supply was essential, so our first encounter with the new régime proved conciliatory. They wanted to regularise supply and we wanted clarity on the excise duty payable. Over an afternoon we reached an acceptable compromise: dealers were allowed access to their bank accounts and a new duty structure was agreed.

To reinforce this rapprochement between the old and new, James arranged a cocktail party and invited both the international community and senior Pathet Lao. The latter all turned up dressed in fatigue green and stood together on the lawn in silence, clutching untouched orange juice in their hands. The head of the UNHCR, who spoke fluent Lao, attempted to engage them in conversation but with limited success.

What was beginning to look like a wake rather than a party was saved by the arrival of a young Lao, arrayed in the flamboyant formal dress of a member of the royal family. His consort touched my outstretched hand with hers, as delicate as a feather, while looking into my eyes with an expression that sought to know whether I was trustworthy. She provided another facet of the mythology I had created about Laos: that it was infinitely desirable but unreachable.

I fell instantly in love but never spoke to her again, as her paramour guided her across the lawn to engage with the Pathet Lao. Within ten minutes they were laughing, smoking and ordering whisky. I never found out who the paramour was (there were so many of them) but he could have been the son of Souvanna Phouma, the neutralist prime minister, or his brother Souphanouvong—the Red Prince and a Pathet Lao founder member. Whoever he was, he turned what might have been a dirge into a convivial occasion.

In contrast to my first visit, I felt increasingly comfortable in this strange country, though Vientiane gave the impression of physical impermanence. Sacked by the Thais a few years before the French protectorate, only the *wats* (temples), endlessly reconstructed after countless invasions, gave hints of the past, scattered among and often obscured by more modern buildings. The 500-year-old That Luang, the national monument, recently redecorated in yellow and white paint, looked as though it had been built in the previous decade.

The French colonial influence stretched only to a handful of official buildings, a colonnaded square and the two main streets, Samsenthai and Setthathilath. Where these converged with the Avenue Lang Xang was the city's only set of traffic lights, and it did not work. Up Lang Xang beyond the Talat Sao was the Lao version of the Arc de Triomphe, distinguishable from its Parisian version by various oriental motifs attached to its bulk. It was known as the Vertical Runway, having been built in the Sixties with American-aid concrete intended for an extension to the airport. There were only 800 kms of paved roads in the country. All suburbs were served by dirt tracks.

The Americans built many more buildings but tended to locate them outside the centre. Their rectilinear design, air-conditioned functionality, apparent solidity and preoccupation with security was the antithesis of the Lao style of open verandas, sweeping curves and wood construction which dominated the spaces in between. Vientiane often seemed like a village in which aliens had landed. Many of its houses were raised on stilts. Below them were miniature rice paddies, complete with snuffling pigs and even the occasional water buffalo. The families sat on their verandas, watching the world go by or chatting to neighbours.

This sense of provisionality was sealed by the unspoken reality that Vientiane was now an island, the only part of Laos outside Communist control. I tested this by driving out on the road north to Luang Prabang. At the first line of hills some Pathet Lao soldiers emerged and blocked the road, pointing their rifles at me. I had brought all the necessary papers and waved them out of the window. They neither moved nor spoke. I reversed the car and drove home.

Travel to other parts of the country required special permits. These would not be forthcoming to anybody who did not have a specific need to go there on a mission with governmental approval. Only aid workers were allowed out. The reality was that the Pathet Lao were now in undisputed control of the country except for Vientiane, where the myth of a coalition government still held sway.

Vientiane seemed a town of temporary tracks. But I found a home there. This was a place I remember fondly. It was a strange construction of a concrete blockhouse base, where the housekeeper lived with her family and the kitchen, on top of which was a wooden superstructure with large eaves and a balcony on three sides. Inside all this was an air-conditioned en-suite bedroom and a large living room with rattan furniture. Steps down led to an open-air dining area, where I had breakfast of coffee and papaya every morning. More steps down to the garden, planted with hibiscus, oleander, bougainvillea and palms, at the end of which was a wooden 'sala' perched over the banks of the Mekong.

The housekeeper and her family were discreet, but whenever I needed something, they would appear. The old man, presumably her father, was always at the gate to let me in when I came home. I was never sure if he spent the whole day there after I left or, by some preternatural instinct, knew of my imminent arrival.

Occasionally the evenings were enlivened by some Thai military posturing. There was a pattern to such occurrences. Firstly the bars on the far bank would turn their loudspeakers up to maximum volume. Thai pop music is not a pleasant experience under any circumstance, but over-amplified across half a mile of river it is torture. Then the shooting on both sides of the river would begin. This felt more like a ritual than a battle so I would sit on the *sala* and watch the tracer streaking across the night sky. One evening with sundowner guests, it started up again and they ran inside, leaving me questioning whether I had become over-accustomed to this place.

Through my new colleagues at work and home I began to understand Lao values. Driving into town one evening, a Honda 90 motorcycle with father, mother and infant aboard appeared suddenly in front of me in my headlights, having none of its own. I hit it very lightly and the family were tipped into the road, without any serious injury. A royalist policeman appeared and the mother harangued him, pointing out the cut on her arm. He noted the details and we all went on our way.

I then received a summons to appear before the local court. The chief clerk, a Vietnamese named Vieng Kham, accompanied me. To my mind there was no doubt about it: an unlit motorcycle had attempted to cut across in front of me. The judge did not agree and told me to pay the family 500,000 kip. Vieng Kham explained that the motorcycle's violation of the Highway Code, by driving without lights, was immaterial. I was in a car, so I was rich; they had only a motorbike, so they were poor. It's for the rich to pay the damages. This seemed fair so I did and everybody was happy.

The same principle applied to the marriage of the daughter of a staff member. This took place on a smallholding on the outskirts of Vientiane. It was a modest affair, held under a purloined American parachute. The bride and groom held centre stage, both highly made-up and looking more like an androgynous couple than man and woman. My contribution was an envelope of cash, which I had been told was expected. Once I handed it over, I relaxed and found myself in a series of conversations with the relations, in French or English or sometimes sign language. I enjoyed it and I think they did too.

My state of mind watching gunfire across the Mekong stemmed from a not uncommon sense of immortality among the young. But the Lao by nature were both risk-averse and resigned to their fate. I noticed that though everyone drove very slowly they made no attempt to avoid accidents. I watched two cars bump into each other outside the Talat Sao at a combined speed of about 20 kph. Both drivers got out, inspected the very limited damage, checked that nobody had been hurt and continued on their way.

Thus I began to understand the Buddhist premise that fate was beyond control and that the best that could be done was to gain merit for one's future lives. A more prosaic explanation is that there were no longer any insurance companies to make a claim against. Whichever the truth there was no point arguing about it. In these uncertain times paying to release birds from their cages to gain merit, first observed in Thailand, was the Lao equivalent of buying a lottery ticket.

This may seem patronising; it is not intended to be. Life is complicated enough and these simple mantras serve to anchor a belief system that reflects both Lao history and religion. It is as far away from individualistic liberal democratic free market principles as is possible. The reality is that the Lao, from top of the tree to the bottom, have for centuries had no say over their collective or individual destinies. It is difficult to distil this into words but the absence of malice, the sense that all problems will pass, the welcoming of others who understand their point of view and their resistance to hardship seemed something worth emulating, a place where being is more important than achieving.[3]

A loose amalgam of friends and acquaintances found reasons to get together, severally or in couples. One evening I took a French girl to the best restaurant in town, hidden down a lane off the road to the airport. We chose the most expensive items from the Western menu, with the top claret and cognac to finish. It cost me $5. Social life was full and cheap.

But things were changing, as everybody knew they would,

---

[3] There is evidence that these values have been around for a long time and are reflected in the nineteenth-century journals of Henri Mouhot, *Travels in the Central Parts of Indo-China (Siam), Cambodia and Laos*: Vol 2, CUP (1864), Norman Lewis's *A Dragon Apparent*, Jonathan Cape (1951), reprinted by Eland in 2008, and Oden Meeker, *The Little World of Laos*, Charles Scribner's Sons, New York (1959).

though they clung to the hope that change would be tolerable. The fiction of neutrality was particularly strong in diplomatic circles, where sterile cocktail parties ignored what was happening outside.

The Pathet Lao became more visible, with senior cadres driving around town in the purloined private cars of the Americans. The saddest sight was an obviously cherished classic MGTF, now often seen on the streets, crashing gears. The foot soldiers wandered around the Talat Sao, fingering radios, watches and calculators, wondering how they worked but too impoverished to buy them. They looked as dazed and confused as the rest of the population.

Revolutions are supposed to be dramatic, with the new order imposing its will as soon as it has gained power. In Laos the transformation felt like a clumsy waltz, made worse by the absence of any reliable information. It was on 23 August 1975 that Vientiane was 'liberated'. I still have the T-shirt imported by the Indian traders on Samsenthai to prove it. We knew that something was going to happen but nobody knew what. James closed the office and everybody walked into the town centre, curious and fearful. The Pathet Lao army rolled into town in their trucks, dropping off a soldier in green fatigues every ten yards on the major highways. As the Royalist army had effectively disbanded itself, this was more akin to a Boy Scouts parade than a liberation. The soldiers stood facing the road with their Kalashnikovs at the ready and would not engage with the curious crowds that had emerged to find out what was going on. A few hours later the trucks came back, picked up the soldiers and disappeared. And that was it. For the next six weeks, life continued just as it had been before.

Thanks to Stuart-Fox I can date the triumphant Victory Parade at That Luang to 12 October of the same year. The previous night there had been a rainstorm. The parade began with military equipment which churned up the parade ground into a sea of mud. Then followed the foot-soldiers who managed to keep some semblance of formation despite the conditions underfoot. After that were the patriotic cadres, who not only lacked the military discipline but, in the case of the women, were all wearing the then fashionable platform shoes (very popular with the Lao who were largely of diminutive stature). They started to fall over and all semblance of military precision was lost. At first there was an embarrassed silence then the crowd and the participants began to giggle. Meanwhile the officials in the grandstand stood ramrod straight, saluting the passing rabble. It became uncomfortable to watch, and slowly the crowd, including me, began to slip away.

Although the 1973 Coalition Government had not been dissolved, this unopposed show of strength marked a watershed. The exodus of the educated and prosperous accelerated. Vieng Kham was criticised for listening to Shostakovich's 'bourgeois' music by the newly formed neighbourhood committee and disappeared a few days later. My housekeeper and her family told me that they had been instructed to report any deviant behaviour of the *falang* they worked for but they promised me they would not do that.

My monthly trip to Bangkok—a reward for working in a hardship posting but also a necessity for all but diplomats, as only thirty-day Lao visas were being issued—changed in character. Each departure required a *baci* ceremony, with a local *bonze* (a monk) in charge. They were always Thursday to Monday, as I had to lodge my passport with the Lao Embassy on the Friday to get the new visa on Monday morning before taking the early afternoon Thai Airways flight back.

One problem with this was that as the visa took up a full page, the entry stamp half a page, the exit visa a full page and the exit stamp half a page, my standard passport would run out of space in three months. In a manner that is impossible today, however, a couple of phone calls to the British Embassy in Bangkok allowed me to collect a new ninety-two-page passport without disrupting this schedule.

These trips took on a greater significance for the remaining Vientiane expatriate community. On taking over Six Click City before I arrived, the Pathet Lao had turned off the electricity supply to the refrigerated store. The resulting stench of rotting food wafted over the entire city. As the familar restaurants and shops closed down, only the Talat Sao was still able to offer fresh food, albeit of a limited range and questionable quality. I began with one cool box and ended up with four as I became, among others, one of the few means of providing desirable, and sometimes essential, fresh food to those left behind.

Vientiane became a more uncomfortable place to live in. Loudspeakers on every street corner broadcast the thoughts of the new leaders, interspersed with patriotic songs from 7:00 am to 7:00 pm. Favourite restaurants shut down. Western music was banned, as was dancing, except for the traditional Lam Vong, a folkloric courtship ritual of appropriate revolutionary modesty.

Many Lao officials of the royalist régime, both civil and military, lined up passively, as instructed, to be taken to *samanas*, or re-education camps. They were told that their stays would be of short duration. (Others, more sceptical, chose the Thailand option.) Lower echelons had to attend similar sessions closer to home. The civil service, such as it was, ceased to function. Laos had never enjoyed efficient, effective and dispassionate governance; now there wasn't even any pretence of it. The intentions of the Communists were never proclaimed except through ideological jargon or by some process of osmosis. What was permitted yesterday was banned today. Lights out.

I was asked if I wanted to renew my contract but the magic

of the posting had gone. I too crossed the Mekong but on a
Thai Airways flight, my wrists covered with good-luck strings
from the farewell *baci* ceremony. Over time the strings dissolved and, back in London, my stories of Laos were not appreciated; ambiguities about foreign affairs were of no interest.

It has only occurred to me while writing this that my experience of Laos was unique. I was resident during the only period in the country's recent recorded history when there had been no foreign occupation. The Americans had gone and all the excesses of their invasion had collapsed. The girly bars had no girls. The rich generals had fled. What remained were ordinary people trying their best to survive in difficult times. People were frightened, but this was not an unusual state of affairs: Laos had been close to annihilation many times before. There was a moment when this could have turned out differently. The overwhelming majority of Lao of all ethnic backgrounds were of neither capitalist nor Communist persuasion; indeed 60 per cent of them were illiterate.[4] As Lane-Fox argues the Pathet Lao were victorious as undisputed rulers of the entity of Laos but they failed to unify it. Communist dogma took precedence over nation-building.[5]

LIVING IN LAOS had a lasting impact on the way I look at the world. In this verdant underpopulated land, anybody could create a reasonable living by building a house from a nearby teak tree, digging a rice paddy and buying some chickens, ducks and a buffalo. There was no merit in being rich, nor any purpose; being left alone to do as one desired was the only

---

[4] M. Brown and J.J. Zasloff, 'First Faltering Steps Towards Socialism', *Asian Survey* (1997), cited by M. Stuart-Fox.
[5] Martin Stuart-Fox, ibid, p. 166.

requirement. The last thing anybody needed was another imposition of ideology.

I had glimpsed a way of life that was the antithesis of my upbringing and was disappearing into history. I committed to memory various mythical qualities of this country and conveyed them to anyone who would listen. I conveniently forgot that I had not experienced Laos as a whole, just its ephemeral capital city. Only later did I realise that it was what had happened in the countryside that had had a much more profound effect on political outcomes throughout Indochina. It is now generally recognised that Laos suffered the highest density of aerial bombing of any country, ever, though it may have been nudged off the Number 1 slot by recent action in Gaza.

LIVING IN SINGAPORE in the late Eighties and working for BAT (British American Tobacco) gave me an opportunity to return to Laos. To do so required meeting a highly dodgy Thai MP whom I had seen passing a thick brown envelope to an opposition MP. We met in Bangkok, where he informed me that the Lao government was considering a joint venture with a multinational for its tobacco monopoly. I agreed to look it over but insisted that I would only return the way I had originally arrived, an indication of how deeply the Lao myth had wormed its way into my head.

The politician's French sidekick accompanied me by plane to Udorn Thani, then by car to Nong Khai and then across the Mekong on a *pirogue* indistinguishable from that of my first visit. I insisted on staying in the Lang Xan, a fortuitous choice as nothing had been renovated and the ancient bellhop was still there and pretended to recognise me. My visit to the tobacco factory convinced me, erroneously, that there was nothing of interest for my employer, as everything was sold to the factory manager's brother at below cost price—and what it did produce seemed to me to be rubbish. My Singaporean colleague, Wang Tee Fock, reached the same conclusion, that this was not a prospect worth pursuing.

Perhaps our unenthusiastic response coloured a subsequent meeting with what I assume was the Foreign Investment Committee. No name cards were exchanged, either because the regime valued secrecy or because we were were not committed enough to ask for them. Whatever the reasons, the most we exchanged was platitudes, and Wang Tee Fock left soon after with the Frenchman, returning the same way he had come in, on the easier Thai Airways flight to Bangkok.

Imperial Tobacco, for whom I worked subsequently, decided we were both wrong and made a lot of money (in Lao terms) from doing so, as did the government.

As for the man who seemed in charge of proceedings, I realised that he was the same person I had negotiated with fifteen years earlier on the fuel excise debate. I tried to remind him of this but he would not be drawn. As we left he grasped my proffered hand with both of his own and *sotto voce* said in French, 'I hope we have the chance to meet again.' I still do not know who he was.

I DECIDED TO revisit old haunts and took the fifteen-minute walk along the Mekong back to my old office. I walked in unannounced, to be greeted as a long-lost son by Khan Kao and her sister, Khan Kham. Out of the offices came others, many of whom I recognised but whose names I could not remember. Finally the general manager emerged and, to my shame, I cannot remember his name either. I suppose he liked me, for he invited me to stay with him for a few days. Or may be he was just bored by his regular existence. But I was glad to stay over with him.

With no other agenda, there was time to talk. I discovered that the GM shared my fascination with Laos. This was his second secondment and he knew David, the replacement aviation superintendent who had left only the year before. When I knew David he was in his mid-thirties, with his wife and two kids back in Birmingham. Laos was his first overseas job. He was a nice chap with a friendly open manner and got on well with the local staff.

After I left, he stayed and took up with a young Lao woman whom he claimed was my ex, which was impossible as I had never had a Lao girlfriend, except in my head. For whatever reason, the woman, like some ten per cent of the population, decided to cross the river into Thailand and ended up in the Nong Khai refugee camp. 'Out of sight, out of mind' seemed now to trump 'Absence makes the heart grow fonder,' and he soon found himself another girlfriend, though she too decided to make the same journey as her predecessor.

Meanwhile communication home became less and less frequent. One weekend, David went to the refugee camp and was met at the gate by his wife, then by the first girlfriend and finally by the second. Both girlfriends were obviously pregnant. This was the first time any of the women had met. He quickly re-crossed the river to the safety of Laos. The *ménage-a-quatre* was eventually resolved by his leaving the country to set up a bar in Cyprus with the first girlfriend, or so I was told. The Shell GM had to clear up the pieces, including handing back his rented house. In doing so he discovered two other women residents, at least one of whom had decided to store coal in the bath (though why she would have needed coal in a tropical country is anybody's guess). If the first girlfriend had been my mythical princess this demonstrated an alarming deterioration of standards. But it also reflected a French colonial saying, 'If you send a man to Laos for more than two years, he'll be unemployable anywhere else.'

VIENTIANE SEEMED UNCHANGED. I have a residents' guide from the period and it highlights new restaurants and hotels to visit, but there was little else to do—a bit more than when I had left but far less than when I had first arrived. In addition, the British Embassy had closed and its affairs were now handled by the Australians, who had a club beside the Mekong a few kilometres south-east of the centre.

My host got me invited to an expatriate's house for dinner with other guests, where I listened to stories of how difficult it was to live in Laos and discovered how little understanding there was of what the government was up to and who was in charge of what. The mood was one of making the best of it while treading water.

My host also arranged a party for the office staff at which I was the guest of honour. It was an enjoyable occasion which took me back briefly to the days, fifteen years earlier, before the troubles began and to the sense of belonging I'd had with the same people at the time. But I began to detect a sense of detachment that had been previously absent. In my absence, I had escaped the strictures of an orthodox Communist state; they had not and, while hoping for better times, they were sceptical. I expect that many had experienced family trauma while I was away and did not want to talk about it.

My information is therefore drawn from secondary sources. Members of the royal hierarchy were among those dispatched to primitive camps beyond the Plain of Jars and close to the Vietnam border, where all contact with them was lost. Some, including the king and queen of Laos—the last to occupy the country's thrones—as well as the crown prince died there from malnutrition or lack of medical assistance, as did very many others.[6] Many of the survivors found, when they were released, that their partners had remarried. In terms of realpolitik, these were minor tragedies, but they were real and human and personal, and yet were never disclosed or used to

---

[6] Christopher Kremmer, *Bamboo Palace*, Flamingo (2003).

elicit my sympathy. Why not? I think the reason is embedded in what I have written above: the past, for the Lao, is strewn with disasters. Better to forget them, enjoy what is good today and hope against hope that tomorrow will be easier.

The last part of this reunion was their insistence on another *baci* ceremony on the day of my departure—and that was when what I had thought of as a charming superstition turned into a genuine expression of inclusion that stayed with me long after.

The day before I had borrowed a car to look for my old house. I was sure I could find it: halfway between the centre and Wattay airport on the Luang Prabang road. Turn left down the lane past the wat, then left again onto the *levée*, then right through aluminium-framed meshed gates. But nothing seemed familiar as I trundled in ever-widening circles. There was no trace of it. It was only much later that I made the connection that the legacy of centuries of pre-colonial warfare between Laos, Thailand, Burma and Vietnam had led to homes being regarded as only temporaray shelters, a custom built on the expectation of chaos rather than progress.

I revisited all the old sites, acquired some better-quality weaving souvenirs than I had been able to procure in 1975, and left in the conventional manner through Wattay. The terminal was exactly as it had been before, but the security had been upgraded. My suitcase was examined by customs before check-in. I then passed through the metal detector and put my hand luggage through the x-ray machine and found my way to the departure lounge, where a sign at the rear pointed to a café up some stairs. I mounted these and found myself in an area that anybody could access, whether landside or airside. Here Kalashnikovs and heroin could be safely handed over, for there was no other check before boarding the plane. Official incompetence remained a very Lao trait.

Despite the disappearance of my old house, Vientiane

seemed unchanged, with no obvious development. Fifteen years earlier, everything that did not fit Marxist-Leninist orthodoxy got closed down. That policy had now been reversed, at least in terms of the economy, but the speed of change was glacial. Before, there had been anxiety about the future; now there was anger about the recent past. My Shell colleagues had been protected by their employer and they knew they were lucky—the fact that they were still in post after half a generation proved that—but they all had their stories of injustice that could only be told to those they trusted.

TWENTY-SIX YEARS later I returned again, wondering what was in store. It was nothing but a four-day visit and was confined to Luang Prabang, a place I had always wanted to visit but had been unable to without a *laissez-passer*, which was not then available to Westerners. Now, in the twenty-first century, this backwater, a UNESCO heritage site, had been reborn as the acceptable face of Laos for tourists.

What I read up about the country ahead of my visit did not reassure me. The mixture of crony capitalism and an unaccountable and still secretive government was unsettling. I was prepared to find nothing of what I had remembered so fondly forty years earlier. I was just another visitor who would leave with new impressions but no greater understanding.

I knew the geography of Laos and could follow the flight path while we were in the air. But when we were where I supposed we were going, there was nothing to be seen, save a few buildings poking through the vegetation. Then the plane turned and began its descent between steep hills, covered in forest. Occasional scars of slash-and-burn cultivation by local hill tribes dotted the mountains. This was indeed Luang Prabang, with a new Chinese-built airport terminal, already falling to pieces after only eighteen months.

Our hotel was the Maison Souvanna Phoum—this odd

name, missing the final 'a' of the ex-prime minister's name, apparently required by the government so that reference to the previous régime could be avoided. It was a colonial residence of both stature and charm. The guest rooms were in the *dépendances* with the main house containing the reception and dining rooms. I am sure it was the prime minister's old residence in the royal capital, conveniently located opposite the provincial office and only a short walk to the palace.

Though the town was now set up to service the tourist trade—the only, and growing, industry—it had none of the commercialism of Thailand or Siem Reap. The hotel welcome seemed sincere and included an edited version of the *baci* ceremony. The instinct to please seemed intact. Wandering that evening through the night market, I found this impression cemented. Nobody hassled, conversations were tentatively suggested, wares offered only if you showed interest. A sale was a blessing, not a pressing need. By modern-world standards the people were poor but did not seem distressed about it. Also noticeable was the mix of ethnicities: Lao Lum, Hmong with mongoloid eyes, and other hill tribes with more angular facial features. They seemed to rub along well enough, whereas in 1975 women from displaced hill tribes would sit in disconsolate huddles on the periphery of the Vientiane market, trying to sell distinctive hand-woven fabrics that were nearly as shabby as the clothes they were wearing.

Our guide, Wong, had been born in a village 80 kms northeast of Luang Prabang and had spent four years in a wat in Vientiane. Over the days we spent together, I found he had no obvious axe to grind. In the royal palace (built by the French and now a museum) I remarked that the king's possessions seemed to have been remarkably modest. 'Maybe', he said, 'but a lot of his relatives are rich.' I guess that this is what he had been told but he had no proof of it. He could also not corroborate something I had read about an unsanctioned group of people getting together at the Royal Wat to pay homage to the king and queen. It was clear that for him, the monarchy was an irrelevance; he would in any case have only been a toddler when the royals were deposed.

By contrast, our guide's preoccupation was ecology, and he announced gravely that Laos's primary forest had been reduced from 65 per cent of the land area to 25 per cent today. I am no forestry expert but it seemed to me that indiscriminate logging had had less effect on the forests than the slash-and-burn that I had seen from the air. Even then, the forests of Luang Prabang still seem abundant. By contrast, there is virtually no forest left in Madagascar, as my single visit there made clear.

One thing that struck me was that Wong regarded teak as the Laotian equivalent of pine. It seems that other, more valuable trees like ironwood are much more at risk from the rapacity of the loggers.

ALTHOUGH LAOS IS a one-party Communist state, the ruling party seems almost bashful about imposing its will. There is no evidence on the street of its attempting to control the people, save for the occasional revolutionary poster and, more often, national and Communist flags. The government is opaque in its intentions. The *Vientiane Times* prints only generalities in its weekly edition: the front page headlines when I was there were, 'Parliament urges improved tax collection' and 'Local authorities prepare for That Luang celebrations'.

It was not always so. Initially, all the apparatus of Communist ideology was imposed from the formation of party cells down to village level—bans on anything that could be considered imperialist or decadent, constant propaganda broadcast through loudspeakers in villages and towns, an attempt to impose collectivisation of agriculture (which was spectacularly unsuccessful) and the suppression of the

Buddhist Sangha, the religious leadership. One by one these strictures have been abandoned, though signs at the Phousi waterfall outside Luang Prabang still insist (at the time of writing) that bathers must be modestly dressed, with no bikinis and no exposure of torso by either sex. These admonitions are ignored with impunity.

What does this government stand for? It seems like a pale shadow of the Chinese model of free markets with political orthodoxy, coupled with vague pretensions towards the legitimacy of rule. The banknotes now carry the image of Kayson Phomhivane, the now-deceased leader of the Pathet Lao, instead of the deposed, and equally dead, king. A myth of revolutionary struggle and the historical inevitability of eventual triumph is rigorously adhered to.

There are rumours of shady deals by government and army, none of which can be verified because of the opaque nature of the political process and the absence of a free press and of an independent judiciary. No doubt there is corruption —the government has not enough money to pay its officials properly—but it seems that this is both culturally acceptable and modest. In Laos, it is just another bureaucratic hurdle.

There are a remarkable number of Chinese-registered cars on the streets of Luang Prabang but their investments, many of which seemed to be white elephants (resort hotels and golf clubs), were hidden away in the suburbs.

Had it not been for the French, Laos would have disappeared as a state. The glory days of the kingdom of Lang Xang ('a million elephants') were 500 years ago. When the French arrived in the 1800s, what is now Laos, which then consisted of three vassal kingdoms (one of which is now within Thailand), was insignificant and remains so today. What interests me is the resilience of Lao culture against imported wars of conflicting ideologies, and the people's powerlessness to do anything about it. Their way of looking at their condition has to do with possibilities, not principles. At my advanced age I consider this a more intelligent response than the binary political kneejerks that govern Western politics. I would trust Lao opinion, however uneducated much of it is, over that of government. Stability and security seem to be fundamental Lao values, rooted in a history of constant invasions. This is why religion and ritual play such an important role; if you cannot control your own destiny, you have to look to higher authorities to protect you from harm. The Western obsession with 'want, own, be', the driver of economic progress, has a Lao alternative: 'be, want, own'. For me, as an ambitious young man wedded to the former concept, it was the glimpse of another way of looking at life that led to my attachment to Laos. Returning, I was less disappointed than I had expected to be. It remains a place apart—but for how long?

The $5.8 bn Chinese high-speed rail project (part of its global Belt and Road Initiative) that joins Yunnan with Thailand is designed to make landlocked Laos 'land-linked'.[7] A government that remains cash-strapped, as domestic tax revenues are small, depends on foreign aid, with little choice over where this is spent. Such an enormous sum could address local infrastructure needs of health, education and communications. Instead, trains will plough through mountains and run over valleys at enormous speed, while subsistence farmers above and below gaze on, initially, at least, in astonishment. Some may have gained from temporary construction work; others may have suffered from having their land sequestered, but ultimately the project will add nothing of permanent value to their lives.

From the glory of the Land of a Million Elephants, through

---

[7] Peter Frankopan, *The New Silk Roads: The Present and Future of the World*, Bloomsbury Publishing (2018).

decline to a client state of Burma, Siam and Vietnam, to the territorial salvation of French occupation, then a war zone of a global ideological conflict ended by the imposition and subsequent failure of a rigid and foreign political orthodoxy, to an increasingly culturally homogenous backwater with no particular place to go, is a leitmotif rather than a failure. The trouble with being small and unimportant is that foreigners feel they can do what they want with you.

Sharing a border with China creates challenges for Laos but I suspect that the imposition of Han cultural values, if it comes to that, will be received with equanimity, and then quietly ignored. The Lao are the world's experts in how to do that.

CHAPTER 3
Vietnam: 1988 to 2018
Death and Rebirth

Leaving Laos for the first time was like walking out of a cinema halfway through the feature. I was an expert on one nation in South-East Asia, or so I thought, and assumed that everywhere else in that region was more or less the same. Then my work with BAT took me elsewhere—to Latin America, Finland and New Zealand—before a posting to Singapore in 1998 gave me the chance to fill in the gaps.

I suggest that it was the Vietnam War (or, more correctly, the Second Indochina War) that provoked the first collective sense of moral conscience about events far from home for Western baby boomers (of which I am one). That awakening has in no small way influenced attitudes towards the rest of the world. What it lacks, however, is nuance.

Vietnam, viewed from afar, became a land of myths. It was the first war that became public property: the photos of the monk immolating himself; the naked girl-child running from a napalm raid; the Vietcong officer being executed in the street by a bullet to the temple, capturing that instant between life and death; and finally the last helicopter on the American Embassy roof, above a rickety ladder, with hundreds of terrified people below, scrabbling for the last remaining seats.

How the mighty had fallen. It was a land of terror and trauma, and those exposed to it constructed their own stories as well as they could to make sense of what they had experienced. On 30 April 1975, nearly thirty years after Ho Chi Minh's declaration of Vietnamese independence in 1946, it was all over. Nearly thirty years: an entire generation.

Graham Greene's *The Quiet American* had influenced my teenage impressions of what Vietnam was like. This was a place of moral ambiguity where a man could live as he liked but remain in danger. Experience taught you how to survive but made you more cynical and callous in the process. I liked this idea of being tested, to find out what moral backbone I had, if any. And I could almost smell it—the humidity and the heat and the sight of black-clad figures emerging from the tree line with AK-47s blazing.

I had got close to this in Laos, but too late to witness it. Returning home, I discovered that my well-educated friends were not interested in my stories. The people had won and America had lost and that was that. The world is a complicated place and the temptation to pigeonhole anything from afar as good or bad is often the most convenient solution, but also the laziest. Vietnam had become a hermetically sealed, hard-line Communist state.

But I still wanted to go there, an interest piqued not by retracing the Second Indochina War's road to ruin (though it remained a preoccupation of those who had lived through it) but by what happened once the Stars and Stripes were lowered for the last time, folded for the last time and placed in the helicopter that departed Saigon for the last time.

The announcement in 1986 of a new policy of Do Moi, an opening up of Vietnam's doors to the outside world, provided commercial opportunities that would foster a socialist-oriented market economy. By then I was in Singapore, and married with three small children. Since the fall of Saigon little had been heard of Vietnam, save the invasion of Cambodia to overthrow the Pol Pot régime, and the refugee crisis of the 'boat people' who risked their lives in barely seaworthy fishing boats to get out of the country. That event, which captured the world's headlines for a few weeks, now seems forgotten. Two million 'disappeared', never to be reported on again, to make the best of their new lives overseas and became collectively anonymous.

The one pro-Western country with flights to Ho Chi Minh

City was Thailand but there were just two flights a week, and entry visas were only obtainable in Bangkok. The embassy proved to be an unkempt little bungalow, almost invisible, tucked away down a *soi* off Sukhamvit. Surprisingly, it proved efficient. I and my most adventurous colleague Wang Tee Fock, the production director, were expected, and our visas would be ready the following morning.

We flew to Ho Chi Minh's Tan Son Nhut airport on Friday, 23 September 1988, arriving at dusk, having flown over the Mekong Delta, which seemed to be three-quarters water, in paddy fields, rivers, canals or bomb craters. Photography was forbidden both in the air and on the ground. The plane was parked in a corner of the airfield next to an abandoned control tower and we waited in light rain for the ancient DeSoto school bus to take us to the terminal. An equally ancient articulated fuel truck rumbled past, none of its lights working but the faded Shell logo still discernible.

The terminal was the second indication of a time warp. It seemed to be imperceptibly dissolving into its own foundations. This seemed of no consequence to the officials, who performed the formalities efficiently. Outside, far too many people were awaiting the few passengers. We were met by the Vietnamese delegation and loaded into a newly imported Japanese microbus. The only other four-wheeled vehicles were remnants from pre-revolutionary days.

Our destination was the Rex Hotel. This had been reserved for US officers during the war, and in consequence had its bar on the roof, beyond the reach of hand grenades. My room was a time warp; it looked as if nothing had been touched since 1975, with a colour scheme—dark brown highlighted by orange—redolent of that bygone era. A functioning Carrier box air-conditioner was fitted into the window frame. The bathroom was swathed in blue micro-tiles and the fittings were universally American: stained but functioning. I was half-convinced that I was being monitored and I looked for signs of concealed microphones, but found nothing. The following morning I took care to leave a hair in the lock of my suitcase to see, when I got back, if it had been disturbed while I was out. Despite the dilapidated state of everything, I still believed that this authoritarian state took a close interest in the activities of all foreigners, and we were few and far between at that time.

My room felt initially like a prison, though later it became a refuge. It was here that I wrote up a journal of the trip and my retelling of it—my first trip to Vietnam—relies heavily on my notes and thus has a veracity and immediacy that I may not have captured in what I have merely remembered of other places that I spent time in. Looking back at what I wrote, what stands out for me is the feeling of having been a stranger in a strange land. This was not an unusual sensation but it was amplified here, where everything except time had simply stopped.

Wong and I arrived at the rooftop bar almost simultaneously. Heineken and Coca-Cola were available in cans at a dollar each. The bar had several tanks of tropical fish and a couple of silently shuffling waiters but no other customers. It was Friday night and the centre of the city was silent. There was no traffic, dark save for a few weak light bulbs, no revellers, no bars or restaurants, no activity at all but for a few figures slipping silently through the shadows.

On the building next door was a faded wall advert for Sanyo, across the street another for Ho Chi Minh. Nothing was new, everything seemed to be seeping into a netherworld where nothing ever happened, and it was impossible to tell whether you were dead or alive. The beer buried the unease and, having spoken to nobody else save the fearful waiters, we went to bed.

The next day's itinerary was bewildering, following neither

a Western-type tour of the sites nor what I had assumed would be a Soviet Intourist-style schedule of visits to revolutionary monuments. It seemed, instead, to have been designed by a committee whose members could not agree on what its aims were, save for the objective of generating investment interest.

A tour of the city revealed many small-scale workshops with artisans hammering away, people sitting on the sidewalk with perhaps a bicycle pump and a spark plug, and street vendors selling vegetables, cigarettes and glass bottles filled with goodness knows what. In a private moment, our guide, Kiet, said that a monthly salary lasted ten days.

Then out of the city to a tobacco factory in the adjacent Dong Nai province. Of it, I wrote:

> A satanic mill choked in dust and grime. Filthy machines clank and spit while workers shuffle about sweeping up the detritus with makeshift brooms, only to throw it all back in again. ... It is sadly ineffectual—dealing with the symptoms but never the problem—[and] perhaps that is true of the country as a whole?

I began to sense that there was something utterly defeated about this society, which was hardly surprising, after all that had happened.

> And the expression in their eyes as they stare at the foreigners, if they have courage enough, chills with its deadness. Even the pickpocket seemed resigned to failure, obvious in her movements and signalling her intentions by her lack of commitment.

The final destination that day was Vung Tau, which the French called Cap St Jacques and where, in the absence of a hotel for foreigners, I ended up with 'A four-poster bed in the master bedroom of an ex-ARVN's general's house'.[1]

Unlike my room in the Rex Hotel, the American appliances here served only as decoration; none of them worked. I spent a sweat-soaked night, interrupted by half-dreams, to awake at dawn, shower and shave in cold water and be just in time for a seven-o'clock breakfast.

> After thirty-six hours of leaden skies and rain the weather had improved. 'Sunday, sunny day,' said one of the delegation, smiling at his English joke. So off to the beach.

The absence of Amerasians had puzzled me the day before, because there were estimated to be 100,000 offspring of GIs and local women (all of whom were shunned equally by the Americans and the Vietnamese) but here they were out in force, along with the amputees:

> The war casualties are the beggars and the hawkers; the beach provides relatively rich pickings. There is a clear pecking order. The Russians form a large circle like a corral and face inwards and are largely ignored by the beggars and salesmen. (One Vietnamese joke at the time went, 'What is the difference between Americans and Russians? Nothing, except that the Russians have no money.') The Vietnamese sit in the regimented lines of the deckchairs. The occasional paunch is noticeable through its rarity. Slowly the lines begin to dissolve as the rice wine and beer begins to take effect. Men and kids use

---

[1] ARVN stands for the Army of the Republic of Vietnam—that is, South Vietnam—which had a conscript army of 150,000 troops at the founding of the republic in 1955 and over a million by the end of the war twenty years later.

inner tubes to splash in the sea—the women stay covered up in the deckchairs. Apart from the heat it could have been Brighton in the 1950s.

I wonder where this analogy could have come from but then remembered the very English restraint and consequent decorous behaviour in public places; one acknowledged others but did not converse with them.

I took my camera on a stroll along the beach but ran out of film before a Vietnamese shyly asked me to take his photograph. He was sorry he asked, as if it were his fault. Then a small boy attaches himself to me and follows me round at a respectful distance, without saying anything. The sense of being an alien, not just a foreigner, becomes more intense.

This is interrupted by the banquet. Most of the cast are already slightly tipsy. We are honoured guests and offered every expensive delicacy the South China Sea can offer. We are also required to toast on a regular basis, alternately praising us as welcome guests or us praising them as wonderful hosts. This goes on for a long time until we are propelled to the steam baths. The plumbing was ancient but they were pleasant enough.

I was then ushered to a wooden cubicle, the sides of which extended to about head height and left a gap to mid-thigh below, for a massage.

My masseuse asked in extremely bad English if I would like a 'real message'. 'Yes,' I answered, misinterpreting the offer. 'You give me money, not desk.' 'I have no money.' 'Ask your friend.' And so on. This was an offer not difficult to refuse, given both where we were and my near paranoia about doing anything that would compromise me.

The reality of Marxist Vietnam became apparent over the next two days. My stay had begun pleasantly, had had a gut-wrenching middle and now ended with my writing these thoughts in the now-welcome sanctuary of Room 405 of the Rex Hotel. What I experienced can only be described as appalling.

> What brought this about? Nothing I can write is adequate to convey the sense of hopelessness, once beyond the cracked varnish of sophistication of Saigon. Bollocks to the notion of the noble savage living on scarce resources, at one with nature. This was a raw, hopeless, venal and selfish battle to simply survive. A moment's relaxation from attention to what might sustain you could be fatal. Why bother to clean anything if I am going to die anyway? And their awful blank eyes know something I had never seen before—that there is no point to anything except getting through to the following day. This concentration camp of misery was not heavily policed. There was no need as nobody has the power to move anywhere anyway. Not even charity has any benefit—it simply creates animosity among those who do not receive and envy of the receiver.
>
> On the road, we began joking that the horn is the most essential piece of equipment. After a while Wong says, 'They don't care if they are run over,' and he is right. Bikes, bullock carts and cows are pushed into the position of greatest hazard, like a game of Russian roulette. For we are privileged [to be] in a Japanese bus and therefore a source of compensation: 'Nobody should enjoy anything if I can't. And if you kill me then you will have a problem.' No happy smiling natives here. They know that they can never get to safe ground, so why bother to make the effort for the danger of an instant?

I remember two occasions when mothers threw their babies into the path of the bus. On both occasions the bus stopped in time. But the journal makes no mention of this. It does, however, refer to a Virgin Mary shrine which I had forgotten about. It carried the graffiti in English: 'What is happiness?' These inconsistencies of memory I can only put down to the turmoil engendered by what I had experienced. I had nightmares about it for weeks.

Outside Saigon, the state had ceased to exist in any practical fashion. What complicated this further was there was no reliable information. Our trip from Saigon to Dalat, in the highlands, and back was planned on the basis that all possible requirements should be obtained before departure. An official delegation had some cash but a truck driver none. The US embargo prevented the import of spare parts for this pre-revolutionary fleet and so, in the absence of reliable diesel supplies, many of these trucks had been converted to coal-powered, with a boiler hanging out back and steam injected into the engine to provide a maximum speed of about 20kms per hour.

A bigger problem was the lack of spare tyres. All through this journey we saw buses and trucks stranded on single bottle jacks where, in the absence of cell phones or internet, it was a matter of luck when assistance might turn up. At the nadir of independent Vietnam, this had become a dog-eat-dog approach.

This was reinforced by the accident we encountered on our return from Dalat to Saigon. A truck had crashed into an ancient school bus on a bridge and had had ripped its side off. The bus was now suspended over the parapet. Two of its passengers lay dead in the road; many others were injured. The survivors sat in glum silence. I asked where the nearest Red Cross or First Aid centre was. Down the road they said. I saw it before the driver, and asked him to stop. All he did was to blow his horn and point back up the road. My intended charitable intervention was pointless, as I was quietly informed that the centre had no transport, doctors, medical equipment or pharmaceuticals.

It was a silent journey back to the hotel and the choice of that night's farewell dinner, at a restaurant of endangered species, seemed less than appropriate, even though there was no recognisable connection between what we had experienced and the dire condition of the Vietnamese, save the very Western sensibility about killing wildlife.

Later I recognised that the restaurant's existence was a function of the country's starvation. There was very little left of conventional foodstuffs; twenty years later, there were very few birds in Vietnam.

Something changed for me after that. Until then, I had just been a tourist, fascinated and absorbed but only in an impersonal sense. Afterwards I felt it was my duty to help, not to retreat into the safety of a flight home. This fitted my conviction at the time that free markets and liberal democracy provided the solution to everything. I could do nothing about the latter but the mission of proving the value added of economic cooperation could alleviate this disaster. This was not an immediate decision but a conviction that finally overrode a strong desire never to see anything like this again.

On our way home Wong and I discussed what we had encountered. He said he wanted to kiss the ground when he got back to his native Singapore. I felt the same but for different reasons. He saw his kin struggling against impossible odds; I saw the 'bigger picture' of the bankruptcy of political orthodoxy. This was a holy alliance: he had the practicality to work out how he could help, I had the conviction that this was something we should do. I could deal with things at the London end; he could get things done on the ground. The alternative was to accept that the company for which we both worked would remain directionless. It would not be easy but it might be rewarding.

In retrospect I also wonder what was going on in the minds of our hosts. My assumption at the time was that they were adherents of the new *Do Moi* policy. Perhaps they were on the surface—they had to be, because this was the new political orthodoxy—but I now suspect there were other emotions that influenced their interpretation of it. It was clear from the outset that Kiet was the outsider, untrusted because of his pre-revolutionary history, but a necessary addition as the only one who spoke sufficient English to act as translator. He was my potential ally, but stuck resolutely to the party line, at least in public.

I now find it hard to believe that my assumption of a common agenda had any credibility. Instead I think the tour was a test. The Vietnamese experience of foreigners was universally bad, from Chinese vassalage up to the twelfth century, French colonialism from the 1880s until 1954, then the Americans until 1975, and finally the Russians who were now deserting the country and had left it in ruin. Nobody could have designed this programme in the belief that it was a sightseeing tour; all our hosts must have recognised that, living through their homeland's declining spiral into penury. It was a test of our resolve and character, from being required to eat things that never appeared on Western menus to seeing at first hand the destitution of the country. We passed, but that did not mean that our potential partners shared our vision of how to proceed. We were still foreigners.

Re-reading my journal, I recognise that I have ignored the obvious, consigning the war to a sideshow between what I then believed was a doctrinaire fight between Moscow, Beijing and Washington. That is a myth. Max Hastings makes a compelling case that the North Vietnamese régime was more ideologically rigid than that of either the Soviet Union or China, both of which were focused on global politics and urged restraint.[2] Ho Chi Minh and Le Duan emerge from this as ruthless pursuers of ideological rectitude, no matter the human cost. The American reliance on technology had the same effect: it depersonalised the war. On the ground, you lived or died through circumstances entirely beyond your control. Personal survival, at the expense of others if necessary, became hard-wired into the Vietnamese mentality.

Our invitation had come from Vinataba, supposedly the tobacco monopoly for Vietnam, but our visit to the Dong Nai tobacco factory had made it clear that it operated its own agenda. The urgent arguments by Vinataba to ignore this pathetic upstart only made this clearer. We decided to hedge our bets and work with both while keeping our cards behind our backs. This seemed to me an eminently Asian solution, allowing us to follow the wind rather than draw lines in the sand.

Over the next two and a half years I returned to Vietnam at least once a month. We started with a technical assistance agreement which involved our loaning them some redundant making-and-packing machinery, which was nevertheless a step ahead of the Czech Škoda equipment they were using and allowed them to start producing products of equivalent quality to the cheap contraband brands that dominated the market.

We also sent our supervisors and technicians to train the Vietnamese, and there was great enthusiasm among our staff for these assignments. When I turned up to inspect the first complete line in the Saigon factory, both the Vietnamese and Singaporeans made it patently obvious that they thought this a marriage made in heaven.

---

[2] Max Hastings, *Vietnam, an Epic Tragedy*, 1945–75, Harper Collins (2018).

We set up a similar arrangement for Dong Nai, though on a smaller scale. Mr. Hiep, the Dong Nai principal, was skeletally thin, had an addiction to Scotch whisky which rendered him incapable after just a couple of glasses and displayed all the manners of a Vietcong guerilla. It quickly became evident that he had no aptitude for business, and Vinataba's eternally enigmatic Mr Thuy and Mme Trinh, who had no love for each other but knew when it was wise to act in concert, ran rings round him.

We ended up as the equivalent of a specialist consultancy, assisting on every aspect of tobacco. We sent agronomists to help with local tobacco cultivation, marketing staff to improve their branding, salespeople to examine their distribution systems, accountants to overhaul their costing systems, engineers to plan production expansion and supply-chain experts to ensure they had the right raw materials at the right price. From year one we made a profit, to everybody's surprise, as did Vinataba, which could now charge more for better products.

For those uninterested in commerce, these details may sound dull; for those opposed to the tobacco industry, they may even sound criminal. But the story is significant because of the light it throws on economic progress. When I had first arrived in Vietnam, nothing worked. Local industry was starved of resources and it produced nothing but unregulated trash. The only items of any quality were contraband, which was only available to the few who could afford it and operated beyond the reach of the excise authorities, thereby denying revenue to the government. Nearly all Vietnamese men smoked in those days, and what we did there was to create an efficient and profitable local industry that served the local market and operated legally. It is now down to the people and government to decide what they want to do with it.

I offer this up not as an excuse for but as an example of

how commercial collaboration across ideological barriers can add value and bring about lasting positive change. Given that Vietnam was emerging as a strong baby from the toxicity of Marxist-Leninist orthodoxy in the time I spent there, this seems to me a good thing. No doubt other sectors were experiencing similar transformations.

What made us successful was our mutual sense of interdependence. That does not mean that we understood their system—it remained opaque—but we were flexible enough to adapt to their short-term requirements while maintaining the integrity of our own approach. That most of my colleagues were Chinese helped this. It was never a trust-based relationship: culture, politics and language caused constant alarums, and there was incessant pressure to grant all our intellectual property. They needed us more than we needed them and we were smart enough to never refer to this directly.

Ultimately, our dealings with them worked, and that in turn made it fun for both sides. There were countless banquets, partly to disguise our awareness that many of the people we were working with needed a square meal. The banquets may have boosted the catering sector but they were mainly seen as milestones of progress, which was important to the obscure and austere hierarchy above them.

For Westerners, socialising could be embarrassing. On one occasion I was required to dance with a Vietnamese young woman of diminutive stature; the top of her head was level with my belly button.

Ceasing to be a problem in this rigid political state meant that, by default, they earned more freedom.

AT HEART THE Vietnamese are capitalist by nature. Unlike the Khmer and the Lao, they have a history of revolting against their leaders, be they local or colonial. Having a geography whose eastern border is the sea, they have been an entrepôt state for centuries. Added to that, high population density demands the creation of a merchant class for individual advancement. The seething intellectual debates of the twentieth century and the violent opposition to colonial rule are evidence of this strongly nationalistic but also individual sense of being Vietnamese.

By circumstance, I arrived when the collectivist Marxist ideology, imposed as the result of a military victory, had proved to be a dead-end street. Though a one-party state remains, the economic reforms of the 1986 Do Moi policy opened the floodgates to a better future, seized gratefully by all who could.

The rapidity of this transformation is best explained by the story of Kiet, the suspicious translator whom I met on my first visit. Initially he was circumspect in responding to my questions. At the same time I got the feeling that he wanted to express his own version of what had happened to Vietnam since 1975, but feared that doing so would get him in trouble with the authorities, who could do him untold damage

It took me several visits to earn his trust but, when I had, he told me a story very far removed from the political orthodoxy. I have no way of verifying his account and I am sure that it was calculated to secure my sympathy but it rings true in its generality, if not necessarily in the detail.

Kiet and I were about the same age but had lived very different lives. The partition of Vietnam in 1954 had prompted his mother, a Catholic, to flee south, taking him with her. His father, a Viet Minh officer, had stayed in the north with Kiet's elder brother. This suggested two things to me: first, that they were a family of means, rather than peasantry, which made the division economically feasible; and that this was probably an arranged marriage where the marital bond was not strong.

Kiet prospered in the south and was offered a scholarship at an American university to study English. Having graduated, he returned to South Vietnam but was required to become a captain in the ARVN, acting as a translator between the American military advisors and the South Vietnamese troops. By this time he was married and owned a newly built apartment on the outskirts of Saigon.

By 1975 he was not important enough to be airlifted out but was interrogated by a colonel in the NVA (the North Vietnamese Army) who turned out to be his brother. How this happened he did not explain but the outcome reflected the paramountcy of political orthodoxy over familial ties. He was then sent for re-education, which, in his words, was nothing more than being dumped in the jungle somewhere close to Dien Bien Phu, with a group of others, all of whom were left to their own devices.

Eight years later, he was released and sent to Can Tho province, in the delta, as an agricultural labourer. What work he had was not enough to feed himself, so he made his way back, illegally, to Saigon and his wife, who told him to go away or she would report him to the authorities. He ended up as a cyclo driver. 'Where did you sleep?' 'On my cyclo.' When did you eat?' 'Whenever I had a fare.'

This story ended with a tirade against authority and Communism. Finally I understood the enigmatic statement he had made when I first met him: 'Do not believe in appearances.'

Two years later, I learned that a Vinataba delegation had finally gained permission to visit us in Singapore, an invitation that had been offered for at least that time. The interpreter was to be Kiet. I was anxious that this carefully constructed alliance could be derailed if Kiet chose to defect while in Singapore. I explained this to him. He laughed. 'You do not understand: I'm important to these people now—and I've got a new apartment and a girlfriend and a motorbike, so why would I want to throw all that away now, to live in Singapore?'

He came and I noticed how his relationship with his

bosses had changed. He remained as deferential as the culture required but he was no longer fearful. He had regained his status and his self-respect. When he went home with the rest of the delegation, maltreatment was now a memory, not a burning resentment.

I left Singapore in early 1991, which meant no more Vietnam. What I left was a country that still had no substantial inward investment, and remained a one-party state. The latter did not bother me much. Would a genuine democracy have done any better? I doubt it. A case can be made for the benign despot with the interests of the people at his or her heart. But attitudes had changed. A land of oppression had switched to one of opportunity; those who had the wherewithal grabbed it. And numbers had risen. Bicycles remained the main form of transport everywhere but now there were millions of them and in downtown Saigon they posed a potential hazard for pedestrians trying to cross the streets.

RETURNING TO VIETNAM at the end of 2016 I found Saigon unrecognisable. As my wife Kathy and I arrived by boat down the Saigon River, we saw a city of skyscrapers emerging from the morning mist, glistening in the rising sun. New-build apartment blocks and housing estates marked a massive expansion of the city, which was now connected by superhighways and soaring bridges over the river. An even larger population—75 million in 1998, over 100 million today—and an economy that thrived on manufacturing, construction and trade had produced a city that was visually indistinguishable from Bangkok, Kuala Lumpur or Singapore for a first-time visitor.

The journey from the Cambodian border through the Mekong Delta had shown that this society had changed. Everywhere there was activity: in the fields, ploughing and planting; in the markets, more shoppers, and vendors selling a cornucopia of food, cosmetics, medicines, clothing, toys, religious and festive fripperies, furniture, white goods and electronic equipment; wholesalers vending fifty different varieties of rice; on the river, fishing boats, dredgers, barges carrying building sand and coastal merchant ships going who knows where with who knows what?

What I was witnessing was the obverse of my first trip. This was now a consumer society, not one of famine and despair. It was also a place where the heavy hand of government had quietly been withdrawn, so that there was less interference and more public-sector facilitation. Vietnam was now a country of entrepreneurs.

Despite this, the new Saigon was a shock. Where had its history gone? On the old Rue Catinat, I had purchased rare colonial banknotes at a fraction of their catalogue value, and poor-quality silver-plate animal effigies from the shop-houses that lined both side of the street. All had disappeared, as had the food stalls that had stood in the gutters. It was now a pedestrianised street of boutiques in the standard lexicon of global urban design.

Our posh hotel was just off this street. It was fourteen storeys high, with a swimming pool on the roof, and it could have been anywhere. Below ground, a metro system was being built with Japanese help. From our bedroom window, we could see that a few unexceptional pre-revolutionary buildings had been left standing but they would clearly not last long. The major landmarks were, on the face of it, still intact but they served as concrete examples of a politically correct version of history.

Despite this, we managed to find the places we had known in 1989. One of these was the Continental, which seemed unchanged and was probably still government-owned, given its lack of guests. I had taken my family here for a grand reopening during which over-use of the generator had fused it for the rest of our stay. On that occasion, our younger flame-haired daughter had made friends with the little boy who opened the door to guests without their having a word in common; the children played under the table of the Vinataba boardroom on a felt floor-covering sprayed inaccurately with emulsion paint; the ancient vacuum cleaner did not have a lead long enough to reach the bed; and my wife had her measurements taken for an *ao dai*—Vietnam's national dress: a long, split tunic worn over silk trousers—which was presented to her on a Vinataba visit to Singapore a couple of months later.

However, the Bamboo Bar—where I had once negotiated to buy a replica embroidered waiter's shirt that had turned out first to be far too big and then far too small—had gone, as had the original restaurant where we ordered fried rice times five at every meal.

Across the street, the Caravelle now had an extra eight floors. The Rex had moved upmarket, its balcony bar much extended, its fish tanks removed, its smartly dressed waiters offering beer at ten times the old dollar price (but at least you got a saucer of nuts with it). As we returned to the lift I recognised Room 405. No point in asking to see it; only the number remained.

As somebody remarked at the time, fifty years of war had brought the people a Louis Vuitton shop with a Communist flag flying over it.

It forced me to acknowledge me that the nostalgia of a pensioner wanting to revisit his past is on a par with the vanity of vanities mocked in *Ecclesiastes*. The history of Vietnam, like Laos and Cambodia, in the latter half of the twentieth century was horrific. Better to bulldoze it to the ground and build anew. And that is what it is doing.

A FURTHER POSTSCRIPT. Three years after our 2016 trip, I visited

Vietnam again, this time crossing the Red River border from the Chinese province of Yunnan. The sense of relief as we went over the bridge was shared by all, and stayed with us over the following week, in the highlands around Sapa and then in Hanoi. We found China's surveillance society, supposedly built on the revived Confucian principles of harmony, order and meritocratic hierarchy, as stifling in both detail and principle as a Covid lockdown.

Max Hastings asserts that unaccountable one-party Communist régimes are, by definition, evil. That does not fit with my experience. Rigid Marxist orthodoxy brought Vietnam to the brink of existential collapse. *Do Moi* opened the gate for aspiration and the transformation has been extraordinary. Would democracy have done any better? The evidence in East Asia is that *dirigiste* régimes are a precursor to more open societies, not necessarily a permanent obstacle to them.

Today Vietnam is by and large content. Material advancement is the driver but not at the expense of its neighbours. The government is secure in power but admits its failings. It wants to eradicate corruption, and I am glad to have played a minor part in developing the practices necessary for it to do so. It may not be democratic in the Western sense of the word but it is in the service of its people and a firm but benevolent hand, like that of Lee Kuan Yew in Singapore and Syngman Ree in South Korea, can guide such a nation towards higher horizons. As our guide said, 'Vietnam is a one-party state which practises "flexible Communism".'

The first Vietnamese Professor of Archaeology, Tran Quoc Vuong of the University of Hanoi, ended his conversation with another interested Westerner in October 1989 by saying, 'The human way is always and must be between heaven and earth. We are animals, we are angels, we are both, we are neither. But when capitalism and socialism do meet, there will be a synthesis of all the perfumes of humankind from primitive times until the present—perfumes which include liberty, fraternity and equality.'[3]

What draws me to this quote are the metaphors that could only come from someone deeply embedded in the culture of their country. At the time his interviewer was as baffled as I would have been. Thirty years later, I find this a good approximation of the course that Vietnam has followed.

---

[3] Justin Wintle, *Romancing Vietnam: Inside the Boat Country*, Viking (1991), p.133.

CHAPTER 4
Cambodia: 2016
Exploitation

Cambodia completes my Indochina circle. My wife and I went there only once, travelling as tourists, and thus made contact only with those who looked after us.

Siem Reap is now the tourist capital and serves as the gateway to the twelfth-century temple complex of Angkor Wat. Our guide was Kiong, a tall and impressive man in his early forties. He had classical Khmer features: a broad nose, high cheekbones and full lips. He could have been a direct descendant of King Jayavarman VII whose visage, it is said, represents that of Buddha on all four corners of the Bayon temple he built. He who sees everything.

Once we and our fellow Western tourists were on the bus, Kiong wasted no time recounting what he remembered of the Khmer Rouge as a small child and revealing the anger that its devastating repression had instilled in him. He moved on to castigating the government: 'It is corrupt and controls everything and that is why we are poor. Thailand today has 28 million tourists; we have only 4.5 million. Teachers should be paid $1,000 a month, not $200.'

His sense of injustice extended also to us: 'You are ten times richer than we are,' he complained, underestimating quite considerably our relative wealth. As a guide, however, he was professional, knowledgeable and approachable. Perhaps he was just letting off steam because he knew we'd be sympathetic; or maybe he thought we needed to have our noses rubbed in a little guilt.

A string of modern hotels lines the road from the airport into Siem Reap. Ours was called a boutique hotel because it was smaller than most. The view from our room's balcony was of another boutique hotel across the road. Occasionally a tethered balloon could be seen rising behind it, hired out to provide aerial views of Angkor Wat beyond.

The hotel's hospitality drew on the Thai *wai* model, which was nothing more than a tourist ritual designed to encourage tips. All hotel staff wore exotic 'national' dress (never seen on the streets), were heavily made up and carried fixed smiles, remembering to keep eye contact as they bowed deeply, with palms together and fingers upwards.

There may be only 4.5 million tourists but they all come to Angkor. Its 'iconic' sites now resemble a 900-year-old theme park with no crowd control. It is impossible to take a good photograph because there are too many people in the way. Getting there means running the gauntlet of children selling knick-knacks: 'only one dollar'. Until they are seven, they play this as a game but after that it becomes a wheedling, insistent, importuning habit that turns them into dependants and you into their unwilling benefactor. As I wrote at the time, 'What I hate about this is casting kids into a victim mindset. They resent your not buying, without understanding that the more their resentment shows, the less inclination for you to buy—a sentiment more eloquently expressed by Geoff Dyer.[1] And this was only Day One.

We spent four days in Angkor Wat with a respected archaeologist/anthropologist. Through his focus on the past, we were able to appreciate the extraordinary skill of the country's craftsmen, the ingenuity of an irrigation system that allowed for three rice crops a year, with all its subsequent wealth, and the reason for temple structures being their only permanent buildings.

At about the same time as the building of Angkor Wat, Chartres Cathedral had been built on the only hill in a flat

---

[1] Geoff Dyer, *Yoga for People who Cannot be Bothered to Do It*, Canongate (2012), pp. 39–42.

landscape. I had always felt that this was not a homage to Jesus but a demonstration of the power of the king; Chartres dominates its surroundings and its size makes it not just imposing but threatening for those who live within its shadow. Angkor seemed another version of this, an impression reinforced for me by the fact that successive kings built additional temples, purportedly in honour of their religion (which switched from Hinduism to Buddhism over time), all conflating the divine with the king, and very much to the latter's benefit. Temporal power was reinforced by the spiritual and that perpetuated the myth that absolute rule was God-given. The Sun King would be another French analogy.[2]

As a result of successive grandiose projects, Angkor is enormous. We covered less than a quarter of it in our four days, but that was enough: we were templed out, particularly as the urchin street vendors were to be found in the most obscure locations. Angkor, disappointingly, is no longer surrounded by impenetrable jungle. Tourism has cut down the trees. I suppose I expected nothing more and nothing less from such an internationally famous UNESCO world heritage site.

THE REST OF our Cambodian travels were made by boat. Tonle Sap is a natural reservoir that takes the overflow from the Mekong in the rainy season. It is navigable only when full, which might explain why our journey to Phnom Penh was under cloudy skies and nearly constant rain. Tonle Sap may have a romantic ring about it but is in fact just a very large brown lake with no visible horizon. A few trees raise their trunks from the water but there is nothing else to see. At night the boat's lights attract swarms of insects that coat the decks with their dead and must be regularly swept overboard.

---

[2] Meeker (ibid) pp. 170–193.

Our boat was a converted rice barge, a ponderous vessel with cramped accommodation. As a fellow passenger said, 'A bit like *Death on the Nile* but without the luxury.' It took four days to get to Phnom Penh but the crew were cheerful, helpful and friendly, something of an antidote to Kiong's resentment.

Phnom Penh is where I started to make some sense out of this experience. Before that it had just been a not-very-enjoyable tourist trip, which I had prepared for by reading Joel Brinkley's *Cambodia's Curse*.[3] What I found was a damning indictment of the Hun Sen régime, and my first instinct was to dismiss it as a relentless search for all that was wrong with the country, made from the self-righteous heights of Western liberalism. There were several reasons for my scepticism: the government was financially broke, and what limited resources it had were spent on repressing opposition. In the absence of any competent governance, it was hardly surprising that mutual back-scratching had become the accepted way of getting things done. With over 2,000 NGOs, all with their honourable but specific agendas, it is hardly surprising that Brinkley diagnosed Cambodia as inefficient. Whether liberal democracy might have been more appropriate for a people with no experience of it, I very much doubt.

Visiting Phnom Penh made me think that maybe Brinkley had a point. The city is now home to 3 million of a total population of 15 million, which gives the lie to the claim that the country is 90 per cent ignorant peasants, who need to be controlled, for their own good, by an autocratic government. It is also not a very pleasant place to be in. The waterfront on the Mekong has new shops, bars, hotels and restaurants—but step off the main boulevards at night and you're back in the parasitical economy of the 1970s, when the Americans were in

---

[3] Joel Brinkley, *Cambodia's Curse: The Modern History of a Troubled Land*, Perseus Book Group (2011).

charge: hundreds of girly bars, most without customers, with a few portly middle-aged tourists scouting around—men you'd not want to be seen with, let alone converse with. While my Scots Presbyterian background may have influenced my attitude, this suggested that, for its poor citizens, any sense of a moral compass had disappeared. It was here that Gary Glitter was finally arrested.

The Royal Palace has been preserved, with a new *stupa* dedicated to Prince Sihanouk, who is now portrayed as father of the nation, having valiantly resisted the excesses of both Communism and American imperialism. In truth Norodom Sihanouk regarded the Cambodians as children to be ruled over autocratically and unpredictably ('mercurial' is the most common adjective used to describe him), while brutally suppressing any democratic opposition.[4,5] He had been ousted in a coup in 1970 and fled, returned as head of state in 1975, was put under house arrest in 1976, was freed by the Vietnamese in 1979, fled again and was restored as king in 1993. In 2004 he was succeeded by his son, Norodom Sihamoni, whose purpose was to act as a symbol of the continuity of the great Khmer Empire, to distract the populace from their sorry state and provide a fig leaf of respectability to the Hun Sen régime.

It is a reasonable assumption that after the Khmer Rouge was overthrown in 1979, life must have got better, because under an unhinged isolationist philosophy that sought to return Cambodia to its historic agrarian roots and ended up massacring about a third of its population in a little over three years, it could not have been worse. It is the only holocaust in modern history to be inflicted by a regime on its own people,

---

[4] David P. Chandler, *The Tragedy of Cambodian History: Politics, War and Revolution since 1945*, Yale University Press (1991).
[5] See also Meeker (ibid) pp. 141–169.

except perhaps for that of Stalin's purges. It was supported by the Chinese Communist Party and its then leader, Mao Zedong.

The transition from the Khmer Rouge to Hun Sen's régime was long and messy and not helped by the UN Security Council, where both the US and China used their veto to create deadlock. What emerged at the end was a one-party state without any aspirations for its people but with the staging of elections to sanitise the continuing flow of overseas aid from countries wishing to be assured of Cambodia's democratic credentials.

The bespectacled Hun Sen seems like an avuncular leader but in fact wears his glasses because he lost the sight of one eye while serving in the Khmer Rouge. He fled to Vietnam under the threat of the killing fields as the increasingly paranoid Pol Pot turned on his trusted lieutenants. (It is claimed that most of those killed in the last year before the Vietnamese invasion were Khmer Rouge cadres.) Hun Sen maintains his dominance by disbarring opposition parties, rigging elections and assassinating political opponents, normally in unidentifiable drive-by shootings which saves the charade of having to bring the perpetrators to trial. He has no identifiable political philosophy except that of remaining in power and garnering the riches that come with it. Unsurprisingly he has proved reluctant to call former Khmer Rouge leaders to account for their atrocities; he was one himself.

In Phnom Penh, two landmarks of the Khmer Rouge era survive, because recognition of the horrors of the Khmer Rouge régime helps oil outside aid and compassion, though the current régime would like to sweep both under the carpet.

The first is the old Tuol Sleng high school converted by the Khmer Rouge into a prison with a notorious interrogation centre. It is in the middle of town and overlooked by other buildings. As the entire urban population had been force-marched into the country to begin life again as revolutionary peasants, its being overlooked was not a concern. Now known as the Tuol Sleng Museum of Genocide, it contains photographs of all who were brought here, evidence of an obsession with record-keeping reminiscent of the Nazis, but otherwise its rooms are empty, save for some of the apparatus that was used to extract confessions. An interrogator would sit behind a high-school desk, a suspect would be strapped to an iron bedstead. Each interrogation room had an electric socket wired to the bedstead and prisoners were electrocuted when their answers were judged unsatisfactory—or, presumably, for any other reason or none at all. Prisoners were also waterboarded, beaten, burned, suffocated, cut, mutilated and used for obtaining body parts. The dormitories at Tuol Sleng had crudely constructed dividing walls within each classroom. Bunks were stacked five high. Each had shackle attachments.

On liberation there were only eleven prisoners left alive, every other inmate having been executed. The survivors now make a living from being trundled out to answer tourists' questions. I do not doubt either their motive or sincerity, but to witness it seems like a tale told once too often.

The second landmark is the Killing Fields of Choeung Ek, about a thirty-minute tuk-tuk drive from the centre. Those found guilty of crimes against the state, in effect all of them, would be transported here for execution. At the centre of the site is a tower, filled entirely with human skulls; around them, the ground is full of bones brought to the surface by the rainy season. For reason of economy, executions were carried out in the simplest way possible. Adults had their heads stove in with shovels, children were simply smashed head first against a tree trunk.

To get any sense of the Khmer Rouge régime, a visit to both places is recommended, but it's no picnic. It was here that I began to formulate the unoriginal thought that atrocities like this depend on leaders categorising the enemy by what they are thought to represent collectively, erasing recognition of them as individuals. This is a theme I shall return to later.

Our trip to Choeung Ek was a private excursion, not included in the tour itinerary. Our tuk-tuk driver was awaiting us when we came out. It was a Sunday, theoretically a day of rest. In the tuk-tuk I faced backwards, towards the traffic behind. I saw a sea of blank faces on bicycles, mopeds and in cars, concentrating only on the road ahead. In poor countries, tourists are usually greeted with at least a little feigned enthusiasm, but here we were ignored—as was everyone, in fact. It seemed that Cambodians had retreated into a private world, having learned that this was the safest way to survive, a reminder of Vietnam in 1988.

The Khmer Rouge régime was a living hell. Personal accounts are readily available in pirated editions at any bookstall.[6] There are several accounts by Westerners of the victory of the Khmer Rouge, all harrowing, including one by Jon Swain,[7] an acquaintance in Laos. The definitive book is by François Bizot.[8] He was the only Westerner to be captured by the Khmer Rouge and released. His interrogator was Duch, who moved on to be commander of the high-school prison referred to above. Duch was finally convicted of crimes against humanity and sentenced in old age to life imprisonment, as have been a couple of the surviving higher echelons who are well past their sell-by date and therefore useful fodder to throw to the international community.

For Cambodians, life has improved, but by much less than it could have. Their government has failed to address the

---

[6] One such is Loung Ung, *First They Killed My Father: A Daughter of Cambodia Remembers*, Harper Collins (2000).

[7] John Swain, *River of Time*, Heinemann (1995).

[8] François Bizot, *The Gate*, The Harvill Press (2003).

trauma engendered by the Khmer Rouge and done nothing to provide the necessities for transition from a peasant society to a prosperous agrarian one. Tourism provides better returns for the hotel owners and government ministers, in the form of *baksheesh*, of course. In consequence, tour guides are paid quite well, teachers very little and peasants nothing at all.

While I was there, the *Cambodian Times* (an English-language newspaper) ran two headlines: about the release of four Hun Sen bodyguards after less than a year in gaol, having been convicted of grievous bodily harm against two opposition MPs, and the government's decision to expel a UN agency on the grounds that it continued to criticise the exile of Sam Rainsy, a veteran opposition leader. I suppose that this paper continued to be published because few Khmer could read it, and because shutting it down would only lead to complaints from the international community.

Despite being officially a multi-party democracy, Hun Sen and his party were the only politicians visible during our journey through Cambodia, with offices and billboards in every village. In Phnom Penh there were those who were happy to reach an accommodation with this régime to make money. On a one-hour journey across the city I spotted six brand-new Rolls-Royces. Patronage of the régime makes the nomenclatura untouchable. I saw no evidence that they had any interest in the population at large.

I suppose this explains the blank faces in the Sunday traffic. People must feel that Cambodia is not their land, because it all belongs to the government. This feeling was reinforced by a visit to a granite outcrop near Chau Doc on the Vietnam Cambodian border (incidentally the place where an American official first saw evidence of Khmer Rouge brutality: every village in sight was burning).[9] On the Vietnamese

---

[9] Chandler (ibid).

side, every piece of land was cultivated, sturdy houses stood beside well-kept roads, and adults could be seen at work or travelling into or out of town while children made their way to school: it was a hive of activity. On the Cambodian side there was just a swamp.

Initially I imagined that what I was seeing was just the deadening effect of a repressive régime and said so to a friend who had been HM Ambassador in the region. 'We stopped giving aid to Cambodia because none of it got to its intended recipients,' he told me. 'In Vietnam, about 90 per cent got through. In Cambodia, if you are a peasant farmer, there is also no point in improving your land. If you do, it just gets confiscated by the ruling party.'

This is, I think, a just indictment of the Cambodian government but not of its people, whom I never got to know. With more time and involvement I am sure I would have had access to stories and narratives from many with different perspectives. Instead I have had to rely on the views of others, almost all Western. I am left with the image of the blank faces on that tuk-tuk ride.

Some claim that Cambodia is stuck in a collective PTSD but, unless this is inherited, it should not apply to the over 50 per cent of the population who had not yet been born when the Khmer Rouge was overthrown. A better explanation may be that the Hun Sen régime is merely continuing to exercise the right to absolute rule that once belonged to the ancient Khmer kings.

IN CONCLUSION THE Indochina War has left the three countries in very different situations. Vietnam is now a fast-emerging economy, engaging with the world at large—the consequence of its history as a seaboard mercantile state. Laos remains wedded to the tradition of the path of least resistance and seems content to remain a backwater. Cambodia is a damaged society and, despite being the only one of the three which is not a one-party Communist state (at least in theory), is the most despotic of them all. All political opponents to Hun Sen were banned from participating in the 2018 elections, which of course he won, again, with an overwhelming majority.

A theme of this narrative is that the legacy of history has a very long tail. A travel book first published in 1951 is prescient about the different paths these countries have embarked on, once free to make their own choices.[10] You can interpret this as fatalism, or the playing out regional psychologies, or the imposition or indoctrination of fixed habits of mind, or as a failure to grasp the innovations and freedoms of the twenty-first century—or simply that the condition that Indochina finds itself in reflects its own exceptionality. But step back. The Indochina War began in Paris, Washington, Moscow and Beijing, not in Saigon, Phnom Penh and Vientiane. The most destructive war in the latter half of the twentieth century began and was continued in foreign capitals. To blame Asia for the effects of foreign interference would be as contemptible as any type of victim-blaming.

In other circumstances, Indochina would have merited little more than the occasional mention in the foreign pages of our broadsheet newspapers, rather than headlines. In the West we have enjoyed over seventy years of peace and seen our living standards rise to levels undreamed of by our parents and grandparents. Part of that is explained by our fighting our wars on other people's territory. Indochina took the brunt of it. It is something of a miracle that these states survived at all.

---

[10] Norman Lewis, *A Dragon Apparent: Travels in Cambodia, Laos and Vietnam*, Eland (1982)

Chapter 5
Myanmar: 1989 to 2018
Back to the Beginning

Myanmar used to be called Burma and many in the West still call it that informally. Defence of the old name arose partly through custom and familiarity but partly also because the new name had been invented by a military dictatorship which was, according to Western media, wrong in everything it did. Name changes by unsavoury régimes elsewhere have been received with far less opposition, either because the régimes in question were too important to upset or too unimportant to bother with.

Changing a country's name makes very little difference to the lives of its inhabitants and is often an indication of the bankruptcy of ideas of its government. In the case of Burma, the adoption of the name 'Myanmar' only gained notoriety because the events of 1988 made the country into a *cause célèbre*, catapulting Aung San Suu Kyi into global consciousness as the personification of a democratic movement. When she failed to stand by the Rohingya, Myanmar became a pariah state again, severely tarnishing her reputation. Back in gaol, she has regained iconic status as the symbol of the democratic resistance to military rule. But it is not as simple as that. Nor is the name change, which does have the virtue of not conflating the name of most of the population, the Burmans, with the state. It now also has historical legitimacy.

HAVING VISITED ON only a few occasions over thirty years, I had not been intending to write about Myanmar at all, but witnessing the changes since 1989, when I first visited, to 2014 when I first went back, and ending with another journey from which I returned days before writing this, I realise that I have an eye-witness perspective which is of some value.

In 1988 Burma hit the headlines with huge popular protests demanding the return of democracy; the protesters were suppressed with indiscriminate gunfire and mass arrests which in turn gave birth to a new round of armed opposition to the military dictatorship.

The events of 1988 did, however, foster a change of direction for the country's dictatorship. On seizing power in 1962, Ne Win had embarked on an isolationist policy which effectively closed off Burma from the outside world: foreign companies were expelled; Indian immigrants were deported (even if they had been there for generations); the army (Tatmadaw) took control of the economy; and all available funds were diverted towards the twin aims of imposing peace on a country that had been in civil war for decades, and of entrenching the rulers. The result was an economic disaster.

It could have been otherwise. At the end of the Second World War, pundits had predicted that the Asian cities with the best economic prospects were Shanghai, Saigon and Rangoon. In the last thirty years the first two of these have finally realised their potential. Rangoon has not. By 1988, Burma had sunk into the category of Most Impoverished Nation.

I have often wondered why the foot soldiers of the Tatmadaw obeyed their officers and shot down their fellow citizens indiscriminately in the streets: after all, what they were putting down was not an armed uprising but merely a mass protest by civilians. I now have a hypothesis for why the troops behaved as they did, but will leave that till the end.

The isolationist policies of Ne Win's dictatorship extended to absolute state control of information. Different perspectives on political science were simply not available. Burma's pre-colonial history was unremittingly one of autocratic rule by revered or weak kings, the difference being how successful they were on the battlefield—not that dissimilar to English history as taught in my schooldays. In Burma, the natural order of things could not even recognise concepts like representative democracy. One Burmese analyst has even suggested that the arrival of bootleg VHS videos and their depiction of luxurious lifestyles may have been a driver of the 1988 protests.[1] In the land of the blind, the one-eyed man is king.

In line with this myopic perspective, the new government was called the State Law and Order Restitution Committee or SLORC, about the ugliest acronym one could think of. This demonstrates the naïvety of a régime that had been inward-looking for forty years and its absolute belief that it alone knew what was best for its people. In turn, the Tatmadaw became almost a theocracy, bending only with the wind of self-interest while remaining convinced of its legitimacy as ruler. Burma has, at its best, only even been the most sham of democracies.

Ne Win's retirement provided an alternative: that of opening up the economy in the hope that economic growth would placate the populace.

I was now working for BAT—British American Tobacco—and it was at this point that I met Tay Choon Hai of Singapore (see next chapter). Mr. Tay was BAT's general export agent and he came to me with a proposal that BAT resuscitate the country's moribund tobacco industry. He had cultivated important relationships within the Myanmar military and his suggestion was not one that I could refuse, not least because it would have caused him to lose face. In the middle of the rainy season in 1989, I boarded another Thai Airways flight and flew from Bangkok to Mingaladon Airport.

My first visit to Vietnam had been cathartic and my return to Laos nostalgic but the one to Myanmar was just depressing.

---

[1] Christina Fink, *Living Silence in Burma: Surviving Under Military Rule*, 2nd edition, Zed Books (2009).

Mine was the only international flight. The airport terminal (still the domestic terminal) was, like Tan Son Nhut, decrepit, mouldy and dim but there were no waiting crowds, few cars and not many bicycles. Arriving at nightfall we were ferried in the rain to the Inya Lake Hotel, a Soviet jerry-built dormitory that served indifferent food at exorbitant prices and was off limits to Burmese without connections.

It was still raining the following morning. A Burmese with a care-worn face and rheumy eyes introduced himself with only the faintest glimmer of a smile on his downturned mouth. He wore the traditional *longyi* (a tightly wrapped sarong of near floor length) which restricted his walk to a shuffle, making him look like an old and rather sad penguin. We were escorted to a private house in an exclusive residential enclave. It was spacious but uncared for. The last coat of whitewash must have been applied several rainy seasons back. Black mould streaked down from broken drainpipes, and creepers had taken hold of the eaves and were now threatening to encase the building, like the strangler figs of Angkor Wat. The sky lowered with a thick and even blanket of raincloud. Inside, a few low-wattage lightbulbs emphasised the gloom of a house that was marooned in the 1950s and gradually reverting to the earth it had come from. Though there must have been servants' quarters, we appeared to be on our own.

Nothing happened for hours and there was nothing for us to do—no mobiles, no internet, no laptops. Our host, whose deference failed to disguise his misery, wandered off, now and then, before returning with a wan smile and collapsing back into an uncomfortable chair. Either the landlines did not work or nobody bothered to answer them. We just had to wait until we were summoned.

Eventually we were called to a dinner on a concrete reproduction of a legendary Burmese war boat permanently 'anchored' on Inya Lake. Our hosts all wore uniforms with the number of medal ribbons on their jackets providing a reasonably accurate indication of their seniority—as did their girth. These were the only fat men I met in Burma. I sat opposite one with five rows of medals. The drink of choice was Johnny Walker. The rate at which this was consumed suggested that these gentlemen regarded a good night out as a recreation of a military mess evening.

It was a stiff meal, not helped by my lukewarm response to their invitation that I join them for a round of golf, their other passion. Looking back, I was piqued. I had wasted a whole day waiting for this meeting and they seemed to have little interest in talking business—but this was another Western delusion; in these societies the priority was to find out who you were dealing with before you dealt with what they wanted. When I plucked up the courage to ask what BAT could do for them, I was told that there were magnificent opportunities for foreign investors. What these were remained unspoken, however. I had yet to pass the test. It was all very polite and the parting salutations were designed to offend nobody. But that was that.

The following day was devoted to sightseeing and we headed to the Shwedagon pagoda, arriving in the evening.[2] Our minder became more animated. We were allowed into the foreigners' lift but were advised to ascend the stairs if we wanted to experience the pagoda properly. Doing so we were surrounded by Burmese at their devotions. The minder explained the rituals and etiquette. I took it slowly and found myself moving from a world of frustration and impatience into something soothing and calming, a reminder that there

---

[2] The Shwedagon is the most sacred Buddhist pagoda in Myanmar, believed to contain relics of the four previous Buddhas of the current cycle of time (calculated as 4,320 million human years).

were other things to appreciate in this world than the preoccupations of a striving executive. Gradually a little light broke through the day's worsening mood of depression.

That change of atmosphere permeated everyone present. The most important Buddhist shrine outside India inspired reverence and served to remind the Burmese that there was something above their daily travails. Perhaps this too contributed to their forbearance. It reminded me of Laos. During that visit, Shwedagon was the only place I saw a Burmese smile.

Everywhere else it was miserable. Look at somebody and they would turn their eyes away. Their revolution had failed and life had got worse. Downtown Rangoon had been caught in a time warp, with colonial buildings showing decades of neglect as a few ancient British trucks, buses and cars rumbled past.

Tallying up the pros and cons of investing here did not take long. Everything was negative. The generals had no conception of the needs of a commercial organisation, expected a cut of all profits, waffled on meaninglessly about JVs (joint ventures), failed to provide any investment guarantees, and offered nothing in terms of fixed assets or technical manpower, all in the context of a currency that was unconvertible and subject to bizarre and unexpected decrees, such as the one that demonetised banknotes that were not divisible by nine. Foreign investment was not government policy, just an idea dreamed up by some generals over a glass or two of Johnny Walker, as a means of getting some money in.

They had not considered that FTSE-100 companies might be concerned about their reputation, nor that they were now regarded as a pariah régime by the outside world. I therefore suggested to Tay Choon Hai that if he wanted to pursue the opportunity he had brought to me, I would have no objection, and we would help, as long as our involvement remained under the radar.

The investment model was that the military would provide the permits for foreign investments in return for a substantial equity stake. The advantage for them was that they would gain future revenue from dividends which, in turn, would reinforce their monopoly on foreign income. Given their reputation, only Thai and Chinese investors were prepared to play ball, though this was not uncommon in developing economies in the region. To potential Western investors, there was usually a moral question about whether their funding would benefit the country as a whole or only those holding the purse strings. The Chinese, who dominate the Thai economy, were not encumbered by such concerns. Quite what arrangement Mr Tay and BAT arrived at, if anything at all, is unknown to me.

I had hoped that this was the end of the matter. It wasn't. I had not known that the chairman of BAT had been born in Burma. Although shipped off to guardians and boarding school in Australia at the age of three—a revealing insight into why he behaved as he did—he was anxious to revisit the country of his birth.

He seemed not to share my reservations about the régime during his twenty-four hours in Burma. He got on well with the generals but steered clear of making any commitments. The highlight of his trip was finding his father's name on the list of captains of the Rangoon Golf Club, where he enjoyed a round with the military élite, as fanatical about golf as they were. The evening dinner, again on the concrete boat, was more convivial than before, and his hosts turned up to bid him farewell at Mingaladon Airport the following morning. I went back to Singapore, forgot about Burma and then got transferred back home.

In the following twenty years, Burma only occasionally aroused my interest; I felt no connection to it. In Laos and Vietnam I had invested time, energy and perhaps a part of my soul; any commercial ambitions we might have had in Burma, by contrast, became a cycle of glimmers of hope followed by renewed disappointment. Aung San Suu Kyi was awarded the Nobel Peace Prize and then put under house arrest again. Elections were held and the results either rigged or ignored. A new constitution was promised but the commission entrusted with its creation was boycotted or suspended. Burma was admitted to ASEAN (the Association of Southeast Asian Nations) and two months later violently suppressed a protest led by Buddhist monks. The West imposed sanctions.[3]

Those were the stark headlines but was day-to-day reality any different? When an opportunity arose to join an expert-led tour of Burma in 2013, we found the invitation impossible to resist. What had happened to this dismal place? Had the country opened up to the outside world?

The first surprise was on arrival. A glossy new terminal at Mingaladon, rebranded as Yangon International Airport, now served international visitors. Immigration and customs facilities, in themselves useful markers of the state of a nation, were efficient and courteous. The airport road was now a traffic jam. Billboards dominated every intersection. New buildings were under construction. An entire infrastructure for servicing tourist needs had been created from nothing. Our hotel lived up to the five-star standard that it claimed. But the biggest surprise was that people were smiling.

Our tour leader was Sydney, chair of the national tour-guide association and an open critic of the military. His parents had been political activists and both he and they had suffered in consequence. It was he who gently pointed out that what is seen on the surface is not necessarily what is going on underneath. I noticed that recognisable Western brand names were conspicuous by their absence. None of the hotels was part of an international chain.

---

[3] Rory Maclean, *Under the Dragon*, Tauris Parke Paperbacks (2008).

A glimpse into this labyrinth occurred when we reached a hotel in Pagan. The staff were gathered outside the foyer and failed to express any delight at our arrival. Sydney disappeared to investigate. On his return he reported that the staff had attempted to go on strike and had now been dismissed, with the ringleader arrested and put in gaol. Sydney then arranged for us to be shown to our rooms and before excusing himself again to deal with more important matters.

Later he explained that the strike had been called because the employees received only a dollar a day and all tips were kept by the management. A hotel guest would be charged $30 per half hour for a massage but the masseuse would only get the basic wage, no matter how long she worked.

The following morning an army colonel arrived by sleek speedboat from Mandalay and attempted to browbeat the staff before Sydney intervened. He spent the whole day in negotiations. How this was resolved I do not know, save that the strike leader was released and restored to his job and the others went back to work, seemingly happy with the outcome. The colonel, however, was not best pleased; he scowled at us and stomped off to his speedboat, vowing vengeance, I assumed.

There is a prison visible from the road to Inle Lake in the Shan Hills. Sydney explained that it housed thousands of inmates who had been imprisoned without charge and whose only hope of release was the whim of the government. Most had been arrested because of who they were, not what they had done. There was no independent judicial process and so they just sat there. This was how it had been since independence. If you were a student, a political activist, a member of an ethnic minority or just somebody the authorities did not like, this is where you would end up.

For those who managed to stay out of jail, life was certainly better than it had been twenty years earlier, as it was for

Sydney, who had achieved sufficient prominence to inure himself from arbitrary arrest. Freedom in Myanmar was not an absolute right but did at least provide a bit of breathing space. For most of the population, this was the first time since independence that they could experience anything approaching what we in the West would regard as normality and it was a pleasure to be among them. They were full of hope and welcomed us with broad smiles, no doubt made even broader by the prospect of making another dollar from us—and that was also uplifting. They were seizing the chance to build a better life. From then on, I became emotionally invested with these people and started to follow the country's progress with more interest.

Five years later, things got better; then they got worse.[4] The 2015 elections had given the National League for Democracy—the NLD—an absolute majority in both houses of parliament, despite having a constitution that guaranteed the military a minority of seats that could be used to block anything that restricted its role as guardian of the nation's security. Aung San Suu Kyi was debarred from occupying an official role because she had been married to a foreigner and was thus regarded as not a reliable national citizen. The role of Special Counsellor was invented for her and passed off as the equivalent of Prime Minister. Another NLD representative with purer blood lines was made president, a largely titular role. To the outside world this looked like democracy. Myanmar now had a free press and a supposedly independent judiciary. The forces of reform were in the ascendant. But the military was not a spent force. It had significant economic interests to protect and the backing of the constitution in guaranteeing its role.

---

[4] Benedict Rogers, *Burma: A Nation at the Crossroads*, Ebury Publishing (2015).

What led to the Rohingya crisis is debateable but the army's actions in forcing over 740,000 people to cross the border into Bangladesh would seem as clear a case of ethnic cleansing as one could find—another example of objecting to who one was, not what they had done. Aung San Suu Kyi's failure to condemn the army's actions severely damaged her international reputation; the military was already beyond contempt but she had been Southeast Asia's icon of democracy.

Since then it has only got worse. In theory there is a free press but any journalist who questions the military can be prosecuted for bringing the institution into disrepute. There were two celebrated cases of journalists accused of this offence. The first was given a long prison sentence; the second was remanded for trial. Aung San Suu Kyi responded that this was simply the due process of the law.

I find it difficult to believe that one who had previously shown huge resolve and personal sacrifice merely abandoned her principles. Maybe her silence reflects the uncomfortable compromise between her and the military. She had a title but no official position and was certainly not the de-facto leader that the Western press ascribed to her. If she had had more power, would she have acted in the Rohingya's support? As things stand, she has not given any sign that she would.

In October 2018 we arrived in Burma again, this time in Mandalay. The last time I had been there, I had revelled in the new sense of optimism that we had encountered. Now I was not so sure. It turned out that the Burmese had become equally equivocal but more pragmatic in their expectations.

An unscheduled visit to a village on the plains down muddy pathways revealed the reality. It had power lines but they were not connected to the grid. The villagers' expectation was that we could provide the $10,000 necessary to install a substation—but that would go straight to the Tatmadaw, of course.

Another side to this visit was more encouraging: there was an emerging compact between Burmans and their ethnic-minority neighbours which was undermining the Tatmadaw argument that only military force could keep the country united. Ironically this compact had been created by the development of a national language. Only twenty years earlier, members of one of the hill tribes crossing from one side of a mountain range would have been unable to converse with people they met on the other side.[5] But now everybody was taught Burmese, as ceasefire agreements had been reached—at least in principle, if not in practice—with all dissenting minority groups.

To understand this, it is helpful to make use of the recent concept of 'zonia', which applies to all the mountainous borders of Southeast Asia. Simply put, it means looking at a map horizontally, rather than from above. The more-established Burmans, Lao, Vietnamese, Thais and Chinese occupy the lowlands; other ethnic groups, arriving later, have to occupy higher latitudes. Each successive wave of immigration involves another shift in population in the zonia hierarchy. These groups come from different ethnic and language groups and have moved because of displacement. They have no interest in central government because, as minorities, they have no investment in it and therefore expect nothing from it. Their sense of self comes instead from their language, tribal myths, customs and social systems; even their clothing acts as a way of differentiating themselves from their neighbours. Typically they are subsistence farmers and in some cases continue to grow rice as the main crop, despite being moved to higher elevations. The extraordinary feat of terracing on 60-degree mountain slopes in Southeast Asia is their legacy. Not

---

[5] Pascal Khoo Twee, *From the Land of Green Ghosts*, Harper Collins (2002).

only is this backbreaking work but also subject to the law of diminishing returns. Three rice crops a year are the norm in irrigated valleys. Above 1,600 meters only one is possible. Above 2,200 meters, rice will not grow at all.

As the market economy continues to develop and education expands the horizons of younger generations, there are more lucrative opportunities. Even labouring pays more. Increasingly these high terraces are farmed by grandparents who also take on the role of guardians of their offspring's children, while their parents are making cash elsewhere.

At the same time, social attitudes are shifting. When I was first in Laos, the generic word for hill tribes was *miao*, which roughly translated as 'barbarian'. When we asked our local Burman guide if she would consider marrying into a different ethnic group, she said, 'Of course,' and insisted that it was her decision whom she married, not her parents'. Another guide was Indian but had a Shan grandmother. A third, Shan by ethnicity, had taken a Chinese as his fifth wife.

The upside of all this, throughout these borderlands of Burma, Laos, Vietnam and China, is that in the future, everyone will have a vested interest in the state they happen to live in, taking from it but also giving to it, to a much larger extent that they currently do. The downside is that the allegiances, customs and costumes of these various ethnic groups will merge and disperse so that, in a generation or so, all that will be left is folkloric shows put on for tourists.

Five years earlier, the Burmese seemed to feel that they were emerging into the light of freedom; they were now more circumspect. When asked about the Rohingya crisis, our guide expounded at length on an incompatible series of excuses for the actions of the government, while trying to maintain the fiction that Myanmar was a peaceful democratic country. This was made worse by her obvious discomfort in what she was saying. There was a visible tension in her effort to retain her belief in freedom and respect for others and her acceptance of her subordination to the authorities.

What was clear was that negative coverage in the world's media had dramatically reduced tourist numbers. In 2013 it had been difficult to find a hotel room. Five years later, we met not a single Western tourist group when staying in Pwin-Oo-Ling (Maymo), the once-British hill station above the plains of Mandalay. This impression was confirmed by our local guides. In an emotional farewell, our sweet, intelligent, naïve and determined young guide implored us to come back.

At the time I found her entreaties moving and persuasive. But things changed with the February 2021 coup, which was denounced by the world—but not by China (which described it as a 'cabinet reshuffle'), Thailand (another sham democracy geared towards protecting the interests of the élite) or Cambodia (ditto). Chinese and Thai investors, in which the bone-headed generals are silent partners, see democracy as a threat to their financial interests.

The military coup proved that democracy in Myanmar was always a sham. The Tatmadaw is the largest army in Southeast Asia with over 400,000 men at arms. The military encampments spread 50 kms out of Rangoon and 20 kms from Ne Pwe Daw, the new capital. Since independence in 1948 it has fought white- and red-flag Communists, ethnic militias, nationalist Chinese armies and drug lords, in the name of protecting national integrity.[6] It has also become inordinately rich through its control of investment. That process, and the history that proceeds it, suggests that the Tatmadaw considers itself not just the protector of the nation but a class apart, and the main beneficiary of the nation's riches. It has become a dynasty. No wonder Tatmadaw soldiers shoot civil-

---

[6] Norman Lewis, *Golden Earth: Travels in Burma*, Eland (1983), originally Jonathan Cape (1952).

ians if they do not behave; they preserve their position by keeping the mass population subservient and fearful.

History tells us that stasis of this kind will eventually create so much societal tension that it falls apart, but rarely without major conflict. The tragedy of Myanmar is that Aung San Suu Kyi and the West imagined that it was possible to create a democracy in partnership with a military dynasty that had vested political, social and economic interests that it was unwilling to forego. They were very wrong.

CHAPTER 6
Singapore: 1987 to 2009
From Small Island to Nation State

For some in post-Brexit Britain, Singapore has become a role model. Described as a flawed democracy by those Western think tanks who like to rank these things, Singapore has been ruled by the People's Action Party since breaking away from Malaysia in 1965. Officially, at least, it has abided by democratic protocols, holding free elections regularly and quietly using the courts to sideline those who supported one racial group over another from standing for election. Though Malays, Chinese and Indians remain separate in custom, culture and beliefs, the state has been impartial.

The architect of this was Lee Kuan Yew. He was by profession a lawyer and by conviction a gradualist and not a revolutionary. One might accuse him of arrogance and paternalism, but he proved to be an astute judge of the condition of his proto-nation and guided it through its development by an even-handed treatment of its racial mix and an economic and social policy that created a common focus on wealth creation. This was *dirigiste* in style and narrowed the envelope of acceptable public debate. Once the prime objective of personal enrichment had become the leitmotif of the nation, he began to loosen the social if not the political chains, a policy continued by his elder son, Lee Hsieng Loong. Singapore's GDP per capita is the world's second highest (Britain's is 28th);[1] it is the only state in Asia to enjoy a triple-A credit rating; one in six householders are US dollar millionaires; and it continues to enjoy strong economic growth. There is now even an opposition MP.

Is this all a tribute to Singapore's autocratic government?

---

[1] www.worldpopulationreview.com (2022).

Yes, though it was also a feature of economic growth in countries such as Japan, South Korea, Taiwan and Finland, where such policies used to be defended as protecting infant industries. All these nations' governments were driven by an ambition to improve the material wealth of their citizens.

Since such a model has provided a remarkable turnaround in fortunes for Singapore, could it work in the West, as some have advocated? I doubt it. The entire political and cultural background is different, and Singapore at independence had an average per-capita annual income of $500. Britain, at least, is in a very different situation.

I was resident in Singapore roughly in the middle of this transformation from colony to supercity. At the time, the country's ex-colonial masters were still treated to a show of deference. I lived in a grand house on the most expensive residential street, was a member of the best clubs, had a bevy of domestic servants and a suitably expensive car in which a chauffeur drove me to work, and enjoyed a network of well-connected contacts which gave me, as a foreigner, privileged access to all but the highest levels of Singaporean society. Admittedly, much of this was a legacy of keeping up appearances. Many of the Singaporeans I met were earning a lot more than I was. Still, there were enough expatriates around to maintain the fiction that we were still in control.

My job was to run a tobacco business founded in 1904—hardly the most attractive investment in town, though it was listed on the Singapore stock exchange. Financiers were more interested in high-tech stocks. Next door was Seagate Technologies, at the time a principal provider of hard drives for the burgeoning PC market. The factory was made up of nothing more than rows of women screwing together component parts—a sweat shop, in short. But from such basic underpinnings a high-tech economy emerged. Seated at the tables in the local McDonalds were students who preferred to study for exams for hours over a Big Mac than in their Housing Development Board apartments, which were too small and cramped. In consequence, Singapore's young are the best-educated in East Asia. They put up with less-than-ideal conditions for reasons that were utilitarian; they wanted to better themselves, and the raising of technical capability was an economic growth driver. There are lessons in the rise of Singapore and the decline of Britain, which lacks Singapore's sense of drive, but those lessons do not lend themselves to simplistic political solutions.

Nor is there anything exotic or challenging about Singapore: it is safe and sterilised, especially in its remnants of colonial times, and has air-conditioning to combat the constant heat and humidity and to ensure that commercial activities can be enjoyed in comfort. Singaporeans' national obsession is shopping and the country has invested in tourist attractions to keep all shoppers busy. Every possible taste is catered for. Only a few years ago, most tourists were Western; they are now outnumbered by Asians. Our travel history was about exploration; theirs is about sightseeing and the focus of investment has been to cater to that market.

Nothing wrong with that but the attraction for me is the food, for Singapore has the widest range of cuisines of any place I have ever visited. If you are a foodie adventurer, you can eat very well in Singapore, often at very reasonable prices.

When I sold the company house, I rented another just up the road. It was as grand as the first because entertaining was still an important part of the job description. We retained the gardeners, reallocated the watchmen to the factory, made the chauffeur available to all management and released the maids, replacing them with a new hire of strong-enough character to discipline our children when they needed it.

Not many expatriates at the time would have regarded this superfluity of domestic staff as unusual. A seven-year-old marching up and down the sidewalk outside Tanglin School shouting 'Where's my driver?' suggested that a sense of entitlement remained deeply instilled, not helped by the persistence of colonial culture in the submissive attitude of the local population.

Our children, like the Singaporeans', attended multi-ethnic schools. One day our son asked whether his friend Ken could stay over. 'Who's Ken?' I asked. 'He's a bit shorter than me and a bit fat, with black hair.' None the wiser I agreed. Ken turned up. He was Thai, something that our son had not thought worth mentioning. At playschool, similarly, our youngest's best friend was a Tamil Sri Lankan girl. Bringing up our children in this racially diverse environment made them all colour blind.

I HAD INHERITED a company that was in gradual decline. The relatively new factory was operating on less than half a shift a day. I was greeted at my first management team meeting by a group of expectant faces, all but one of whom were Chinese. They expected direction but I turned the question on its head. 'I've been here forty-eight hours and I haven't got a clue. If this were your company, what would you do with it?' It took a while to convince them that this was a genuine question. Eventually they agreed to work among themselves and come back in a fortnight with an answer. I deliberately absented myself from their discussions.

When they reappeared, they were not enthusiastic about what they had come up with, though it was radical and made eminent sense to me. There were three reasons for their hesitancy: the fear that head office would never permit what they were proposing, that they would lose face by presenting something unacceptable, and that it was traditionally the preserve of the boss, not of his underlings, to make critical decisions, something not unusual in Western commercial enterprises either. That was where I stepped in. I reached an agreement with London that I could do what I felt was right, provided I did not blame them if I failed.

The result exceeded all our expectations. Within nine months, the company was operating at three-shift capacity, had sold all its non-core assets—including our house—and had returned over $100 million to its shareholders, 20 per cent of whom were Singaporean, through capital reduction.

Only one member of the board was less than enthusiastic. He was the export director but preferred congenial visits to Brunei, an established territory for us, rather that this risky and uncomfortable foray into a new market. The other directors thought what we were doing was exciting and were happy to cover for him. His purported role had in any case become redundant. I therefore asked him into my office to suggest that he might consider retiring, as he was in his late fifties. To my consternation, he burst into tears: his title was more important to him than the generous retirement package I was offering. 'Face' was critical to self-confidence in collective societies and I had not treated him with the respect he felt he deserved, so we fudged it and created a largely fictional advisory role which mollified his loss of status.

As a country of commerce, Singapore was (and probably still is) a place where socialising is an important lubricant to trade. The Chinese demonstrate their social advancement through lavish weddings and other gatherings. These operate on the belief that those who can help and those who can harm need constant and personal reassurance of their value to the host. We attended many weddings of people whom we had never met before and enjoyed what I always counted as eleven-course dinners until I was told by a Chinese colleague that there were only ten. The final course was rice or noodles and it was considered impolite to eat them, as doing so indicated that the guest was dissatisfied with what had gone before.

Gifting was part of this culture and each New Year I was given XO Cognac or expensive Scotch whisky, in quantities that made them impossible either to consume or refuse. But as I too was expected to entertain, my functions proved a useful way to reduce the stock.

The West began to take corruption seriously after the collapse of Communism. Corruption destroyed the prospects of many states—and these I will come to later—but suffers from a very Western, narrowly moralistic attempt to legislate against it. Both the US's Foreign and Corrupt Powers Act (FCPA) and the UK's Bribery Act (2010) treat lavish entertainment and gift-giving as malign; but this was how business was always conducted in this part of the world—perhaps in any part of the world—where relationships were more important than contracts. It is simply a fact that social glue is paramount in societies with collective cultures, and this seems to me sensible. Business is not a science and does not conveniently conform to the classical economic theory of perfect competition and supply-and-demand equations. All business partnerships enter uncharted territory; to reach a mutual agreement rests on each party's trusting the other to deliver its side of the bargain, and that typically involves inducements of trust, invariably through the exchange of tokens of good will.

ONE DAY AT work, I received an unannounced visit from two police officers. An anonymous whistleblower had written to them about questionable events that had taken place over a decade before my arrival. I was told to present myself at their offices the following day for interview. I consulted Michael, my finance director. He looked at their calling cards and fell silent before saying, 'This is serious. It's the CPIB' (or something similar; everything in Singapore has an acronym). The Corrupt Practices Investigation Bureau, or whatever it was called, was charged with investigating civil, commercial and political crime and had a deserved reputation for its zealotry. The whistleblower's letter claimed that BAT had paid backhanders to senior ministers in return for tax breaks. That was all I had been told; no names and no dates.

Michael and I went back through the history of excise, profit and tax incentives for the new-build factory and found nothing amiss. I duly turned up at the meeting the next day with little of substance and was politely but insistently grilled for three hours, despite my explaining that I had no personal knowledge of events that had taken place ten years earlier and that a search of our files had revealed nothing unusual. I was then dismissed with the comment that they would be in contact again in the event of new developments.

This episode told me that no accusation of malfeasance, no matter how ancient, would be ignored. Singapore is rated in the top ten of least corrupt nations.

Tay Choon Hai, whom we met in the last chapter, is an exemplar of what it meant to be part of Singapore's success story. He had got to know so much about the world of shipping and maritime trade in and out of the Port of Singapore that BAT gave him virtually a free hand to expand the company's activities into any Asian market that was not already spoken for. Not many questions were asked about how he carried out his commission as BAT's general export distributor but, in his defence, the world he dealt with was a murky one in those days.

For example, the import of tobacco into China was at the time controlled by the People's Liberation Army (PLA), not the government in Beijing. As with opium in the nineteenth century, demand for cigarettes far exceeded the quantity that government could make or was prepared to import. The PLA also had a sideline in the import of luxury cars. These were stolen in Hong Kong, loaded into sealed rubber containers that floated just below the waterline, and towed up the Pearl River by tugs to Canton (now Guangzhou) for eager customers. The whole process took less than a day. I learned about this from a subsequent employer, Inchcape, a multinational conglomerate, which held the Hong Kong franchise for nearly all the most prestigious car marques. I was told, also, that the record for a new car hijack was less than forty minutes from when it had been delivered.

Liberalisation of the Chinese economy under Deng Xiao Peng unleashed an explosion of entrepreneurship, exploited with few scruples by most and, in particular, the PLA, the second most powerful organisation in the nation. The first stage of China's economic revival has been labelled as 'crony capitalism' and was accompanied by a wave of corruption, leading to an 'informal' economy for goods that were undersupplied by the government. The PLA always preferred to make a fast buck rather than behave with moral rectitude, as did other players. Such trading practices continue to this day and are not confined to luxury cars and cigarettes. The going rate for Johnny Walker Black Label in Saudi Arabia is currently $400 a bottle.

Mr Tay was then already around seventy. A short man with little command of English, he was always smiling and always accompanied by an assistant called Janet, who acted as his interpreter. Janet turned out also to be his mistress, a fact that I was slow to pick up on. There must also have been a Mrs Tay, as Mr Tay had four sons, but she was never mentioned; as for Janet, she would have been about the same age as one of the sons.

I had no commercial relationship with Mr Tay, because export belonged to a part of BAT that I was not involved with. Still, there was a connection and Mr Tay was keen that we become good friends, which we did, though there were times when our different cultural backgrounds and expectations put our relationship under a lot of strain. Mr Tay's business world was all about networks; mine was about three-year plans and head office expectations. He was lavish in his hospitality and generosity; I was more wary of strangers bearing gifts. His world was fluid; mine was proscribed and controlled.

We had met by chance on the road one Chinese New Year. After the usual friendly greetings, Janet went back to his car and presented three red envelopes to our children. Each envelope contained S$400—the equivalent of £150—which was more cash than any of them had ever had. I think my wife and I managed to convince them that this was better in a savings account.

He also bought a boat which he named *Ruby Queen*, after a brand with which he had much success in export markets. But his eldest son, Hong, had no interest in his father's business and had a low opinion of the boat: 'Has air-conditioning, big fridge-freezer, washing machine, television, everything. But no depth sounder or radar. Stupid.'

The other sons had very different personalities. Philip was an accountant and said very little. William had followed his father's profession, but not his advice, and reportedly ended up in gaol in Cambodia with a finger cut off, though he returned to Singapore eventually. This left Arthur, who seemed to me more attracted to the symbols of success than the means of achieving it. I met him in 2000 at the Malaysian Grand Prix, which he had driven to in his Ferrari, with other Ferrari-owning friends. He wanted me to be impressed and I pretended to be, and maybe he deserved more praise than I offered: after all, with Singapore's levels of tax, this car must have cost him close to US$1 million.

I sometimes wonder what happened to the business. I heard a rumour after Mr Tay's death that family members were at loggerheads with Janet but also split among themselves—all a bit like *South Fork* or *Succession* but with a Chinese cast. Mr. Tay's final legacy to me was the 'opportunity' in Burma.

Mr. Tay preserved his Chinese given names. Of his sons, only Hong did. An anglicised given name was thought to give the possessor more credibility. Some experiments with given names had unintentional consequences. My favourites were Ringo Wee, in Singapore, and Bacon Ho, in Hong Kong. The aspiring to Western identity indicated cultural insecurity. Though the British had long gone, English was still the *lingua franca*, a sensible choice since the racial mix of Chinese, Indian and Malay had no common language. What has happened is that Singapore has developed its own vernacular, or pidgin, now recognised as 'Singlish'.

The assumption made about me was that I was considerably richer than they were. That was only true in the sense that I had phenomenal benefits in kind, all the legacy of the colonial era and designed to impress the locals that I was—or we were—still in charge. I am confident that the fiction of Western wealth has now been demolished. As for my own salary, it was modest and the idea of buying a boat, as Mr Tay had done, would have been entirely beyond my means.

My experience of life in Singapore was the diametrical opposite of that of Paul Theroux, the travel writer and novelist, whose insights have often caused me to question my own lazy assumptions about those parts of the world that we both had visited.[2] We are of course temperamentally different: he is comfortable with being an outsider and relishes confrontation; I prefer to immerse myself in a culture and to suspend judgement. He regards the Singapore régime as rotten to the core and offers in evidence quotes from friends revisited after thirty years, all *sotto voce*. In Singapore he lost his job; that

---

[2] Paul Theroux, *Ghost Train to the Eastern Star: On the Tracks of 'The Great Railway Bazaar'*, Penguin (2009), pp. 309–333.

rankles. What he seems to have been looking for is evidence that supports his sense of injustice. With that attitude you get the answers you want. I suppose the difference goes back again to C.S. Lewis, whom I this time quote, rather than paraphrasing: 'What you see and hear depends a good deal on where you are standing: it also depends on what sort of person you are.'[3]

In a much more secure position, I enjoyed a vibrant social life in a society that seemed to have no losers. My wife kept amusing clippings from the *Straits Times* (whose editor was a neighbour of ours and a social contact) about people arrested for urinating in lifts or 'offending modesty'. Such anodyne titbits kept Tiananmen Square off the front pages. Liberal instincts might object that this was censorship but the BBC World Service was openly available on FM radio for the government had decided that making a civilised and inclusive society was a priority for, indeed a precondition of, democracy. We put up with fly-tipping, knife crime and an increasingly angry social discourse in the name of free speech and respect for the individual. These are not values I would give up lightly but nor would I criticise the government of a fledgling nation for trying to instil social norms that are to the benefit of its diverse population. The proof is in the pudding. There are only a few Singaporean outliers who rant against their government; the rest enjoy the fruits of their success.

We left without regret and with admiration. The road to democracy is long and has clearly been well handled by an authoritarian government that, with some exceptions, has had the best interests of its own citizens in mind.

---

[3] C.S. Lewis, *The Magician's Nephew*, Chapter 10, Bodley Head (1955).

CHAPTER 7
The Political Systems of East Asia
Some Thoughts

The vignettes in this section cover a mixture of democratic and authoritarian régimes with different histories and outcomes. There are, however, some overarching themes that explain how political systems have developed in adjacent societies which have interacted through people, trade, migration, invasion and religion for well over a thousand years. In that context, colonial rule was a short interregnum which briefly papered over the cracks by stopping the clock.

Western empires were built on technical superiority, giving the colonisers a notion of themselves as 'advanced' and of those they colonised as less so. Such a notion was felt, by the colonisers at least, to justify the presence of the French in Indochina; of the British in Burma, Malaysia, Hong Kong and the Indian sub-continent; of the Dutch in Indonesia; of the Spanish and Americans in the Philippines; and of the whole lot in trying to control China. These were primitive countries not then ready for representative government, in their opinion.

Post-independence, six of those countries are classified as functioning democracies: Japan, South Korea, Taiwan, Indonesia, Malaysia and Singapore, but this is just a Western tickbox exercise and reflects a post-colonial mindset. If you asked Far Eastern nations to rate the effectiveness of each government in terms of how it serves its citizens (a more meaningful measure), I suspect the list would be different. That raises the question of whether liberal democracies perform better. I believe that they probably underperform. Democracy is a process, not a solution, and none of these countries had any experience of it before independence. 'A firm hand at the tiller', directed with good intent, has led to dramatic improvements in living standards which now match or even exceed those of the West, aided and abetted by a near-universal belief that the purpose of life is to improve one's material circumstances, now that the colonial yoke has been lifted.

There is another factor that raises questions about the desirability of democracy and the attraction of its ubiquity. Asian societies operate on the principle of communal responsibility rather than individual freedom. One's place in society is determined by parentage. How one behaves is subject to strict social norms and these begin with the family (where respect for age, experience and knowledge are expected) and then extended to clan and society. As a coach I have worked with several Asian clients and learned that a better question than, 'What do you want to do?' is 'Can you think of anybody who has done something different and show how successful they were?' These inbuilt constraints contrast with the Western approach of one person, one vote.

In purely material terms the Far East (another Western construct based on the Greenwich meridian) has nothing to learn from the West and, beyond geo-political conflict, requires no lectures on how to govern itself.

PART 2
AFRICA

CHAPTER 8
Nigeria: 1965 to 1999
An Unsettling Introduction

Nigeria for me as an adolescent was a disturbing encounter and left a legacy of assumptions that remained unchallenged for decades. It was the start of my many visits across sub-Saharan Africa that eventually erased my generic fear of Africans but did little to suggest that the African continent was not benighted. Over and over again, success stories collapsed into conflict, a pessimistic view that was reflected in everywhere I went. Botswana, Zambia, Namibia, even perhaps Rwanda and Uganda, have better trajectories, but I have spent less than a couple of days in any of them. The same applies to what look like failing states in east and southern Africa. I will focus, however, on West Africa and Ethiopia/Eritrea because I know them better, ending with a model and the challenge of how to incorporate its principles into government policy and action.

Arriving in Lagos, it took a long time to get through the entry formalities, despite the best efforts of the local fixer who provided the equivalent of a fast track for favoured passengers. I had hoped to re-encounter that extraordinary smell I had first experienced on arrival in Indonesia three years earlier, but while there were hints in the streets of spice and steaming vegetation, these were overlaid with something more repellent: perspiration, shit and piss. And the noise was deafening: everybody shouting, pushing, shoving, declaiming their right to proper treatment to anybody who would listen—and nobody did listen. I stood there, drenched in sweat, holding out against an encroaching sea of bawling humanity. This was the tropics of a different sort: ugly, abusive and scary.

It was relief to get into the car at last for the night drive to a new home. Air conditioning and closed windows provided some insulation from the world outside, but I looked with growing anxiety as the car passed through Surulere and Yaba towards Lagos island. People here lived like ants, crawling all over each other, importuning, beseeching, screaming insults right onto the carriageway. Mohammed, the driver, constantly sounded his horn to clear this zombie-like mass of humanity. He thought he only needed an inch to get through, a margin I felt was insufficient for, if he hit anyone, I was sure that the entire mob would turn its anger on us and that nothing would placate it.

This frightened me; for Mohammed it was an everyday experience. And nothing happened. We crossed the bridge to Lagos Island and into comparative peace. It was a shell of a city. Flanking the lagoon, it could have been something marvellous. The newer buildings suggested that this had been the intention but could not hide the broken footpaths, the stinking drains, the piles of refuse and the slum shacks of those trying to make a desperate living from those with just a bit more money. It was like a churned-up cemetery, interspersed with skyscraper tombs. On occasion, I returned there in daylight, which was, if anything, worse.[1] Clogged with people, every journey became an obstacle course, the lagoon was an opaque brown sludge carrying corpses of animals, and occasionally humans, down into the Bight of Benin.

On neighbouring Victoria Island stood the Federal Palace Hotel, commanding a vista over the lagoon, isolated among the sand and scrub. The hotel had been built, I suppose, to demonstrate that the masters of the newly independent state could manage grand projects. Six years on, nobody stayed there. The sand-blown parking lot contained a collection of General Motors cars, all painted in patriotic green and white.

---

[1] Ryszard Kapuściński, *The Shadow of the Sun: My African Life*, Allen Lane (2001), pp. 98–117. Offers a more in-depth description of what it was like to live there.

They were rusting hulks, never to be driven again. It was incomprehensible. Back in England, my father had bought his first car only a couple of years before: a 1953 split-screen Morris Minor. How could a nation that was demonstrably poorer than its ex-colonial master let all this expense dissolve into rust? This was the beginning of my understanding that régimes are not necessarily in service of those they rule.

Our house was in Ikoyi, near Thompson Avenue, on the corner of what was then Waring Road—not just the best part of town but one of its most expensive districts. There wasn't a beggar in sight. The house conformed to the colonial model of large rooms and overhanging eaves to protect against sun and rain. Upstairs were the air-conditioned bedrooms, one for my parents, one for me and my brother. My mother recounted the story of their first night there: the steward asked what they wanted to eat. 'Scrambled eggs,' she replied. 'And what wine shall I serve?' A pillar of imperialism was a refusal to bend one's standards to accommodate the locals; that left one above and beyond the masses. My mother's practical, no-nonsense approach perhaps served to undermine, if only in the smallest way, the presumptions of supremacy.

Outside the house was a large garden surrounded by a standard suburban wrought iron fence on concrete pillars. My mother wanted something resembling an English garden. The gardener knew only about growing tropical crops. Their joint efforts were not considered a success by either party. She found she had to stand over him to make sure he did as he was told and this was not conducive to a happy relationship.

Were these the halcyon days before things fell apart? Well, not exactly. There were islands of safety where life was pleasant but the surrounding sea was dark and foreboding. Perhaps that first drive from the airport influenced how I felt. Every Nigerian I met was friendly, open and curious. It was those I did not meet that worried me.

We occasionally stayed overnight at a house on Tarkwa beach, across the lagoon, or further up the creek. Both locations could only be reached by boat. By day they were fun, by night disquieting: no night watchman, no iron bars on the slatted glass windows, no fence, and no air-conditioning, because the generator was switched off when we went to bed. I would lie awake sweating, listening to the wind thrashing and creaking through the palm fronds, alert to any extraneous noise that might signal danger. Nothing ever happened but that did not convince a fifteen-year-old white boy that he was safe.

English prejudice about Nigerians being unreliable was reinforced by the opinion that they were also incompetent and 'tricky'. Certainly they exhibited a logic that we found difficult to comprehend. My mother was teaching Julius, the second steward, how to drive. He drove into the garage and put his foot on the accelerator rather than the brake, hitting a ladder that fell forward and smashed the windscreen. 'You will have to pay for that,' my mother told him. Later he sheepishly asked if it was not possible to patch the windscreen rather than replace it. Only at a distance does his failure to understand the physical properties of glass seem explicable, as windscreens had played no previous part in his life.

Similarly, the occasion when a director from London changed his plans and had to have dinner with us twice in succession became part of family history. My mother had told the cook, Tom, to 'brighten up' some stew he had cooked earlier. He proudly presented it covered in Hundreds and Thousands, the brightly coloured sugar morsels used in cake decoration. It was not until long after that we were able to admit that my mother's choice of language had been idiomatic and misleading, and that the blame was hers.

My experience of Nigerian food was limited to a few mouthfuls of *garri*, a spicy hot confection of rice concealing a few bits of tough goat meat. I had no idea that you were supposed to hold the meat in your cheek while you consumed the rest; for the average Nigerian, goat was very expensive and so you kept it in your mouth for as long as possible. I was no more tempted by Nigerian land snails, which are regarded as a delicacy but which my mother described as having the taste and durability of a car tyre. If these meals failed, I now realise that Tom was cooking meals he had never eaten, but no such generosity of interpretation was offered at the time.

In fact, stories of this sort became part of expatriate folklore. I have several times been told the story about the suckling pig and the Nigerian cook. The pig should have an apple in its mouth and be delivered through the serving hatch. Inevitably the cook puts an apple in his own mouth while trying to manoeuvre himself and the dish through the hatch. Such stories always came with the assertion that 'I witnessed it myself.'

Such casual racism seems appalling these days. At best, the people recounting these anecdotes would have rejected such criticism, saying instead that it was simply the collision of two uncomprehending cultures—except that those belonging to the more 'sophisticated' culture made no attempt to understand the behaviour of the other. That was their error, for they had a duty to try and understand, but it only becomes obvious in hindsight. I recently re-read Chinua Achebe's *Things Fall Apart*[2] and he explains it better than I could, and from the perspective of an African. His tolerance, humility and desire to understand why colonisers had a different perspective encourages me to think that meeting on equal terms still represents the best opportunity for reconciling inbuilt prejudices on both sides.

After that bit of moralising, another story, told by my

---

[2] Chinua Achebe, *Things Fall Apart*, Heinemann (1958). First read at age sixteen in Lagos.

parents. The transistor radio in the study went missing. It had to be an inside job. My father called all the domestic staff together—and there were a lot of them. If the radio was back in its place the next morning, he said, no more questions would be asked; if not, there would be hell to pay. Next morning, no radio. Another meeting was convened. Nobody would admit responsibility. Then Mohammed came up with an idea. All the staff should go to Yaba to consult a witchdoctor to determine who did it. The master of the house thought this was nonsense but it seemed reasonable to everyone else and so, in the absence of any ideas of his own, he reluctantly agreed. They piled into the Chevrolet and disappeared.

They returned several hours later triumphant, except for one. Mohammed, as the spokesman, exclaimed with some satisfaction that they had identified the guilty party. He went on to explain that the witchdoctor had said that he would take a stone from the fire and place it on everybody's forehead, one by one. If anyone's skin burst into flames from the hot stone, this would prove that that person was guilty of the theft. And that person was (pause for dramatic effect) Ben, the chief steward.

My father dismissed the rest of them and then told Ben to put the radio back 'and we will hear no more about it.' But Ben protested, 'I did not steal the radio.' 'Then what explanation do you have?' Ben paused and then admitted, 'I am not so young anymore and I have difficulty getting the ladies. So before I go out on my day off, I put Kiwi boot polish on my head to hide my grey hairs and that is what caught fire.' Ben kept his job and the radio was never seen again.

As a postscript, the staff came from different ethnic backgrounds (Yoruba, Hausa, Fulani, Ibo and Igbo) and different religions (Muslim, Christian and Animist). They always got on well together, or that is how it seemed to me. And nothing was ever stolen again.

My brother and I spent days at the Ikoyi Club, still dominated by white members. Outside the Ikoyi Hotel, there were hawkers selling their handicrafts to passers-by and on our way home, we would stop to bargain with them. Without even thinking about it, we entered into a tacit contract on the basis that we had more money than they had, and were therefore under a social obligation to buy some wild animal figurines, inexpertly constructed from hide and bone. On a later visit I bought two bronze lions of infinitely superior artistic merit. I liked to think that this represented an improvement in artisan skills but maybe the makers moved on to brass because there were no more bits of animal left to work on.

My father took us on a chartered flight to the north but I cannot remember whether we were introduced to St Elmo Nelson in Kanu or Kaduna. He lived in a typical Hausa compound consisting of a series of interconnected square rooms with domed roofs constructed of wood and daub. St Elmo was the last of the white colonial officers still employed by the federal government, and his value was that he was the only person who could negotiate reliably between the authorities in Lagos and the semi-feudal emirs of northern Nigeria, an appointment that says much about the difficulty of governing a country as divided as Nigeria is by polity (tribes and feudal states), livelihood (subsistence farming in the tropical south, nomadic cattle herders in the Sahel), religion and culture.

St Elmo's dress uniform was a cockaded white hat on a white uniform emblazoned with medals. He was less formally dressed when we met him, but had maintained the language of a typical colonial officer—somewhat brusque but ornamented by the often-repeated, 'don't y'know?'

My brother and I were sitting on opposite banquettes built into the wall, while father sat facing St Elmo across an ancient partner's desk at the head of the room. After a general chat, which left both of us bored, father enquired, 'Where is Britannicus?' 'I'll call him,' St Elmo answered, and bawled out the name. The door was opened and a two-year-old lion bounded in, sat on my bench with his massive paws on my lap and proceeded to lick my face with his sandpaper tongue. His feet were the size of side plates and I could feel his claws extending and retracting on my thighs as he welcomed his newfound friend. I stroked his emerging mane, unable to think of any other appropriate stratagem.

'He's a gift from the Emir of Sokoto. Thoroughly decent pet, though he killed a chicken this morning, don't y'know? Don't fret, he might get upset. Shame, but I think I'm going to have to send him to Longleat. All arranged of course, but it's been a lot of fun having him around. Darn sight more intelligent than most of the people I have to deal with, what?'

Something like that. I don't quote him verbatim, nor am I implying that St Elmo shared the sense of infuriation which Colonials typically visited on those they considered damned, recalcitrant natives. He must have dealt well enough with the Nigerians, for how else could he have managed so well as an honest broker? It may have been his sense of decency and fair play that endeared him to the Lagos government but that and his old-fashioned style made him an impossibility.

Another trip was in the Chevrolet to Dahomey on muddy, rutted laterite roads that carved a wide brick-coloured pathway through towering dense green jungle, interspersed by small villages with buildings of clay, wood and palm fronds, surrounded by cultivated patches of yams, cassava and other fruits; to call them fields would be an misrepresentation. Roads such as this would be impassable in the rainy season for a car of our sort, which, when it hit wetter patches, slithered and skidded on every dip. We crossed the border, with the usual passing of banknotes to ease the passage.

Our destination was the Hotel Croix du Sud in Cotonou. At dinner I understood why this arduous drive and the relentless inefficiency and confusion of border crossings was considered worth the effort. The hotel pretended it was in metropolitan France, not isolated in a country that had already become a by-word for African instability. The manager was French, the service was impeccable and the food was up to the standards of a Parisian brasserie. With it came French bread and French wine; there wasn't a single African dish on the menu.

The president of Dahomey was holed up in his palace, employing the entire community of witch doctors to preserve his soul—unsuccessfully, for he was assassinated only a few months later. One of his successors renamed the country Benin as an anti-colonialist measure. That was a shame, as Dahomey was the legitimate name of a pre-colonial African empire based exactly where the country was; the ancient kingdom of Benin, by contrast, was in Nigeria.

I like to think that my mother had a more enquiring mind than most of her ilk. She made friends with a missionary—not one of my parents' usual social circle—who took her, my brother and me on a walk through villages in the then outer reaches of Victoria Island. This was not an uncomfortable experience, as I had feared it might have been. Everywhere we went we were welcomed. My only other memories were of poverty, dirt and squalor.

I was out on a boat in the lagoon when a Dakota appeared in the sky above and dropped a 44-gallon drum which fell harmlessly in the harbour. This was the beginning of the Biafra War. A few days later, my father announced that we were returning to the UK by ship, along with other expatriate families. It was yet another experience; I had never been to sea before.

Our first port of call was Takoradi, from where we went in buses to Elmina Castle, a one-time slave-trading port. I remember the Dutch fort on the hill, the slave pens on the shore, the rough iron shackles that had tied the captives together, and the drawing of how they were packed in on the small ships and transported across the Atlantic. I cannot recall what I thought about it at the time. Interested, certainly, and probably saddened but detached: this was history, I was sixteen and there was nothing I could do about the past.

I WENT BACK to Nigeria in 1999. The country's reputation in the interim had sunk to new depths. It was considered corrupt and dangerous.

Unlike most of our party, the finance controller and I took a night flight. We arrived at Murtala Mohammed Airport (named after the only Nigerian president without a totally besmirched reputation) at Ikeja at dawn. The air-conditioning did not work but it smelled a lot better than when I had first arrived here over thirty years earlier. The problem was that there was no one to meet us.

We called the hotel where our colleagues were staying. The call was disconnected as soon as it was answered. I tried again and got the switchboard operator to at least respond. I asked to be put through to the room of our group leader. The phone was answered by an English voice, the owner of which clearly had no idea who I was; the operator had connected the call to an entirely random recipient. The advice of the friendly English stranger was to stay where we were. It was too dangerous to venture outside.

I remembered that there was an international hotel close to the airport and, by talking to some curious and importuning unemployed locals who hung around hoping for a dollar or two, discovered it was still there and only a five-minute taxi ride away. With the reluctant assent of my colleague, I went over to a queue of beaten-up vehicles and negotiated with an old man in a Peugeot 404 who seemed the safest bet. The car was incapable of any speed above 60 kms an hour, but that was a relief as he seemed to have only the vaguest idea of how to drive it. We got to the hotel without incident and the driver was happy enough with a $10 fare.

The receptionist was not surprised that we had arrived without a reservation and gave us a room. It took several hours to make contact with our colleagues and hosts but eventually a car was sent for us and we joined them. Alas, we could not visit the head office in Apapa because there a riot was in progress. A field trip was offered as an alternative. Lagos was now a much bigger city and was more of a nightmare than I remembered, despite the addition of a few more highways.[3] Physically it looked as chaotic as ever, with open sewers, dirt tracks, and shacks made of whatever could be found, topped with a cat's cradle of wires siphoning off unmetered electricity. A few white men wandering around, looking at stalls and shops, did not arouse much interest so it did not feel unsafe.

That night we went to a restaurant on Ikoyi island and passed my old house on the way. As far as I could tell it was unchanged, but that was difficult to verify as it was now surrounded by 20-foot-high concrete walls topped with razor wire. The following day we flew to Port Harcourt, the main outlet for oil exports. It was a smaller version of Lagos, except that oil pipelines ran everywhere and were often ruptured by residents extracting crude oil for their fuel needs. The oil bled into creeks and killed the wildlife and vegetation. It looked like a First-World-War battleground.

We returned to Lagos, where the head office was still off limits due to the continuing unrest. With nothing else to do, we traversed Victoria Island, now entirely built up, to the tour-

---

[3] The intractable problem of the urban poor in Nigeria seems to have got no better. See Chibundu Onuzo, *Welcome to Lagos*, Faber & Faber (2017).

ist village where I bought the two bronze lions.

We made our journey to the airport in a convoy with two Toyota pick-ups manned fore and aft by machine-gun-toting security men. All the prejudices I had garnered from my adolescent encounter with Nigeria were now reinforced. Black Africa scared me and that subconscious prejudice remained an unexamined assumption until many years later. I realised that I was conflating a system of corruption, patronage, theft and brutality with the thought that these values applied to its victims rather than its perpetrators. But the evidence was that I never met anybody who believed in them. It was just a system that they had to accommodate.

At the time of writing, Nigeria continues to totter on the edge of disaster, with ethnic, religious and economic conflicts flaring up unpredictably like the oil platforms in the Bight of Benin. But there are a lot more millionaires. Huge oil wealth has ended up in the pockets of the powerful few. None of it has made any discernible impact on the lives of the masses, who are still wretched in their poverty. The population explosion, though nobody knows how many Nigerians there are, indicates that children are still seen as an economic asset rather than a liability. And that is a sure sign of the absence of sustainable development.

Nigeria is a country that has got used to a state of high anxiety. There is no expectation that its government can do anything in the short term that will alleviate the situation.

CHAPTER 9
French West Africa: 2010 to 2013
From Coups to Elections (and Back Again)

Between 2010 and 2013 I visited most of the countries that make up French West Africa on behalf of Imperial Tobacco, for whom I was now working. Looking back, I find it hard to remember exactly what happened where. I do recall that none of them was a functioning democracy and that nowhere did I encounter any optimism about the future. All seemed stuck in a state of subsistence; the one or two that had enjoyed some progress in the past now only had nostalgia for the good old days. Days spent in local offices were interrupted by visitors who had nothing better to do than chew the fat—'*Comment allez-vous?*'—before subsiding into an armchair, asking for a coffee or a soft drink, and then summoning up the energy to recount recently heard anecdotes. This was resignation with a sense of humour.

The Sahel states are hot and dry. Capital cities are more like expanded villages with a few pompous and incongruous official buildings and boulevards. The dominant colour is ochre, and the Sahara dust blown on the Harmattan wind clouds everything, so that all appears mute, blurring horizons so that figures emerge from the haze like ghosts. The pot-seller appears on his bicycle, piled high with his wares balanced on planks fitted crossways and tied together with string, so that in the distance he looks like a kite flying too close to the ground. Nothing moves in the heat of the day, and only slowly in the mornings and evenings. Little seems to have changed for centuries. Women wear lengths of cloth wound round their bodies and carry their baggage on their heads. Men wear ragged shorts and T-shirts, unless they are high-ranking, in which case the *mode du jour* remains the cotton 'piece', ironically a legacy of the slave trade. The further north you go, they move from printed decoration—perhaps of people or animals—to white, as it is *haram* in Islam to depict life forms.

The main function of the cities appears to be the provision of employment, and thus of an income, for those at the foot of the social ladder: artisans, shopkeepers, domestic servants and security guards who live precariously on the needs of the tiny government and civil service. Outside the cities, life in these harsh climes is nomadic. The landscape is dotted with acacia trees which only goats will eat; water is scarce. From the air the migratory tracks suggest only what has gone where, without any indication of why. They are like scribbles on a sheet of paper.

There is always a small community of long-term and usually French expatriates who make a rather better living serving more sophisticated needs. In this torpid world they at least seem to have more energy. But tourism is dead. Al-Qaeda and Boko Haram have managed to make the hinterland off-limits. The French military is here, though troops tend to stay in their bases. In Chad, Mirage jets took off every night on sorties to who knows where. Our resident manager's wife complained that they could not get out of the city any longer. These were places that had had precious little to offer to a visitor in the first place but were now besieged. The manager resigned a few months later. They were on the edge of nowhere.

There is a stark contrast between French and British government attitudes to their former colonies. The British walked away from their former dependencies, redefining them as part of a Commonwealth that is nothing but an English talking shop for cultural exchange; the French continue to manage and underwrite local currencies. The British only intervene when things get out of hand, as they did in Sierra Leone during the civil war of 1991–2002; the French react to any threat through immediate military intervention, as if they themselves are threatened. The British take principled stands; the French care more about promoting stability. On balance I find the French approach more appropriate—or I used to. They took responsibility for their ex-colonies, at one time even providing boltholes for a lot of overthrown dictators, but this policy is now in retreat as numerous coups have installed military regimes who find the Wagner Group a better option. Not good.

BURKINA FASSO
Lassiné is president of my ex-company's board in Burkina Faso. He is one of Africa's most successful businessmen and regarded as beyond reproach. He is soft-spoken, almost apologetically deferential and respected wherever he goes. He walks a fine line between African reality and Western moral strictures. His mission is to find a means of reconciling one with the other, to the benefit of both. His success is testament to how skilfully he does this.

Lassiné comes from Bobo-Dialassou where our factory was located. He spends his time either in Paris or in the capitals of former French West Africa. Bobo-Dialassou has a population of nearly a million and everybody employed by the factory seems to be related to each other: they are Bobos or Burkinabés, of a tribe that inhabits the west of Burkina Faso and extends into Côte d'Ivoire and Guinea. In spite of that, Bobo-Dialassou is little more than an overgrown village. There are no hotels of any repute, no restaurants worth mentioning, just a few administrative buildings among the mud huts. The expatriate factory manager lives a lonely life, meeting his unspoken obligation of providing meaningful employment for Lassiné's kinsman.

Lassiné knows that economic development is vital, as Africans will only acquire a vested interest in political and environmental stability if they have money in their pockets.

Africa today is a cruel world of droughts, disease, corruption and enmity between tribes and religions. Thanks to Western aid there are plenty of schools—but no teachers: the government cannot afford them, nor can the parents. In many countries, foreign aid makes up the major portion of government revenue and it all comes with strings attached. The other main source of income is excise duty, typically on gasoline, alcohol and tobacco. Import duties are frowned on by the World Trade Organization (WTO) and are ineffectual anyway, as smuggling from Guinea infests the whole of West Africa. Systems of income tax, VAT, corporation tax and business rates exist but can only be applied to the fraction of businesses that are registered, normally foreign-owned.

The economy is therefore based on the absolute power of the president who, paradoxically, has no resources. When a president runs out of money to pay the army, which is unsurprisingly often, he is usurped and another emperor-with-no-clothes assumes the stage. Graft is the only means of survival, at every level. Meanwhile, soft-spoken Lassiné seeks influence, knowing there are riches here in undisturbed mineral deposits.

Lassiné is increasingly frustrated by the strings attached to Western investment. Why can he not make donations to political parties? He supports all of them. He must also deal with the consequences of hypothecated aid. For example, the Bloomberg Foundation donated $1m to the health ministry of a certain country on condition that the money was used to combat smoking. In fact, few of the poorest Africans smoke and those that do so buy only one cigarette at a time and only when they can afford it. In my time, some 99 per cent of our volume was sold in so-called 'stick sales' because the efficient collection of excise duty on tobacco made larger packs too expensive, and the vendors made less than one euro a packet.

So what happens when Bloomberg adds conditions to its

gift? The minister of health promulgates a new measure requiring plain packaging for all tobacco products, lifted off the Bloomberg website, and congratulates himself by buying himself a new Mercedes.

Commoditising tobacco products may be a legitimate public-health policy but serves only to cement the enrichment of the favoured few while doing nothing to ameliorate the hapless lives of the many. One of the things that African governments are good at doing is proposing new laws which serve no worthwhile purpose, rarely get implemented and cost them nothing to enact.

The whole of Africa is beset by the problem of corrupt élites with only tenuous control over ethnically divided people and with insufficient funds to deal with those people's problems. If the money provided reasonable salaries for politicians and civil servants, accompanied by draconian legislation on graft, we might just see the emergence of policies designed to improve the lot of the population, but if these were to have any long-standing impact, they would need to be generated internally, not imposed by well-meaning but naïve outsiders.

I was initially enthusiastic when the press heralded a new dawn for Africa at the start of the twenty-first century. The emergence of democratic principles, a new accountability for those in power who had abused their position, the removal of barriers to trade—it all sounded very promising but proved to be a chimera.

GUINEA
Guinea became a magnet for foreign investors following the election of Alpha Condé as president in 2010 after twenty years of military (and entirely incompetent) dictatorship. I met President Condé in 2012. He had spent most of his life in France and made his career in the trade-union movement. Returning to Guinea he realised that foreign investment was

the key to unlocking the huge mineral reserves the country possessed. He struck me as an intelligent man and committed to social justice but already at the end of his tether. This was emphasised by the head of customs, who was also present at our first meeting. He was wearing some sort of military uniform with cow-hide sandals on his feet. He nodded absent-mindedly when he thought it necessary but displayed not the slightest grasp of the issues involved in attempting to restart a factory that had had to be mothballed because of rampant smuggling. It became obvious that the well-disposed president had no power whatsoever to effect the very minor changes necessary to make this project a reality.

President Condé did not directly refer to what the French call '*les Peuls*'—the Fula or Fulani, a tribal mercantile ethnic group who effectively control much of the economy in West Africa, traditionally pastoralists with an instinct for business but little respect for formal authority. I met several Fulani over the next few days who had made fortunes out of circumventing import duties. Tobacco and alcohol paid less import duty than rice; in consequence they dominated the black market across West Africa. No doubt the racketeers paid the head of customs a pittance for the privilege. He in turn was happy not to rock the boat. The factory remains mothballed.

Bringing this story up to date, I see that Alpha Condé was deposed in a military coup, supposedly by an 'élite division', in September 2021. He has not been seen since. The Organisation of African Unity (OAU) has deplored the coup but will do nothing about it. My guess is that Condé had managed to attract inward investment by offering a transparent environment and was punished for it. The irony is that only those likely to suffer a loss from the introduction of reforms had the power to remove him, and their doing so has renewed the never-ending roundabout of corruption, self-interest and lawlessness, forcing potential investors once again to have second thoughts. It is a tragedy for the people and for a decent man who returned to his country of birth to improve the lives of its citizens. As ever, a downward cycle of poverty and undeserved riches is perpetuated throughout sub-Saharan Africa by self-interest and the improper control of the levers of power.

CÔTE D'IVOIRE

Côte d'Ivoire was at one time held up as an example of what could be achieved in sub-Saharan Africa. Along with Senegal, it had become the centre of *négritude*, a black-led anti-colonial movement that goes back to the 1930s. More of an attitude than a philosophy, *négritude* promulgated the idea that Africans should control their own destiny through a programme of 'black consciousness'. For three decades, Côte d'Ivoire surpassed all other states in that part of the world for economic growth and stability. And then, at the start of the third millennium, it degenerated into civil war between north and south on ethnic and religious grounds.

I feel like something of an expert on civil wars, having been a local observer of many of them. They operate in areas of influence but without hard-and-fast frontlines. Our factory was in the north but managed to keep up our supply to the south through mechanisms I can only guess at but suspect involved payment of unofficial customs duties.

Abidjan, the capital of Côte d'Ivoire and the financial hub of French West Africa, had once been a city of ambition. When I spent time there, it was already sinking back to being just another port town on the West African coast. It had dual carriageways and flyovers but what lay between them was run-down and dingy. Its people had better educational standards than most in this part of the world but their prospects for improvement were few and far between. Our English manager, who had been recently promoted to area director for West Africa, was not in a good state of mind.

He had been in this part of the world for over twenty years. We went out together, just the two of us, to talk about this. In a bar we met one of his, I suppose, ex-girlfriends. He ignored her and she switched her attention to me. She was pretty and likeable, good at conversation and apparently self-confident, but her presence reminded me of a conversation I had had with Lassiné. 'As you grow older,' he said, 'you need to find somebody younger to fill your bed.' At the time I had thought nothing of it; such a modus vivendi for those with power seemed to be standard practice just about everywhere I had worked outside the West, but was not something I wanted to emulate.

As we talked, I started to understand the root of my colleague's disquiet. Here in Côte d'Ivoire he could find himself a girlfriend with very little effort. His status made him attractive and he had played the field but a succession of relationships left him unsatisfied. He had been a lonely expat for too long and yearned for something more familiar, more intimate, than was available here. It may just have been another dream but he resigned and went home. I hope he is happier now.

SENEGAL

I had expected much of Senegal. It has perhaps the world's best climate, with temperatures in the mid-twenties throughout the year. Dakar, the country's capital and largest city, is the most westerly port in West Africa and I imagined that the influence of Europe and South America might have softened the harshness that I had seen in the other African states I had visited.

Perhaps it has done, because other visitors talk fondly of it, but is only a matter of degree: Senegal is a little richer than its Sahel neighbours and benefits from French tourism and a relatively robust electoral system.

My opinion of the country was soured by my visit to our local factory. A making machine jammed and the operator had no idea how to fix it. The foreman intervened by shouting at him. Then the shift manager began shouting instructions, which was pointless as neither the operator nor the foreman knew who he was directing his instructions to. The cacophony reached the ears of the factory manager in his office and he came down to sort things out. The general manager, accompanying me on my tour, then weighed in as well. His managerial style was to shout the loudest. They almost came to blows.

This was not how a factory should be run and I blamed the general manager for it. As a long-term French expatriate he should have known better, I felt, but maybe I knew less. I was assuming that local staff would want to improve themselves by doing a better job. But if you live in a culture that provides only limited opportunities for advancement, perhaps that is a vain hope; and the gulf between the cultures was so wide that maybe the only way to manage was through command. I hope not, though that was clearly the conclusion that the general manager had reached.

SUMMARY

Despite my dismal appraisal of what I found in French West Africa, there was an inkling that change was afoot. West and Central Africa were not without natural resources. The problem was lack of infrastructure to exploit them. Enter the Chinese, fully prepared to invest without regard to any rules of corporate governance. Much easier to gain concessions if you did not criticise those granting them to you. Inevitably Lassiné was intimately involved with many of these schemes, which were far more ambitious than any Western investor would have contemplated. Railway lines were being built that extended hundreds of kilometres inland to where the ore deposits were. What was strange was that the lines were built entirely by Chinese, not local, labour, and serviced by a supply industry that was also entirely Chinese. Those involved, from the investors to the heavy lifters, were a race apart.

What I did not realise at the time was how very large these schemes were in their scope. A brief glimpse of China, where every valley has a project for a four-lane highway or a high-speed rail link, provided evidence of an ambition to tame and conquer the world. But for what purpose? It is a question I still cannot answer, though it seems more about influence than territorial ambition—for now.

What I also did not recognise at the time was that what I assumed were direct investments by China were in fact soft loans. African nations are now vastly indebted to their potential saviours—not that they have had much choice, for no one else seems to have wanted to get involved. I hope it all works out well for them. The West looks very weak in comparison, despite its loftier ambitions and moral qualms.

For the present, the lack of any attempt by China to integrate into the societies they are beginning to invest in suggests that they are more interested in controlling the levers of power rather than running the governments. It reminds me of a story about Afghanistan told me by a Turkish contractor who had won a UN contract. His firm employed local tribesmen to build the road, then knocked it down and started all over again. The Chinese contractor insisted on building their road with no local involvement. They never finished theirs.

French West Africa, like Nigeria, hovers between anxiety and chaos. Mineral wealth has the potential to ameliorate this but it is more likely to remain in the pockets of the privileged.

Working with Lassiné and our local managers both in Africa and in Paris led to the slow dissipation of the unconscious bias I had developed as an adolescent in Nigeria, as did my encounters in the street and markets, my conversations with strangers, and my periods of socialising and relaxation. I found a refreshing lack of malice; any criticism tended to be sugar-coated into a joke. It seemed that in these fragile societies, calm and conviviality were of the essence, and this applied to both men and women, as did a sense of humour and of the absurd. The only times I encountered open animosity were from uniformed officials, but the wearing of any badge of office often prompts officious behaviour, wherever you come from. In Africa, I felt comfortable.

In recent times the region has become more unstable and less governable through the incursions of jihadist groups who operate with seeming impunity in the Sahel and apply the brutal methods promoted by the militant group known as the Islamic State, ISIS or Daesh. Efforts at combatting them are termed a 'war on terrorism' but from a distance, and with no specialist knowledge on the issue, opposition does not look very much like what we would normally regard as a war. The smuggling of weapons and drugs from one side of the Sahara to the other provides a source of revenue that governments cannot match. Kidnapping and people trafficking is another rich source of income.

The inability of governments to protect their own people has created power vacuums, which in turn has led to an increase in military *coups d'état*. Ethnic and religious divisions now denote who are friends and who are enemies. The French have become unpopular for failing to quell these rebellions; in their place, a foothold has been established by the Russian mercenary Wagner Group, which I suspect will make things worse because of its commercial interest in perpetuating the conflicts that it is called on to sort out, and because collateral damage seems be an intrinsic part of its strategy.

Conflict now extends right across Africa to Somalia. I wonder whether the political chaos once caused by the slave trade now has a new driver.

CHAPTER 10
Ethiopia and Eritrea: 1994 to 1995
Poverty and War

For over twenty years, Ethiopia was seen as a beacon of political, social and economic opportunity. No longer—and I cannot think of a better example in Africa of how Western ignorance failed to recognise the fault lines that threatened it.

From 1977 to 1991, the Marxist régime of Mengistu Haile Mariam drove a poor and illiterate peasantry into starvation. The music industry's 'Save the World' campaign provided a palliative but changed nothing. A coup got rid of Mengistu and he was replaced by a more market-oriented régime dominated by Tigrayans. Now the West had something they could engage with. That was why I was there, while working for Inchcape and at the invitation of the Coca-Cola Company, as a potential purchaser of the state-owned soft drinks business.

This was not a hardship visit: I enjoyed a decent flight, an international hotel and a benign climate. Ethiopia's capital, Addis Ababa, sits high in a mountain valley, where flowering plants grow profusely, even in untended patches. Their fragrance mixes with woodsmoke from cooking fires. At night, lights twinkle in the city and the only sound is the barking of pi-dogs. While I was there I would sit on the hotel balcony listening to John Martyn on my Discman. That languorous voice seemed the perfect accompaniment: beautiful, unusual and just enough outside one's comfort zone to be exciting.[1]

The state-owned bottling plant was antiquated and inflexible. It could only produce 25 ml glass returnable bottles and lacked the capacity to meet demand. The commercial opportunity was obvious and only required modest investment.

---

[1] See also Ryszard Kapuśiński, *The Shadow of the Sun: My African Life*, Penguin (2001), pp. 127–136.

The difficulty was that the management seemed unexcited at our arrival. They were polite but resisted any attempt to get on friendly terms. Meanwhile the Scots TCCC (the Coca-Cola Company) country manager, Sandy, kept extolling the potential of this investment.

A market visit into the heart of Addis revealed another reality. Ethiopia was a country of dire poverty where children played football with rolled-up discarded plastic bags, which was why the streets were so clean. Shops were no more than windowsills, stocked with what the shopowners could afford rather than what their customers wanted to buy. The twinkling candles of the city below, the woodsmoke and the silence were only a sign of nothing else to do.

I cannot remember how many times I visited but the size of the delegation and the length of stay increased each time, although our potential management pool, made up largely of Chileans, would shrink as they regularly got food poisoning, despite their only eating at the hotel. Whatever Chileans' many virtues might be, they found the rest of the world uncongenial and Africa particularly so.

THE TOYOTA FRANCHISE was run at the time by the only permanent resident Inchcape manager, a bluff Yorkshireman and divorcé. He was also not a fan of the local cuisine, which was based on a kind of flat bread pancake called *injera* made from *teff* or millet. It had, in my opinion, the look, consistency and taste of carpet underlay. My friend told me it that it was also full of iron, so that 'every time you take a shit, you end up pointing north.' I am glad to say that I was untroubled by stomach maladies while we were there.

This plan of taking over and upgrading the bottling plant petered out, despite main board visits, probably because the idea of foreigners acquiring a controlling interest in even a half-functioning commercial asset was hard to accept. The

Vietnamese model of testing the water through consultancy might have worked but was not part of the brief.

Learning a little about Ethiopia's history, I found that, like everywhere else in the continent, the country had no democratic roots. This was hardly surprising as literacy was the preserve of the élite, ethnic divisions (still reflected in the country's federal structure) were enforced, slavery remained a common practice until outlawed by Haile Selassie in 1942, religious minorities—Muslims, Jews and Animists—were used as political scapegoats, and Ethiopia's passive peasantry was offered nothing better to aspire to. The only things that held the country together were its Christianity and its resistance to colonial domination.

I have never been back to Addis but the city, since my visits, has exploded in size, as has the national population, now estimated at 110 million. This expansion is a function of high economic growth, which the West conveniently assumes is good for everyone while ignoring how fragile Ethiopia still is.

Abiy Ahmed, the prime minister, is an Oromo, the most populous of Ethiopia's ethnic groups. He took office in 2018 with a very Western outlook on what needed to be done to make the country a modern and prosperous state for all, and with a mould-breaking project—the Grand Ethiopian Renaissance Dam (work on which actually began in 2011)—intended to provide electricity for all, but opposed by Egypt and Sudan, downstream of Ethiopia, who feared that water flow in its own stretches of the Nile would thereby be depleted.

The West welcomed Ahmed and he was awarded the Nobel Peace Prize in 2019 for ending the war with Eritrea, but the federal constitution, which came into effect in 1995, continued to grant degrees of autonomy to the provinces on ethnic lines, embedding traditional divisions.

In 2020 Ahmed lost the support of his people following the killing of a popular Oromo musician, with subsequent riots leading to over 200 deaths. Civil war with Tigrayans ensued in a vicious struggle for power.

The only possible explanation for the turnaround in Ethiopia's fortunes is that it was never the settled, placid and unconquered nation that it wants to be seen as. Like Afghanistan, it was left untouched by imperial powers and was only united in its opposition to them. With the death of colonialism its various ethnicities reverted to the internal squabbles of earlier years, built as they were around historical divisions of tribal allegiance, language and religion. What had been an African miracle has become a débâcle.

Intertwined with this was another Coca-Cola investment project in Eritrea, also under the tutelage of Sandy of TCCC. Eritrea was one of the most bizarre places I have ever visited. We landed in Asmara and were met in blinding heat on the airport apron by a man with a computer and printer. He checked our passports and gave us each a bit of paper with a barcode on it. We then proceeded to the terminal where the usual formalities, entirely paper-based, resumed. With stamps duly lodged in each passport and the barcode stapled to it, we emerged again from the ancient flaking building and into the blinding sunlight.

Eritrea was yellow—not the vibrant colour of daffodils but something dirtier, more downtrodden and more subdued. Compared to Addis, Asmara was tiny and had little substance to it: just a few central streets built by the Italians when it was their colony. The most prominent building was the 1930s cinema, Art Deco in design but still in use. The Italian legacy was muted and run-down but I note now that the central zone of Asmara is still called Alfa Romeo. The few people we saw were like shadows. They observed us but kept their distance.[2]

---

[2] Kapuśinki ibid, pp. 306–313. This rings true to me except for estimated distances from Asmara to Massawa.

Sandy, however, was enthusiastic. I could see why when we visited the local bottling plant with its single antiquated line churning out glass Coca-Cola bottles without interruption. A group of women crouched over a trough, deep cleaning bottles too soiled for recycling through the bottle-washing system on the line. 'Some of these bottles are over forty years old,' said Sandy. It was indeed impressive that this plant ran at over 90 per cent efficiency twenty-four hours a day with antiquated machinery. The problem was that it could not be upscaled to meet demand. Unlike in Ethiopia, however, the management was desperate for foreign investment. If Ethiopia had seemed like a good opportunity, this looked like a goldmine, for both us and the government.

The following day we drove over the mountains and down to the Red Sea port of Massawa. On the right of the road were the remains of the Italian 'ski-lift', a cable car for goods and passengers that traversed the 50 kms between the two. It must have been the longest in the world. One could easily assume that the road had made it redundant but this was not the case. The ski-lift went on being used until destroyed in the thirty-year civil war between the Eritrean Liberation Front and Ethiopia, a war which had ended with Eritrea's gaining independence only a few months before my visit.

The destruction caused by the war became evident when we arrived in Massawa—also known as Mitsiwa. No building was undamaged. Around the port, only skeletons of buildings were left standing. Even today, Google Maps shows whole zones of the town as nothing more than faint outline of streets and flattened buildings. It also shows wharves deserted, except for a few trading dhows, a scattering of containers and a disused railway.

My enthusiasm for the Eritrean bottling project was influenced by my recollection of Vietnam, a similarly devasted state where we had built a thriving business. Here was a chance to do the same again, so we returned to Asmara for a meeting with the president, Isaias Afewerki, who had spent the previous thirty years as a guerrilla leader. I had the confidence of an innocent as I walked in with our offer, which had been pre-discussed with the local delegation that had accompanied us. We would give the government a forty-per-cent stake and fund the necessary investment ourselves. Afewerki was disarmingly charming but demanded a sixty-per-cent stake. Our management control was not negotiable and that was the end of that.

As it turned out, it would have been a disastrous investment. Afewerki still regarded himself as the head of state of a country at war. He launched offensive after offensive against Ethiopia and succeeded in making it a landlocked state with the capture of Aseb, but otherwise the hostilities were conducted at huge cost, in terms of the number of lives lost, while leading only to a stalemate.

The Google Earth satellite picture of Aseb is troubling. There is a port with no ships of any kind, roads including a stretch of dual carriageway and a roundabout but with only a couple of vehicles on them across the whole extent of the city. There appear to be a few smart houses close to the shore and the suggestion of a couple of rows of shops on the main street. Elsewhere there are warehouses but no sign of activity and the ruins of what seems once to have been a church. In the spaces between are random scatterings of huts—a twenty-first century equivalent of the ancient cities of Central Asia. It is like looking at an archaeological site that no longer serves any useful purpose, populated only by ghosts.

In the name of nation-building, the president, Isaias Aferwerki, had destroyed his country. All men are conscripted for an indefinite period and the one-party state is justified on the grounds of defending the fatherland. It is a social and economic failure: the images of Massawa and Aseb provide the evidence. Eritreans represent a disproportionate share of those African economic migrants who resort to desperate measures to get into Europe. It was the peace agreement with Eritrea that led to Abiy Ahmed's peace prize but relations between the two countries remain frosty.[3] Oddly, however, Eritrea is an active combatant in the Tigrayan war on Ethiopia's side, something that is difficult to make sense of—except, presumably, for the participants.

---

[3] Meron Estafanos, 'The Nobel Peace Prize was Awarded for a Baffling Reason', *Washington Post*, 19 October 2019.

CHAPTER 11
Mozambique: 2012
The Opportunity

It would be a corporate jolly for the management team, I thought, hosted by our two principal tobacco suppliers. I looked forward to it as a chance to visit places I had never been to, see some big game in the wild, spend time with colleagues I respected and liked, and be temporarily relieved of the relentless and repetitious requests to 'improve our numbers'. In the forty years since I had first visited Africa, my views had crystalised and I was not going to learn anything new.

And so it appeared. The first part of this journey recalled previous experiences. In Malawi we stayed at a hilltop hotel with impressive early-morning views over the Great Rift Valley when the dawn sun lay low and the topography was accentuated. Less impressive were the public tobacco auctions that I attended. Since the prices paid for the crop were determined by these auctions, which in turn were under government control, buyers who might otherwise have invested in better production chose not to. Divorcing buyers from suppliers meant there was no incentive to create added value.

The surprise occurred in Tete province in Mozambique. Tete is close to the country's borders with Zimbabwe and Malawi and had suffered massive devastation and decay as a result of its proximity to the civil war in what was then Rhodesia and through the internal ructions in Mozambique itself when the Portuguese pulled out, following their own revolution. Among its many challenges was the fact that most of its agricultural land had been sown with land mines.

We arrived there on a light aircraft and were greeted by a ritual dance of men dressed as birds of prey. The accompanying delegation dutifully took photographs. I may have done so too—but reluctantly, having experienced a surfeit of folkloric welcome ceremonies over the years.

I had imagined that the turmoil of the Mozambiqan Civil War from 1977 to 1992 would have left it profoundly damaged. That impression vanished as soon as we arrived at the first of the villages. There were good roads, clean wells, schools with teachers and clinics with doctors. Houses had proper floors and roofs of galvanised zinc; some had satellite antennas, others had motorbikes outside the door. The local town had a thriving market selling consumer goods, including clothing of all descriptions, generators, televisions, radios, refrigerators, bicycles—an almost limitless stock of whatever the inhabitants aspired to own. And all the men had a mobile phone. This was a prosperous place.

But that was not what made the deepest impression. Wherever we went, we were greeted with something I had never experienced before in Africa: joy. People were glad to see us and wanted to show us everything; the children wanted to play football with us and were delighted when we joined in and they showed us how much better than us they were. The village headmen, all avuncular figures, showed us also that they were proud of what they had achieved but equally respectful of the communities they led.

The key to this difference lay in their attitude. They welcomed everybody on their own terms, were eager to know what we thought, and treated our mostly white hosts as trusted partners in a shared mission. Never before had I felt so much that all of us—locals and visitors—came together on equal terms. It was an inspiring sensation.

What had transformed this area from a ferocious battleground to a prosperous, optimistic and contented rural community? The answer is not what most people would want to hear: tobacco. Back in the Nineties, the warning signs that Zimbabwe was about to destroy its most valuable export crop through land seizures had prompted Universal Leaf to initiate a project to encourage tobacco growing in neighbouring Mozambique. Tete province had the same climate and soil types as Zimbabwe but it took people of vision to recognise its potential, given the calamitous condition the country was in. It took twenty years to make the project self-sustaining.

How was it done? Essentially it was a no-risk deal for the farmers. They were guaranteed a minimum price for their crop and provided with micro-finance and the assistance of agronomists to teach them how to cultivate. Each year they made a profit (though I doubt Universal Leaf did, at least in the first decade) and slowly, again thanks to Universal Leaf, the farmers gained a reputation for quality in a global market.

Universal Leaf's mission also had a social dimension. It wanted its farmers and families to live in a sustainable environment. It was this driving factor that led to the clearing of mines, the building of roads, wells and schools and the planting of trees. Flue-cured tobacco requires the burning of a lot of wood to produce a saleable crop. Originally this had been provided by the import of fast-growing eucalyptus; today it is sustained entirely by indigenous woodland.

Contrast this with an overseas aid project to encourage the growing of groundnuts in a neighbouring village. It was successful in the sense that the villagers were able to raise a crop or two but there was no market for them because no accessible towns had any interest in buying them. Their women sat by the side of the road all day trying to sell something that nobody wanted.

There are now over 750,000 people in Mozambique—nearly 8 per cent of the total population—who depend on tobacco as their source of income. The success of this project has also halted the drift of population to major urban centres in the hope of employment, and Chinese entrepreneurs have now set up shop in this former backwater. Unsurprisingly,

Universal Leaf is now regarded by the government as a reliable partner and its advice is readily listened to.

What makes this more extraordinary is that Universal Leaf, based in Richmond, Virginia, is not itself a very profitable organisation. Squeezed between growers and the four global tobacco majors, its margins are slim and many similar tobacco suppliers have gone under, or been absorbed by larger rivals. None of them makes much money.

So why did it embark on this highly risky strategy? My guess is that it was down to the people it employed. Most of them were long-term white Africa hands for whom the easy option of returning to Europe did not appeal. One of them had owned the tobacco farm ranked third-best in Zimbabwe until seized by Mugabe. It now grows subsistence crops. I asked him how he felt about this. 'This is Africa,' he said with a shrug; 'you have to expect the unthinkable.'

Such people do not fit the liberal expectation of what it takes to transform society. In many ways they are unattractive: hard-drinking, misogynistic and blunt in their language. Their politics, too, verges from conservative to extreme right. But they love Africa, irrespective of the personal sacrifices they have to make, and that toughness and drive gets results. From what I saw, they respect local opinion and seek consensus with the communities they work with and I suspect that their no-nonsense approach is more venerated by the black communities than the Western conscience is prepared to admit. I admire them.

This is my last Africa story and the most important, because the approach that these farmers take offers a way forward that has too rarely been applied, probably because it is not politically expedient. It embraces many virtues. The first of these is empathy. These white farmers, who in many cases have had their lives turned upside down by land seizures, understand Africa and know how to work with it, even if they are unapologetic about how they came to be landowners in the first place. The second element is know-how, long-term vision and strategy: they possess detailed expertise, the ability to develop plans and the resolution to carry those plans out. The third is that they are mentors, not teachers: they seek to influence the building of consensus and use the results to demonstrate the effectiveness of their proposals. (Tobacco growing is labour-intensive; it is not just the landowners who need to be convinced.) The fourth is that they are interested in the well-being of the whole community, not just a select few. The fifth is they act as an effective conduit between the expectations of the end-customer and global stakeholders and their growers. The sixth is that they are prepared to invest in social infrastructure even though it has no obvious payback: they know that not to improve living standards all round is counter-productive. A seventh element, I suspect, is that a universal trait of African culture is respect for authority and these guys obviously know what they are doing.

The model employed by these tobacco farmers is that of a cooperative in all but its financial structure and, from the little I know, that seems appropriate for Africa, where society is collective, hierarchies are respected, and local or tribal loyalties are strong. The model operates in a sector in which venal politicians have no interest, and which requires very little government involvement. It employs the skills of the people and improves them, and those who do not cooperate are put under pressure from their own clan in what works as a virtuous circle. Growing tobacco in this way shows that a better life can be attained on your own doorstep, in radical contrast to the subsistence farmers who are failed by the model imposed on them by international aid and who flock to the city slums in desperation.

CHAPTER 12
The Political Systems of Africa

When I studied African history in the 1970s, I was supervised by two white lecturers who had never been to Africa and who relied on source documentation that was strongly biased towards European records because there were few written languages in Africa and therefore little in the way of conventional African archives.

Accordingly we were directed to a one-sided narrative that even then I was aware was paternalistic and patronising. The mythology of 'Darkest Africa' may have had its roots in the impenetrability of the heartland's pestilential rain forest but was used to convey the idea that Africans needed to see the light in order to escape their intrinsically barbaric and savage nature.

The legacy of this calumny remains in my account, above, of post-independence Nigeria. What we were not taught at the time was that the woes of Africa were to a large extent the result of Western intervention, and the values and attitudes that the West embodied at the time. As ever in politics, powerful nations determine the fate but also the perceived character of weaker ones.

Since then, the re-evaluation of African history that began in the academic world has become a staple of the popular media. It has also become more contentious, as a wider range of thinkers contribute to it. This book is not about unravelling that historical debate but, because of my conviction that history is never binary, I do wish to attempt a precarious and anti-ideological path of my own, for the purpose of explaining why societies behave as they do. To repeat myself: cultures and conventions have long histories, and detail matters.

One common approach—found today in the GCSE history syllabus—is to lump every aspect of European involvement in

Africa into an unbroken period of exploitation and evil intent. However, there were two distinct periods. The first was the slave trade, which emerged as a by-product of the original quest, first for gold, then goods, in the late-fifteenth century and which ended after it had been abolished by Britain and, later, other mercantile states in the first half of the nineteenth century. The focus of that era was trade, pure and simple, and no African territory of any significance was colonised during that period. The second period—the colonial 'Scramble for Africa'—was a product of the second half of the nineteenth century and was a very different phenomenon.

Slavery was not an imported concept but a pervasive practice in Africa long before the Europeans arrived, providing a source of export income and a solution to tribal conflicts. Populations who were regarded as surplus to requirements or fighters who were regarded as a danger were exported to destinations in North Africa and the Middle East. Africans sent their slaves for sale in the trading ports. On the east coast, the city of Dar-es-Salaam was built on slaving to Oman, nearly 2,500 miles away, at the south-eastern tip of Arabian Peninsula.

Our stereotype of a slave is that of someone bound by shackles and treated by his or her owner as no more than a discardable chattel. Though this certainly applied to those transported across the Atlantic, the treatment of those who had been enslaved was not always so dire. Greek and Roman historians, for example, refer to slaves rising to the highest positions in the state. Some Turkish slaves ended up ruling Egypt. And my tutors suggested[1] that the Ashanti assimilated those they had captured by making it a capital crime to

---

[1] But I have never been able to verify my tutors' suggestion, nor the assertion that the seizure of the Benin Bronzes was justified because Benin was a slaving state.

enquire where a stranger had come from. The fact that there are many analogous systems, such as serfdom in Russia, landless peasantry in Europe, the proscription against Dalits (untouchables) in India and the exploitation of indigenous peoples in the Americas suggests that servitude was a global phenomenon in the days before machines, when cheap labour was, aside from land, the only cost-effective asset.

I have relied on Howard W. French[2] to make sense of the impact of the slave trade and have found in his writings a compelling narrative, written as it is from the viewpoint of an American descendant of African slaves. I recommend it to anyone interested in the impact of the slave trade in the Americas for he shows that slavery's consequences for Africans in America were very different from its consequences for Africa itself, and that poses important questions that are too easily sidestepped.

Physical artefacts of the slave trade can be found in many places on the African coast but there is one visible reminder of it on the street: the aforementioned 'piece'—that five yards of printed cotton cloth. This remains the favoured garb of Africa men and women when dressing up. According to French, a fit slave was worth two of these.

The slave trade must have exacerbated political conflict through the dislocation of populations and the increasing demand for firearms rather than pieces. Its abolition in the first half of the nineteenth century ended a lucrative business for both suppliers and buyers (though the latter were well compensated). As a result, most of Africa was left in a weakened and possibly chaotic state: perfect ground for the introduction of colonial rule. In that sense, colonialism was

---

[2] Howard W. French, *Born in Blackness: Africa, Africans and the Making of the Modern World—1471 to the Second World War*, Liveright Publishing Corp. (2021).

the natural successor to slavery. Notably, the only significant African opposition to colonialisation came from the Ashanti and Zulu; from this it was eagerly concluded in Europe that colonisation was not unwelcome, as long as social structures based on tribal allegiance remained intact. A more considered evaluation is that Africans were in no state to resist.

For those people who were transported westwards to the Americas, social structures broke down almost immediately. The only thing that the enslaved had in common was the fact of their being black, and their owners were assiduous in keeping them separate from their own kin. The civil rights movement of the mid-twentieth century and its twenty-first-century successor, Black Lives Matter, were based on the premise that skin colour was the sole factor that gave rise to discrimination. That is true in the sense that skin colour was seen as validating ill-treatment. But a more subtle abuse was that the cultures of those transported to foreign soils diverged from that of those who remained at home.

The earliest example of this can be seen in Liberia, where an influx of freed and free-born African-Americans, together with a smaller number of Afro-Caribbeans, led to Liberia's declaration of itself as an independent nation in 1847 and thereby Africa's first modern republic. The newly arrived and better-educated cohort went on to dominate Liberia's own indigenous peoples for over a century until 1980, when a coup resulted in two brutal civil wars. In summary, the new black governing class regarded the native people as mere forest-dwellers; so much for the universal black community.

Laudable attempts to create some unification and a sense of belonging in French West Africa, above and beyond tribal allegiances, can be traced back to the late nineteenth century and culminated in the 'negritude' movement, referred to earlier, whose prime (or perhaps most prominent) mover was the poet Léopold Sédar Senghor, who went on to become the first president of independent Senegal, from 1960 to 1980. The movement failed, however, through a combination of vested interests and the same ethnic rivalries that had dominated African politics for centuries.

A recent BBC programme has claimed that black people of African descent in Britain tend to obtain higher starting salaries in the UK than the children of white, Indian, Pakistani or Chinese background. The programme attributed this to a shared belief in education as a means of personal advancement. Having tried to reconcile my own experience of meeting many highly professional and personable Nigerian professionals with the apparent shambles of their government, this came as welcome news: it suggests that a new generation has got beyond foregrounding its centuries of white suppression to justify under-achievement. Less welcome is the news that the same is not true for the descendants of black slaves from the Caribbean. In short—as should be obvious— being black does not mean you share the same values or experiences. 'Black' is not an all-purpose label, and generalisations about being black should only be embarked on with great caution.

Africa was the last continent in the world to be colonised, and colonisation post-dated the slavery years—though King Leopold of the Belgians regarded the Congo as a personal fiefdom where slavery continued in all but name. There was no rational argument for his doing so: there were then no untold riches to be discovered and exploited, the climate was noxious and civil society was anarchic. Leopold's behaviour was about formalising areas of influence in the race for empire: a question of prestige cloaked in the patronising cloth of bringing civilisation to savages.

In the absence of any coherent rationale for their land grab —trade could have been conducted peacably and more productively without making claims on foreign territory—the sub-Saharan colonisers made a bad situation worse by imposing borders that ignored ethnic structures and divisions. Investment in the new colonies was also cut to the minimum after it became obvious that the economic return on colonisation was insignificant. The colonisers' legacy was a bunch of independent states defined only by Western lines on a map, their economies dominated by subsistence agriculture, ruled by a tiny élite of landowning expats and tribal leaders whose loyalty was to their ethnic supporters but with no experience of governance, operating on a minuscule revenue base, with high levels of poverty and illiteracy, and the most rudimentary physical and social infrastructure. People quickly became impoverished and diminished, and independence, when it came, made absolutely no difference to the lives of most of them.

British Prime Minister Harold Macmillan's 'Winds of Change' speech in 1960 positioned independence as a purely moral issue. It was true that colonies had become unfashionable and increasingly difficult to police, and that populist national leaders were painting rosy pictures of what life would be like once the colonists had gone. But when the colonial flags were finally lowered, it marked little more than the symbolic passing of the reins of government to local politicians who had already been dealt a bad hand of cards.

Beholden to liberal democratic values, the West's response was driven, and continues to be driven, by guilt at having left such an unholy mess, by an unwillingness to get embroiled once again in the politics of the ex-colonies, and by a patronising attitude as to what would benefit Africa's benighted populations. In 1984, when the BBC journalist Michael Buerk described the famine in Ethiopia as 'the closest thing to Hell on Earth', it inspired various leading figures in the pop music industry to make a charity record,[3] the finale of which was

---

[3] 'Don't They Know it's Christmas' (1984), written by Bob Geldof and Midge Ure.

'Feed the World'. This notion encapsulated all three responses but motivated the West to embrace the concept of charity as a solution to Africa's ills.

This had two devastating repercussions: the atomisation of appeals for help for myriad disadvantaged groups (not just people but also livestock and nature) and the arrival of megafoundations with their own Western-biased agendas for what the poor most needed. There are myriad stories of how these well-intended initiatives not only failed to achieve their aims but reinforced a prevailing culture of victimhood or extortion.

It is unsurprising, therefore, that Africa's political élites concentrate on enriching themselves and their friends at the expense of Western donors. And why not? It's payback time. In this light, Mugabe's seizure of white-owned farms fitted the logic of dispossessing a small minority with no political power and passing them on to cronies who would forever be in his debt. The fact that it ruined the economy is something he regarded as an acceptable if regrettable consequence. Mugabe's successor and former righthand man, Emmerson Mnangagwa, known as 'the Crocodile', made all the right noises on assuming power but has since settled back to business as usual, having been accused of just the same human-rights abuses and corruption as the man he deposed.

The chaotic polities of self interest and ethnic rivalries have had numerous unfortunate impacts. NGOs now by-pass governments as far as they can, on the grounds that they are either useless or obstructive. They try to concentrate on their mission statement and, as a result, deal only with the symptoms, not the causes. The Gates Foundation, the largest private benefactor to Africa by miles, is dedicated to the eradication of malaria. It has been remarkably effective but in that lies another irony. World population growth is highest in sub-Saharan Africa. High birth rates have been driven both by high infant mortality and the belief that children are economic assets who will grow up to exploit already denuded agricultural resources. This desire for procreation—other than the sheer pleasure of the act—is driven by desperation. Madagascar has had the unique distinction of doubling its population while its gross national product stayed exactly the same. The result is visible: parched earth instead of traditional forest, land leached by monsoon run-off, and another 250,000 acres of forest destroyed each year by desperate peasants. It is a road to nowhere for them and for us.

Meanwhile the West is preoccupied at home by ageing populations and declining birth rates, a consequence of the post-war economic miracle of developed societies in which children became an economic liability rather than an asset. The delegates to COP 26 and COP 27, the United Nations conferences on climate change in 2021 and 2022, spent much time arguing how much the developed world should pay to bribe the rest of the world to reduce its carbon emissions. The reality, however, is that it is not the rest of the world but the industrialised nations that are the culprits. The last thing Africa needs is a carbon-emission reduction programme as yet another barrier to wealth creation.

Breaking the post-independence vicious circle of revolving governments, ethnic and religious conflict, and corruption requires as a first step a conviction among its citizens that government matters and that good government can improve their lives. This must come from below, moving subsistence agriculturalists into a more added-value system that depends on collaborating with others. The means of making African governments more responsive to the needs and expectations of their citizens depends on the West's funding the initiative.[4]

---

[4] Granting €1 billion to Tunisia to curtail illegal immigration despite a new autocrat leader suggests that this is not unaffordable and could address the root cause of the problem, not just the symptoms.

This is not an overnight solution—the values and histories of these societies are highly engrained—but it is the only way out. We cannot expect liberal democractic régimes to emerge from the ground like fully prepared warriors from dragon seeds; but making the connection between citizens and a government that matters to them would be a huge step forward.

Do I take responsibility for anything that went wrong in Africa, whether in the distant past or during my own time? No. The sins of our fathers were usually done with the best of intentions. Nor do I think that cancelling benefactors who profited from slave trading or from colonial rule is anything other than virtue signalling. If liberal democracy has a core value, it is the provision of opportunities for all and that is what needs fixing. Sending asylum seekers to Rwanda seems only marginally better than the slave trade. It is root causes that need grappling with, not their consequences.

PART 3
LATIN AMERICA

CHAPTER 13
Haves and Have-Nots

The Spanish and Portuguese colonies were left to their own devices 200 years ago but Iberian values and Catholicism continue to resonate in Latin America, not least because after independence was granted, expatriates from Spain and Portugal continued to run the fledgling countries on the same lines as had Madrid and Lisbon.

Having worked for a time in Spain, I am reminded that these new republics' cliques of authority, extended families, personal hierarchies and ideas about obligation, all very different from the Northern European meritocratic model, are reminiscent of the cultural practices of Mediterranean states.

In my next chapters I refer in detail to only two of them—one in Central America (Nicaragua) and one in South America (Chile)—partly because those were the only Latin countries I lived in long enough to understand the nuances of their societies, and partly because their propects as nations are so very different.

On a biographical note, I spent most of my time in Latin America as an employee of BAT. During that time I married Kathy in Managua in April 1978; our son, Jamie, was born in Santiago de Chile in October 1980. We went together to El Salvador, Costa Rica, Panama, Brazil, Argentina and Suriname, to the last of which my wife took a particular dislike, an opinion shared by the KLM check-in at Schiphol who, on learning where we were going to, said 'Poor you'. Working later for Inchcape, I returned to Chile and visited Ecuador, Peru and Mexico to investigate Coca-Cola bottling interests.

CHAPTER 14
Nicaragua: 1977 to 1979
Civil War

I set off for Latin America with only the slightest understanding of it. I knew where the countries were on the map well enough but thought that they were all dictatorships, all had regular coups, all were universally corrupt, all suffered insurgencies and that all these patterns were long-standing. I also assumed that all were subject to frequent natural disasters.

My time in Nicaragua did nothing to alter this, for most of the places I went to conformed to the stereotypes. Mexico, Brazil and Argentina, as larger nations, were (and are) more complex but they nonetheless suffered from the dysfunctional politics and rampant corruption of the smaller nations. What I wanted to know, as I travelled across Central and South America, was why these patterns of behaviour recurred—and I think I eventually found out.

At the time I was there, in the late 1970s, the USA regarded Nicaragua not just as a battleground but as the site of what might be the final showdown between Communism and capitalism. This binary view was at odds with what was actually happening on the ground, which was a slowly emerging coalition of those opposed to the tyrant Anastasio Somoza Debayle, who were prepared to put into action their call to arms: '*Patria libre o morir*'—a free country or death.

I hesitated before using the word 'tyrant' in the paragraph above. 'Dictator' is less value-laden but, on reflection, 'tyrant' is the right word. Somoza regarded Nicaragua as his personal property, having inherited the presidency from his father. 'Tacho', as he was called, was prepared to eliminate anybody who opposed him. It is revealing that when he resigned from the presidency and fled to Miami in July 1979, he took with him the mortal remains of his father and grandfather, as well as all the central bank reserves. He was killed by a bazooka in Paraguay a year later. Good riddance.

The USA, however, preferred Somoza and his model of capitalist corruption and after he was overthrown did everything in its power (and beyond it) to reverse the outcome.

Managua, the capital of Nicaragua, was not an attractive place. The earthquake of 23 December 1972 had destroyed most of the old city. All that was left was a gridiron of roads going nowhere with, here and there, a few surviving buildings poking up like headstones in a giant's graveyard. New structures had started to circle the remains of the old. A postcard that I sent at the time is labelled, '*Managua surge de sus cenizas*' (Managua leaps from its ashes). It shows a two-lane blacktop flanked by borders of sand and a series of jerry-built concrete one-storey buildings. The building closest to the camera has the golden arches of McDonald's.

My lack of conversational Spanish, my preoccupation with events at home and a social life lived among other expatriates skilled at keeping out of trouble, left me on the very fringe of understanding what was going on this country. I knew that the reason for Somoza's prohibition on rebuilding the old city —that it was not safe—was spurious and that the real reason was that he and his cronies owned the land around it and thereby stood to make (and then steal) a fortune. I did not know until recently about his systematic looting of humanitarian aid in response to the earthquake, or that his ban on rebuilding had turned a significant proportion of the middle class against him because their modest properties in the old city were now valueless. Protests would have been louder, especially among the younger elements, but the police state kept them silent.

While the Lao had suffered far worse misfortunes, they seemed to remain hospitable, gentle and welcoming. Here I encountered a sullen indifference, a rapaciousness that had no moral compass, save that the poor had to live off the rich in whatever way they could. At the start of every week, after spates of weekend killings, the Government newspaper, *Las Novedades*, would carry pictures of corpses at the morgue on the back page of its Monday edition, with the message, 'if you recognise them, pick them up.' In hindsight, I think this is why I found Nicaraguan society, in so much as it touched me at all, utterly uncongenial.

In fact, there was no 'society', in the way I understood it. Alcohol was the essential element of any social gathering and getting drunk was considered socially acceptable, unless you were a woman, in which case your task was to stay with the other women and make small talk about babies and fashion.

The political reality was oppression: overstep the mark and you too would be on the back page of *Novedades*. The way one lived one's life was conservative and conventional, with well-established gender roles. Women were expected to be stay-at-home mothers while men acted as hunter-gatherers, hunting and gathering, among other things, a *querida* for themselves. Our Nica friend Lionel made a good living from running a knocking shop on the highway to the airport, where cars drew up behind closed curtains and rooms could be had by the hour. But for a woman to be unfaithful outside her marriage—that was unforgiveable.

The women I met conformed on the surface to the stereotype outlined above. One did not: Giaconda Belli,[1] on whom I have relied to put my experience into better perspective. She was clearly a woman ahead of her time. Only one other woman whom I knew had a similar outlook and that was only revealed to me near the end of my stay. Perhaps that is not surprising: before the Sandinistas toppled Somoza,

---

[1] Giaconda Belli, *The Country Under my Skin: A Memoir of Love and War*, Bloomsbury (2002).

anybody who supported their movement was unlikely to admit to it, given the threats that they faced.

Sandinistas were named after a national hero of the 1930s, who was assassinated after a banquet given to celebrate a peace deal. As Salman Rushdie noted in *The Jaguar Smile*, Augusto César Sandino's most recognisable feature, in the graffiti that depicted him with increasing frequency, was his hat: a bowler-like construction with an elevated top and extended sides.[2]

It was only towards the end of our stay that Manuel and Adela, the son and daughter of knocking-shop-owner Lionel, admitted that they were Sandinistas. They arrived at our house one night to report that they had been smuggling guns into town and trying to avoid the intertwined nails in the road (known as *miguelitos*) that would have blown their tyres out. Manuel admitted all this while giggling. He had been stoned during the whole mission and proved it by showing me the stash hidden in his sock. The two of them were the most unlikely revolutionaries one could have encountered. Manuel was running to fat, smoked joints continuously and chuckled when embarrassed. Adela was rather more practical but had never in our acquaintance expressed a single political opinion. It was at that moment that I realised that this was not a civil war between the proletariat and bourgeoisie but a middle-class confrontation with itself. It takes a lot to turn a stoned and self-confessed coward into a gun runner.

To begin with, my time in Nicaragua was relatively quiet. The Sandinistas were considered little more than a fringe opposition, confined to their jungle lairs. The first inkling that they might constitute a threat to the incumbency, which occurred shortly after my arrival, was easily defeated: the

---

[2] Salman Rushdie, *The Jaguar Smile: A Nicaraguan Journey*, Vintage (2007).

raiding of some provincial towns. The only inconvenience it caused in Managua was that temporary roadblocks were set up but they were soon removed.

As a trainee, I had a buddy. Clemente was a Nicaraguan who had been employed in the leaf department but wanted to broaden his career. He was required to teach me how tobacco was grown locally so we drove in a VW Beetle decorated with the company's livery, Tanic (Tabacalera Nicaragüense), into the remote highlands of the northeast, along dirt roads cutting a track through sombre jungle. On the way, the fan belt snapped, which did not seem much of a problem in an air-cooled car but turned out also to service the dynamo. We arrived in what was little more than a scattering of huts in a clearing to discover that a new fan belt could not be delivered until the morning. Clemente was not happy about this, fearful that we might be kidnapped for ransom by Sandinistas who were known to be nearby. However, a meal of *gallo pinto* (beans and rice and chicken), plus copious quantities of Ron Plata, helped us to sleep, and when the fan belt turned up the following morning, we got going. Clemente became a friend until we went our separate ways. I last encountered him in Baku in 2012.

I am embarrassed to say that the political tensions of my host country largely passed me by at the time and I was careful to laugh them off in my letters home. I confess that I failed to recognise what a disgusting régime I was living under. Had I met anybody prepared to discuss with me openly what it meant to be a 'Nica' in Nicaragua, I am sure I would have changed my view—but I didn't. As expats, we lived astonishingly insulated lives, which was odd, given our commercial interest in fully understanding the country we were working in.

My exploration of Nicaragua's neighbours came through cricket. There were no native Central Americans in the teams from El Salvador, Costa Rica and Nicaragua, though some had taken out dual nationality. Those who took part were a mixture of expatriates, the scions of local entrepreneurs from the days when Britain was a world power, and descendants of former Caribbean slaves who had ended up on these shores. English was their lingua franca. The local population watched us play in incomprehension; in conversation, as in so much else, they kept their thoughts to themselves before moving on quickly to more important things, of which there were few.

El Salvador was a carbon copy of Nicaragua, except that it had no ruling dynasty but, instead, a tiny Mestizo élite who ran the country for their own mutual advantage, relying on the labour of the poor (of more Indian blood) to keep themselves in the lifestyle they considered their right. Corruption and crime were rife, the physical and social infrastructure decrepit, except in those isolated pockets where the rich lived and moved, and social services were the exclusive remit of foreign aid organisations and the Church.

My second cricket match there coincided with a power cut across San Salvador, which marked the start of its own civil war, just like its neighbour Nicaragua, but without its ending in a revolution. I never went to Honduras or Guatemala, but had enough chats with those who knew them well to recognise second-hand their similarity.

Three months in Panamá, despite the gloss of high-rise apartments, a thriving entrepôt trade and some very dodgy private and public finances, was just a slightly richer version of the same model.

A much later visit to Mexico showed how this structure could develop a growing middle class and thus an expanding tax base capable of funding at least basic physical and local infrastructure; that has not halted the exodus of Mexicans to menial jobs in the USA, as is well known. Mexico is big and makes the rest of Central America look insignificant, but the absence of any way out for the underclass has created fertile ground for an alternative challenge for power: the emergence of drug gangs. In 1971 the USA declared a War on Drugs. Some fifty years later, it can claim to have nabbed a couple of high-profile drug lords but has achieved little else through its whack-a-mole policy of attacking whatever moves while ignoring the underground systems that keeps moles alive: principally, consumer demand—in the USA and elsewhere in the West.

My wife was hired to take the legal documents justifying the seizure of a Cessna light aircraft which had been transporting drugs to Norman, Oklahoma, via New Orleans. It was supposed to be a there-and-back journey with an overnight stay. Since she was suspiciously only carrying hand baggage, she was strip-searched on arrival in the USA. I suppose that Somoza would have said that this gained some credit with the American government. What was not provided was any official document to explain the purpose of her trip.

I had spent four month in Nicaragua on my own but at the end of December 1977, Kathy, then my fiancée, joined me. I met her from the steps of a Pan Am 707 and a BAT fixer escorted us outside while he dealt with her documents. In a matter of minutes, it seemed, he returned with her luggage and a resident visa. It was a bizarre introduction for someone who had previously been coordinating translations of Amnesty International's report on Nicaraguan state-sanctioned torture. I was delighted at how easily Kathy's transit had been effected but was aware at the same time that only banknotes' changing hands had made this possible. She found it bewildering.

On 10 January, 1978, Pedro Joaquim Chamorro Cardenal was assassinated. He was the editor of the popular newspaper *La Prensa*, the only independent journal in Nicaragua, and was revered for his principled opposition to Somoza's excesses. Although he was imprisoned several times, his stature as an independent observer of events provided the Somoza régime with a cloak of respectability, falsely suggesting that it could countenance opposition. The régime's attempts to place the blame for his assassination elsewhere were universally disbelieved. Mass demonstrations at Chamorro's funeral provided the evidence that Somoza had been feared and not loved. It was a turning point. Somoza now began to lose the outward support of the middle classes, who had only ever put up with him as a protector of the status quo. I never read the Amnesty torture report. I should have done.

To get a break from Nicaragua, we drove to San José, Costa Rica—very different from the rest of Central America. It had no army. What it did have were regular elections, though it was hard to distinguish the difference between the two main political parties. It was also inclusive, as was testified to by our host's guided tour of *cantinas*, where we greeted with tolerant amusement by the *Ticos*. Some referred to Costa Rica as the Switzerland of Central America—an analogy that went no further than that it was small, peaceful and no threat to the USA. In a very un-Swiss policy, it had chosen to attract US retirees with low income tax and cheap housing, on the grounds that their spending would stimulate the economy. This appears to have been successful, as has the promotion of tourism in a country with more ecosystems per square mile than anywhere else in the world. Above all, it is safe. Nowhere else in Central America can claim that. For the increasingly risk-averse Western world, that is its biggest attraction.

In contrast, Nicaragua was a country of barriers: between the *campesinos* (peasant farmers) and the bourgeoisie, between expatriates and locals, between the government and the population. We were advised never to venture into the poorer parts of town.

I had failed to consider that an uncongenial country would not appeal to a new wife who had abandoned a career to be with me. I had a job; she had nothing to do all day. I was occupied by my work; she was frightened by gunfights down the street from where we first lived. She had never lived outside Europe before. Even driving scared her, as there were no discernible rules of the road. This was the Wild West and beyond her experience. However, a move out of town, the kindness of new friends, being forced to drive back from the airport when the alternative was abandoning the car, and her taking on some part-time jobs slowly created some sense of normality for her. Underneath this was a compact: I was the breadwinner, she the housewife. No other contract was available—except that we got a tiny but ferocious dog. That also helped.

WE EXITED OUR first period in Nicaragua in better shape than we had begun it. On 19 September, 1978, we left for San Francisco to stay with friends. It was a strange reunion, summed up by Giaconda Belli's remark that, 'There was no harmony in a world where one could jump in a five-hour journey from abject misery to excess.' Back in the UK we were told that spouses were advised to stay out of Nicaragua.

I returned to a country on the edge. A year before, the Sandinistas had been regarded as a mere irritant, now they were a danger. There were roadblocks on every major highway into and out of the city. The sound of bombs and gunfire in the poor *barrios* of Managua at night became something we got used to. The head of security visited and instructed expatriates on how to hang up a sodden blanket between two washing lines to avoid small arms fire. His demonstration went as predicted: a bullet passed through the first layer, hit the second and then fell on the ground. I never worked out how I was going to fix two washing lines to all our windows. It was also suggested that we disrupt our usual patterns of movement by changing arrival and departure times, using different vehicles and taking different routes. I did the first but there was only one route to the office and we only had one car.

The sense of being under siege became a part of everyday life. It gave rise to a foolhardiness and an adrenaline-charged misapprehension about feeling in command.

A visiting BAT manager stayed at the Ramada Inn, where he was accosted by a distraught young Canadian woman. She had met Tachito, Somoza's son, at a nightclub in Los Angeles, was invited to Nicaragua and had been locked up in her hotel room and repeatedly gang-raped. The Canadian Embassy was apparently contacted and the woman returned home. It was not reported in the media.

There is a whiff of Graham Greene in the moral dilemma of expatriate permanent residents whose livelihoods depended on the status quo. The most obvious example was Somoza's pilot, who had convinced my wife that flying to Norman, Oklahoma to hand over the paperwork for a seized drug-transporting Cessna would be a routine procedure, but failed to provide any official documents to verify this. His attitude was that this was just a job and he protected himself from criticism by expressing little regard for his employer. He seemed to have little regard for anybody when he emptied the magazine of his Uzi sub-machine gun, provided for his protection, into the roof of his living room in the presence of his wife and stepchildren. It was an accident, he explained.

Despite the roadblocks, the curfews and the intermittent sound of explosions and gunfire, life carried on as before. An American teacher was killed in a skirmish. We did not know him but all agreed that he had been silly to be in a part of town at night where there had been unrest, but what did we know?

For unknown reasons, the UK's ban on wives and dependants coming to Nicaragua was lifted (Kathy had been left in England for her own safety when I returned from annual leave). Perhaps the situation had calmed down; it certainly ebbed and flowed. This was no march to certain victory, unlike Vietnam post-1973. My memory of it was of an uncertain decline towards chaos.

Our dog was to prove his worth on Kathy's return. He would perch on the top of the bench seat of our newly acquired but ancient Mercedes and launch himself at anybody who came near. The street kids roaming the parking lots of shopping malls attempted to buy him from us. '*Es muy feroz*,' they said. And he was—a perfect guard dog.

Civil strife might have waned but it was only an intermission. The road blocks, manned by the National Guard, became permanent fixtures and Somoza's resources increasingly stretched. The same guardsmen would be on duty for forty-eight hours, kept going by a supply of amphetamines. These drugged-out zombies became unpredictable. Kathy was driving into town one morning when she was stopped, as usual. The procedure was for the driver to open the glove box so the leading guardsman could take a look inside it while others checked the boot. This time, the leading guardsman made the mistake of leaning through the open driver's window too far, at which point our dog bit him on the nose. It was one of those instants that last an eternity. Fortunately, and unexpectedly, he laughed, '*Muy peligroso el perrito*' (a very dangerous little dog), he said, while rapidly withdrawing. The story must have got around, as Kathy was waved through thereafter.

A side effect of the conflict was that law and order began to break down. Guard dogs and small arms became common accessories for most households but proved not to be effective. Guard dogs, kept outside, could be quickly and silently disposed of using strychnine-laced meat. And thieves knew where everyone kept their guns, which were in great demand, because everybody had a maid, or at least a cleaner.

We had no gun and Ricky the dog slept in our bedroom.

One night we were targeted but he alerted us. The thief fled but had managed to slide my briefcase through the iron grill. I found it the next morning abandoned outside the house next door. All that was missing was a $1 Barbados banknote, that I had kept as a souvenir. Value? About 8p.

We had the situation under control, we thought. We even managed to convince the Costa Rican cricket team to come to Managua for a return fixture. They came for pre-dinner drinks at our new house. I noticed that they seemed uneasy. 'What's that?' one of them asked. 'Oh, nothing! Just mortars and rifle fire downtown. Happens every night.' The following day our public-school bowler got them all out for a total of seven. They got home safely but I doubt they enjoyed the experience.

It seemed that our time in Nicaragua could go on forever in this uncertain, insecure way. Then I was told we were being posted to Panamá. We received a circular dated 29 May, 1979 from the British Consul in Costa Rica, advising all dependants with UK citizenship to leave the country in view of the deteriorating political situation. We framed it and now have it on display in our downstairs toilet.

Our departure was fixed for some weeks later. A round of farewell parties was organised but had barely begun when the general manager called me into his office. 'You're leaving tonight on Braniff.' I drove home and we began to pack: two suitcases, a trunk and a dog.

Two doors down from us lived the head of station of the CIA and his wife. He told us that our moving out was ridiculous, that he had it from the highest authority that there was no risk. I explained that I had no option. He made a disparaging remark about rats leaving a sinking ship—a saying I have never thought of as indicating anything other than the most sensible option—and we parted.

Our departure now seems like a half-remembered dream. The pilot allowed Ricky the dog to travel with us in the cabin, which was kind. I seem to remember an air-bridge at Panamá, as well as long concrete walkways to immigration and customs, but that seems too modern. Panamá was a busier airport than Las Mercedes in Managua but not by much. What I do recall was Ricky cocking his leg at the first pillar he came to and pissing for over a minute. I thought I should clear it up but was overcome with a wave of exhaustion as the rush of civil war dissipated. It was reminiscent of *The Year of Living Dangerously*,[3] but on another continent. A few weeks earlier, in all the stress and disruption, I had snapped at my wife during an inconsequential game of cards, infuriated by her winning all the time. I was confused and contrite. My excuse was that the pressure of pretending that what we were living through was normal and that I was in control of it got ruptured in that moment. How we got to our destination in Panamá, I have no idea.

We must have stayed in a hotel—the Hilton?—and four days later we were reunited with the wife of the CIA man. She had left under fire, evacuated by the USAF from Somoza's private airstrip, the airport already in the hands of the Sandinistas. Incandescent with rage, she told the media that the US government had not only failed to realise the gravity of the situation but had no contingency plans in place for its people. Ours was the last commercial flight out, a precursor of Saigon and Kabul. Why is it always a surprise for them?

The principle that guided Washington's approach to Nicaragua almost to the end of the Somoza régime was the 'better dead than red' nostrum referred to at the start of this chapter. As an adjunct to this, American understanding of what was happening on the ground, not to mention why, was always hopelessly blinkered—even under the presidency of

---

[3] A 1982 movie based on a novel of the same name, concerning the Suharto coup in Indonesia and its repercussions.

the supposedly liberal Jimmy Carter. How else could David Heywood, general manager of a relatively insignificant subsidiary, have had a better grasp of political reality, despite the meagre resources that he had to monitor it and the detachment that I have already commented on of the expatriate business community? I believe the answer was that he had no political agenda and was therefore more open to listening to anyone who was prepared to talk to him, a skill refined by the weeks he spent as a hostage of Argentinian guerrillas. As for the CIA, the Afghanistan *débâcle* suggests that they don't seem any more capable now than they were back then.

I was invited to return to Nicaragua after the Sandinistas had won. When I arrived, my passport was stamped with a poem by Ruben Dario, Nicaragua's most revered poet in a country that regarded poetry as a most distinguished profession. I did not need a visa, and nobody asked me about my political affiliations. Every wall was covered in graffiti with the revolutionary slogan '*Patria libre o morir*' and effigies of Sandino in his famous hat. Red and black bandannas were everywhere. Above all, everybody was smiling. The factory was unscathed. Pretend rifles—black painted broomsticks—had kept the adversaries out until it became a Red Cross field hospital, though everything else along the airport road was damaged.

Steve, the pilot, took his dogs with him on the presidential plane to Miami and telexed his resignation from there.

The outpouring of idealism from the overthrow of a tyrannical régime seemed naïve but genuine. It did not last long. US policy, as recalled by Belli, was 'do what we tell you'. Within a year, civil war had returned to Nicaragua with the 'contras', a mercenary army financed legally and illegally by the US government. This was their 'sphere of influence' and they felt entitled to do whatever they wanted. Until February 1990, death, destruction and poverty continued. Finally caving into US pressure, the Sandinistas called elections under international supervision and lost. Violetta Chamorro, widow of the assassinated *La Prensa* editor, was elected president. Belli puts this down to a general exhaustion with the constant state of war and laments the loss of a vision of a fairer, more inclusive society. Here I disagree with her. As I indicated earlier, this was not a national struggle but a middle-class war. The *campesinos* were largely of indigenous stock, though laced with the bloodlines of the Spanish *conquistadores*. For four centuries they had been treated as the equivalent of cattle, and like cattle they had never complained when being led into the abattoir. While war raged around them, they sided with whoever was least likely to upset their impoverished existence. The Nicaraguan war was not a war in the sense that a European could recognise, just a battle between adversarial élites, not a war between Marxism and Capitalism but between autocracy and aspiration.

How else to explain the irony that Daniel Ortega, the Sandinista leader from 1979 to 1990, re-elected as president in 2007, is now facing a popular revolt for his attempt to create a political dynasty through his wife. Another Somoza? Maybe. Certainly someone who has become more interested in the trappings of power than in any vision for the future of those he governs.

I have never been back to Nicaragua, so this is all hearsay. But friends who have done report of a country with grinding poverty. The circle continues.

Nicaragua, like most of Latin America, is bipolar. The *campesinos* have become habituated to centuries of exploitation and seem resigned to their own political insignificance. The prospect of a better future may have enthused them to support the Sandinista revolution but they were not surprised when it failed to make any difference to their lives. Those in the few urban centres with education and hopes of a better future had a euphoric victory that dissipated in the return to politics-as-usual. The final twist in the rope is Ortega, who has adopted Somoza's methods so he can remain in power. He also has an estimated net worth of $50 million; Nicaragua remains a very poor country.

CHAPTER 15
Chile: 1979 to 2008
A Nation Transformed

This is controversial. Salvador Allende was Latin America's first elected socialist president. He committed suicide in the Almeda Presidential Palace during a military coup led by General Augusto Pinochet. He was obviously a victim—no?—and Pinochet equally obviously his abuser.

It must be so, because the West remembers Allende as a martyr and Pinochet as Latin America's Hitler.

Fair? No. Neither description fits the facts.

Looking back on it, after a three-month break in Panamá, I think I had to some extent gone native in my previous posting. The corruption, incompetence, enervation, misogyny and avarice of the country's self-entitled wealthy class were just the way it was in this troubled part of the world. I failed to make the connection that its turbulent politics were a function of its dystopian culture. I also failed to note that, by and large, these failings were a disease that applied to all of Latin America.

But then we were sent to Chile. Once again, my wife had read the Amnesty report and I had not. Another Nicaragua?

We landed at night in the Chilean winter. Rafa met us. A previously sleepy BAT monopoly was about to face real competition from its rival, Philip Morris, and I was taking on half of Rafa's job. He took us to the Hotel Tupahue in downtown Santiago, where a soldier stood guard by the reception desk. We checked in. Rafa was distressed. 'This never happens. Everything is peaceful here. Do not believe everything that is written about us.'

It was not a great start, stuck in this mediocre hotel with little assistance from my new employer. It was made worse by the fact that my marriage was coming unstuck. The pressure and instability of life in the Americas was becoming unsustainable. 'Get us somewhere permanent to live or I'm going home,' I was told, and home was not here. By chance we found somewhere decent to live and established a connection that led to our introduction into a vibrant Euro-Chilean social world.

It made a welcome change. This new crowd was a stark contrast to what we had experienced in Nicaragua. Not an isolated, exclusive, uncomprehending clique of privileged top dogs but a polyglot of nationalities, including Chileans, with different professions and views of the world. Yes, we all lived above the smog in the middle-class *barrios*, but we did not feel removed from what was happening in the country that was hosting us—indeed we felt engaged and enjoyed talking about it. In Nicaragua I had felt divorced; here I felt involved. Santiago was far more sophisticated than either Managua or Panamá. Without realising it, we had become part of a privileged multilingual community in a country that was actually pleasant to live in. How unusual!

Given the current reputation of the Pinochet régime, this account would appear to be delusional. That was not the case, though my time there did coincide with the high watermark of his rule. I worked in a department without a single English speaker and within six weeks of my arrival I had become fluent in both spoken and written Spanish. Our source of news was the local media: print, TV and radio. I read the papers every day, watched TV when not going out and listened to the radio news on my journeys to and from work in the *collectivos* (shared taxis) that plied the route. I also took the opportunity of questioning everybody I met on how they saw the country's prospects; as a market-research manager, I could be trusted to phrase an open question in acceptable terms.

The vast majority of those I spoke to were happy with the status quo. Their reasons were diverse: that the old democracy was a sham—just the rich arguing about which of them could rip off more than the others; or that the Allende régime had been a *golpé d'estado* (a coup) and that, with only 36 per cent of the vote, Allende had had no right to impose a Communist régime on the country; or that Allende had driven the Chileans apart by favouring the poor and that everyone had lived comfortably together before his arrival; or that Allende had brought the country to a state of ruin, with no food and nothing but strikes all the time, and that it was not surprising that women took to the streets—a reference to the mass demonstrations, ahead of Allende's downfall, in which women symbolically beat empty cooking pans; or that the economy was in chaos—'Can you imagine a situation in which a small car cost more than a big house in a smart area of Santiago?' This was a reference to the widely shared story that the British Ambassador's residence in Providencia had been bought with the proceeds of the sale of a Mini.

Although I did not record these comments, they are, I think, a fair representation of people's opinion at the time, though a British diplomat friend reminds me that my evidence sample is limited because I only tended to quiz the monied and those with whom I had commercial dealings and that there were very many more who had no money and with whom my job never brought me into contact. I acknowledge that, but he acknowledges that Pinochet had very much more popular support than one would have expected, especially if one knew of him only by reputation.

We were sent to Chile five years after the overthrow of Allende and I have had to rely only on what I was told by Chileans who were there before we arrived. However I have recently found out that a lifelong friend from university was in Chile in September 1973. His account of his stay for a few weeks is, of course, subjective but suggests in the round that Pinochet's coup was regarded with, if not enthusiasm, then at least equanimity. His only unusual experience was being blindfolded by some students he met when taken to a meeting place—for his protection, they explained.

The convenient notion that Chile was nothing more than a police state was simply not evident during our time there. After their release from captivity in Lebanon in 1991, Brian Keenan and John McCarthy, both kidnapped in Beirut, journeyed from the north of Chile to the south. Pinochet had resigned the presidency by then but remained the only Chilean that foreigners could name. Keenan and McCarthy went on to write a book, a theme of which was their search for evidence to support their assumption that he was the devil incarnate. They eventually recognised that the situation was more nuanced and that Pinochet was a symbol of a period of Chilean history that was both good and bad.[1]

Under Pinochet, Allende's supporters were rounded up in the National Stadium, among them my former Cambridge University economics tutor, Brian Pollitt, the son of the founder of the British Communist Party. My friend tried but failed to meet him before he was deported. Chileans of the same political persuasion either fled and became part of the beacon of discontent with the Pinochet régime or met a grisly end.

The best estimate I can find of the number killed or 'disappeared' in the coup is 2,500.[2] In this context, I recently had lunch with a Chilean *exiliada* who was a fellow guest at a mutual friend's party. She was the daughter of a professor of Medicine, who was arrested after the coup and then deported. Her interpretation of events was the opposite of my own.

It seems to me that those opposing camps who believe that Pinochet was a tyrant or a saviour cannot be reconciled. For the relatives of those who were killed or arrested, and

---

[1] Brian Keenan and John McCarthy, *Between Extremes*, Transworld Publishers (1999).
[2] www.globalsecurity.org/Argentina Dirty War, 1976–83.

others with a strong belief in socialism, the coup was a traumatic event from which they developed their own narrative—expressed, for example, in Ariel Dorfman's highly regarded play, *Death and the Maiden*, and in the fiction of Isabel Allende, whose father was a first cousin of Salvador Allende, president of Chile from 1970–73. Their words were taken very seriously around the world, because the most outspoken were in exile abroad, but their voices made little impression inside Chile itself.

Those who were personally untouched by the coup developed a quite different narrative. Although violent political upheavals had been frequent throughout the rest of Latin America, Chile had not had one for 150 years. Then, three years after coup, Argentina's 'Dirty War' broke out and at least 30,000 died.[3] Another comparison is the estimated 200,000 leftist non-combatants executed during and after the Spanish Civil War.[4] In the light of these figures, the casualties of the coup were, to those who supported it, the unfortunate victims of a surgical operation to remove those who had destroyed both the economy and democracy. More importantly, Pinochet supporters remained at home and, over the five years before we arrived, witnessed a transformation of their society that reinforced their belief that the coup had been justified. A poll taken on the fiftieth anniversary of the coup showed that 36 per cent of the adult population considered the Pinochet regime a success, though half of those questioned would not have been born in 1973.

The binary notion that dictators are always bad and democracy always good is therefore not helpful to under-

---

[3] Andrew Graham-Yooll, *A State of Fear: Memories of Argentina's Nightmare*, Eland (1986).
[4] Giles Tremlett, *Ghosts of Spain: Travels Through a Country's Hidden Past*, Faber and Faber (2006).

standing what Chile went through. Pinochet's rule was a dictatorship, certainly; a tyranny, probably not.

A well-researched book about the Pinochet era by Constable and Valenzuela reflects Western assumptions about this country in its very title.[5] The authors' fundamental assumption is that dictatorships are evil. But some are more evil than others. Political parties in Chile were banned but free expression in the media was restricted only to the extent of questioning the legitimacy of the régime. And as a friend found out when his business was devastated by the removal of import tariffs, the strict law on the protection of labour continued to hold sway. Our friend continued to record and bring out the works of Chilean musicians, many of whom had an antagonistic view of the Pinochet régime, and we continued to accompany him to concerts without sanction or police presence. The maintenance of a relatively free press and judiciary are not the characteristics associated with dictatorships.

Pinochet hated Communists but allowed debate. His militaristic vision of a fatherland and of nationalism served him well in restoring order after the chaos of the Allende régime but became increasingly less relevant as Chilean society came to terms with itself. His achievement was that he avoided civil war and handed over power peacefully, albeit reluctantly, when a successor, Patricio Aylwin, was democratically elected to the presidency.

I met Pinochet one night in London, when, after visiting Margaret Thatcher, he was unavoidably detained by the Spanish procurator general, Baltasar Garzón, who had issued an international arrest warrant for crimes against humanity.

There is an irony here. Nobody in Spain was prosecuted for crimes against humanity under Franco's régime. After

---

[5] P. Constable and A. Valenzuela, *A Nation of Enemies: Chile under Pinochet*, Norton (1993).

Franco's death, the old Falangist establishment ordered the destruction of state records so that estimates of civilian deaths during the civil war and the white terror that followed it vary widely. The fact that Garzón sought punishment for atrocities overseas while ignoring the amnesty and amnesia of his own homeland suggests either frustration or double standards.[6]

Pinochet reminded me of both my grandfathers: one an honest and upright man who thought it his duty to do his best, the other the possessor of strongly held convictions about right and wrong. Both were more or less of the same generation as Pinochet who, as he aged, seemed increasingly baffled by his transformation into an international pariah. When Ferdinand Marcos rescinded a state visit while Pinochet was already on his way to the Philippines, he returned home to find the route from the airport lined with cheering supporters, including many of our Chilean friends. He appeared puzzled by Marcos's action, but what puzzles me is his naïvety in thinking that cosying up to Marcos would bring him international acceptability.[7]

I think Pinochet had no understanding of the international process by which heroes and villains are made, and thus found it hard to mount a defence for himself but on his return to Chile in 1990, no charges were laid against him. Since he had not profited from taking power, attention moved to his son-in-law who, as an intermediary in Chile's privatisation process, had managed to procure for himself some well-remunerated executive positions.

In many respects, Pinochet was not a politician. He was a soldier and an officer. He saw it as his job to bring order to Chile's social chaos and to ensure that his troops (and by extension the entire population) were happy with their lot. I

---

[6] Tremlett (ibid), p. 82.
[7] His wife demanded that he fire the foreign minister for this affront.

find it difficult to think of any democratic solution to the domestic crisis engendered by Allende, given that the two global political philosophies of that time—capitalism and Communism—were mutually adversarial. In that light, Pinochet could be compared to Lee Kuan Yew of Singapore, though he lacked the latter's political nous. Under his watch Chile was transformed from an inward-looking, insignificant country to a byword for stability and sustained growth in Latin America. He destroyed his own reputation by eliminating—i.e. murdering—or exiling prominent Communist supporters and was not skilled enough in public relations to cover up his crimes. But in his time and place, he was 'good enough'.[8]

Chile's problems were obvious: a typical Latin American society riven by the division between the haves and have-nots, exacerbated by a 'democracy' that had served for 150 years to promote one élite at the expense of another. He initiated a social-welfare programme which focused on housing, health and education. Slums were cleared and replaced by affordable housing; free health care and education were provided for the poor. In my time in Chile I cannot remember seeing a single beggar or homeless person—but perhaps vagrancy was proscribed. Neither France nor Britain has solved its vagrancy problems despite enjoying a per-capita income several times higher than Chile's, so our adopting the moral high ground of respect for human rights rings a little hollow.

Pinochet also inherited a moribund economy, with hyperinflation fuelled by ballooning government deficits and a protectionist stance that diverted investment into sectors that made no sense. All industries were protected by tariff barriers.

---

[8] A reference to the psychiatrists John Bowlby and Donald Winnicott, whose Attachment Theory on parenting argued that 'good enough' was the best that could be hoped for. This would appear to be an analogue of Pinochet's role *in loco parentis*.

Why make cars for a population of just over 10 million in a country with only a tiny manufacturing sector?

Chile's economic policy prior to Allende had been to protect nascent (or even mature) industries behind high tariff barriers. These helped preserve the interests of the owners of capital but at the expense of poor quality and high consumer prices. Although I suspect that Pinochet had a limited understanding of economics, he was persuaded to follow a radically new approach by adopting the ideas of the Chicago School. The Chicago School had two basic principles: monetarism, or control of the money supply, to fight inflation; and an open market, to direct investment where it would produce the highest returns and thus create growth. It did not bother itself with the social fallout that should arise from such an abrupt change of direction.

Fortuitously, perhaps, the solution to the first of these ameliorated the second. Before we arrived, inflation had been so high that salaries were paid weekly and people were allowed to take Friday afternoons off to buy what they needed before prices went up again. The principle was enshrined thereafter in a monthly retail-price-index adjustment of salaries. Money supply then started to be controlled, from 1979 to 1982, by pegging it to the US dollar, as a result of which the rate of inflation fell back rapidly. The next radical decision was to devalue the Chilean peso and then in 1984 to let it float once again within a system of crawling bands. Financial markets (normally quicker on the uptake than the average consumer) recognised this as an improvement and revalued the currency. This in turn reduced the cost of imports and further contributed to the decline in the inflation rate. The economy stabilised, food shortages came to an end and new imported products began to appear on the supermarket shelves.

There were, of course, casualties. I had a friend who was general manager of Fiat Chile. I bought two cars from him, both at a considerable discount on the list price. Both cars had bits missing on delivery. The problem was that a car assembly plant could not survive without tariff protection and eventually the factory became a refrigerated warehouse for fruit and vegetable exports.9

It was because of BAT's need to face new overseas competition that I was sent to Chile. The detail is irrelevant but we ended up with a higher market share than we had started with, and when Philip Morris (our main competitor) gave up and pulled out, I gained some kudos for my part in it. It was only one example of how local businesses proved to be highly entrepreneurial when exposed to competition. The Chilean wine business and Chile's other agro-industries all expanded and are now recognised by the outside world; the same is true of its mining sector. But the impact of greater competition domestically was just as visible. By the time we arrived, Santiago was becoming indistinguishable from other European cities with its growing and sophisticated service sector.

That leaves the question of the social climate. The only anachronistic symbol of the Pinochet coup was the *toque de queda* (curfew) that ran from 2:00 to 6:00 every morning. It seemed unnecessary but was perhaps connected to the incorruptible police force, unique in Latin America. A couple of minor infractions led to my having my driving licence taken away—not much of a hardship as I had an international licence to fall back on. Like Pinochet, the police believed that the law was the law, no matter the circumstances. This was a country of order and principle, which again made it unique.

As far as politics was concerned, there were protests at the Universidad Católica and Universidad de Chile, but little more than I had participated in at Cambridge nine years earlier. A few ringleaders were exiled but none of them 'disappeared'.

---

9 Constable and Valenzuela (ibid), p. 215.

Pinochet put his rule to the test in 1980 by calling a plebiscite to endorse a further nine years in power. To me, this was the acid test. El Mercurio, the upmarket daily (supposedly CIA-funded during the Allende régime), came out as, on balance, opposed: nine years was too long a term. La Tercera, the equivalent of the Daily Mail, favoured stability. Courteous television debates were held between proponents of both sides, who talked about the issues rather than the president. Pinochet, neither a politician nor an orator, was absent, leaving it to others to argue his case. This left the impression that it was truly a decision for Chileans. Voting was obligatory for nationals, voluntary for resident expatriates. We did not vote because it was none of our business. Pinochet won with 68 per cent of the turnout. There were no credible complaints that the voting had been rigged.

A second plebiscite in 1988 produced the opposite result: 56 per cent opposed the extension of Pinochet's presidency. Had I been there on that occasion, I would probably have voted with them, as economic growth had come to a halt when the peso got pegged to the dollar at too high a rate. In response, he stepped down: I suspect that the proud man who had always done his duty was mortified at having lost the vote. After that, Chile became a democracy with a centre-left government until the presidency of the right-wing Sebastiàn Piñera.

I write this on the day of the announcement that Pablo Neruda, the poet and Communist, did not die of cancer twelve days after Allende's end, as had been believed. The implication had been that his death must have been of Pinochet's doing. What I take from this is that the tyrant myth is of more interest to the media than the facts of Chile's fate. Our maid, Marie, made the most telling remark: 'At least he gives us something to eat.'

In Latin America, Chile is an oddity. It is the only country with genuine democracy, a free press, an independent judiciary, a police force that does not take bribes and very little corruption. Controversial perhaps, but it was Pinochet's interregnum as president that catalysed this transformation. As in the rest of Latin America, Chilean politics before Allende was the preserve of the elites. Elections were won by one or other of the two factions (the traditional '*Blancos y Rojos*', known by their colour to help illiterate voters recognise which party they were meant to vote for) but the results changed nothing as, despite promises of reform, their only agenda was to keep things as they were.

This paralysis led to the growth of socialist-leaning parties and came to a head in the 1970 election, a three-horse race which Allende won with 36.2 per cent of the vote, 1.3 per cent ahead of Jorge Alessandri, a former president and main representative of the status-quo faction. This was the first and only time that an avowed Marxist had gained power through an election.

The tradition that the military existed to defend the integrity of the republic rather than acting as arbiter of its politics had long been established in Chile, though hardly anywhere else in Latin America. Indeed, one of Pinochet's predecessors as head of the armed forces had died of his wounds in 1970, when resisting a kidnapping attempt by right-wing officers opposed to Allende.[10] Pinochet took on the role of head of state only reluctantly.

His actions thereafter recognised the political divide between the haves and have-nots, and his domestic programme was a pragmatic attempt to cauterise this wound. He felt he was acting *in loco parentis*, as it were, for his country and wanted to be assured that what he was doing had the people's approval. Paradoxically, that gave Chileans the space to work out for

---

[10] Wikipedia: Salvador Allende—1970 elections.

themselves what form of governance they wanted. It worked —and now they are the envy of the rest of the continent.

This might seem like an encomium, as if Chile was the perfect place to be. Perhaps it was not; its virtues certainly went unrecognised at the time. Chile's isolation also created attitudes that I found unpalatable. One day, when walking down Ahumada, the pedestrianised main street of Santiago, a Chilean colleague regaled me about the iniquities of race relations in the UK, following a couple of brief riots that had appeared in the world press. Then he stopped and pointed at two black people walking towards us and said, '¡Mira los monos!' —(Look at the monkeys). I changed the subject.

I also found group attitudes unattractive. Middle-class Chilean women tended to chorus their approval of what they thought they were expected to like, or their disapproval of anything that upset their conventions, in accents that I felt reeked of insincerity, with fixed smiles on their faces and an intonation that expected automatic agreement from the listener. Our baby was invariably greeted with uniform cries of '¡Qué lindo!' (how pretty). Not everyone was like that but social conformity was obviously a major driver. Of course there were feisty and independent women in Chile: I met many of them and enjoyed their company. But they were rare. I expect that has changed now; having a woman as president—Michelle Bachelet (2006–2010 and 2014–2018)—suggests that it has.

La Tercera offered advice to '*viudos de verano*' (summertime widowers) on how to enjoy themselves when their wives were at the seaside, invariably accompanied by a topless photo of a young lovely—no different from *The Sun* in the UK at the time. At heart, Chile was no different from any other Latin American country: men did whatever they could get away with and women were expected to put up with it and get on with the job of raising their children. As far as I can remember, the most senior woman in the company was the managing director's secretary. Even the HR department, in those days often run by a woman, had a male manager. Forget about a career, become a honking goose.

Working in a dozy monopoly, our managers were not of the highest quality. Some were dismissed after proving themselves unequal to the task but others were transferred to less onerous duties while retaining their impressive job titles and salaries. Rafa cheerfully admitted his incompetence but was unconcerned because he was closely related to the most senior Chilean manager. He was still there when I left.

Perhaps this is the Spanish legacy. I found the same thing when I was charged with integrating an acquired Hispano-French business in 2008. The Madrid head office was overrun by employees seeking favour from on high. I was told, in total confidence of course, that so-and-so was indispensable, even if he did not appear to be so. With few exceptions, Spanish management found the idea of meritocracy unappealing. Few of these deadweights survived very long, though many found new roles immediately with Telefonica, where our chairman found a new job of the same standing in minutes.

As for Spain itself, it had recently been through some very tough economic times, as had much of Latin America. By 2012, youth unemployment in Spain was in excess of 40 per cent, more than any other country in the European Union; two years later it was approaching 60 per cent. A popular revolt seemed a likely reaction. It has not happened, perhaps because the young and not-so-young are looked after by their families. I understand this but did not feel that Hispanic culture was for me. Perhaps this is also a reflection of cultural bias. Despite being derided as class-ridden, Britain is essentially meritocratic (though not so much as the USA) and I find it more congenial. These are some of the reasons I called on to justify our departure: *post hoc ergo propter hoc*, you might say.

Once you leave somewhere of your own volition, it is difficult to go back. On a later return trip, I stood on the balcony of my high-rise hotel and looked up towards the Andes, below which we used to live. As much as I wanted it not to, it felt like a country apart. By then, with its female president, it seems to have laid its ghosts of the past to rest.

There remains a disbelief that Chile can become a genuine democracy, following the protests of 2019–20, a referendum result that initially suggested enthusiasm for a radical overhaul of the constitution, and the election of the young leftwing firebrand Gabriel Boric to replace the decidedly rightwing and old Sebastiàn Piñera as president. Was this a return to typical Latin American politics, with its lurching between left and right? One commentator said, 'Chile's future now hangs in the balance,'[11] when the new constitution was rejected by another referendum on 4 September, 2022. The original Pinochet constitution was out of date, as it favoured private enterprise and limited the role of government in providing social services. Its proposed replacement ended up three times longer and was preoccupied by the need to preserve the rights of all minority groups—in other words, its tone was restricting rather than enabling. The fact that it was rejected by the electorate shows a remarkable degree of common sense.

The Chile experience demonstrates a characteristic that is mostly lacking in the rest of Latin America, in that the centripetal force of compromise remains dominant; and like all Western democracies, Chile gives extreme left and right groups a voice. There are lessons here for older Western democracies which have adopted an adversarial form of politics, none more so than the USA.

---

[11] Tony Wood, *London Review of Books*, 3 November 2022.

CHAPTER 16
The Roundabout

Latin American independence amounted to little more than a handing over of authority to the local management team. As I have observed above, these small élites continued to run their countries in the same manner as the *conquistadores*—for their own advantage, exploiting the poor and powerless, the indigenous and imported labour. These lived a life apart, but they were everywhere.

In Central America, the underclass got drunk and fell asleep in the road at dusk on Sundays: you had to be careful how you drove. In Brazil, by contrast, the rich used helicopters—uncatchable dragonflies of the skies—while the middle classes fumed in traffic jams, with their car doors locked. The poor struggled on in *favelas* (slums) that tumbled down the mountain sides to the security fences of those with their own gardens. At night, the city became their playground.

Campesinos in Colombia have endured decades of violence, starting with *La Violencia*, a ten-year civil war between the two establishment parties that left 200,000 dead, followed by another civil war between the *campesino*-based Marxist FARC and the Bogotá government, with its paramilitary allies from 1960 to 2020 and the emergence of an alternative nexus of control—the drug barons, countered by massive military aid provided by the USA in its 'war on drugs'.

In Ecuador, Peru and Bolivia, indigenous Indians had the stuffing knocked out of them as they peddled tourist knick-knacks or performed Paul Simon's tiresome dirge 'I'd rather be a hammer than a nail'—or is it 'I'd rather be a sparrow than a snail'?—on their reed pipes, until their influence began to be felt at the ballot box.

Some states have managed to develop their economies. Mexico has benefited as the sweat shop of the USA. Venezuela grew an economy on oil and then trashed it. Agricultural and, to a lesser extent, industrial development in the latter part of the nineteenth century in the Southern Cone (Brazil, Argentina, Uruguay and Chile) led to rapid growth: Argentina had the second-highest per capita income in the world before the First World War. But only Chile, Uruguay and Costa Rica made the transition to pluralist democracy. Argentina's Italian immigrants were so numerous that the spoken language reflects their antecedents. Brazil's substantial ex-slave population and its indigenous people of the rainforest stayed marginalised and ignored. Until the collapse of the Soviet Union, Latin American governments were either dictatorships or sham two-party democracies which shared a vested interest in maintaining the status quo.

How the disenfranchised reacted to this has differed. Andean Indians have seemed docile and resigned in the face of the Sendero Luminoso's failure in Peru and Che Guevara's adventures in Bolivia. Slave descendants have made common cause with Black Lives Matter activists. Central American peasants blow where the wind takes them, often at the behest of a drug runner with a pistol at their neck. Industrial workers have used trade unionism as a means of raising their political profile. Peronism remains a core political force in Argentina, though it was an economic fiasco seventy years ago. The division between labour and asset owners remains the defining political issue in most of Latin America, and its roots go back centuries.

Where this has changed, it has been in response to a new approach to Latin America by the United States. The confrontational 'better-dead-than-red' ethos has been replaced by a drive to require liberal democratic principles of national politics. Under US funding pressure, elections have become *de rigueur*, dictatorships unacceptable. Social programmes to improve the lives of peasants and workers have raised literacy rates, and urbanisation and mobiles have brought scattered groups together, thereby ensuring them a more meaningful vote.

One would have thought all of this would have drawn together the fractured social elements in each of these various countries, but in accordance with the law of unintended consequences, this has not happened; instead, the division between rich and poor has only demarcated them more. There is no centre ground and there cannot be, as the divide is so vast. From this develops a pattern in which both sides promise a transformation for their supporters and then fail to achieve it. Tired socialist policies send the economy into decline and free-market reforms get lost in the vested interests of the powerful. In most of Latin America, money continues to be manipulated by the few.

The logjam of having two incompatible political agendas encourages governments to turn to extra-judicial means to achieve their ends. The last four Peruvian presidents have all been convicted for corruption; Alan García committed suicide when told he was about to be arrested for the same crime. This in a country where I was told by the scion of one of them that eleven families controlled 80 per cent of the official economy. Difficult to say no when offered a fat brown envelope by one of them.

The inability to find any centre ground enhances the ability of parallel power structures to tighten their hold on society. Throughout Central America, drug gangs are at least as powerful as governments and their tentacles extend much further, into the south. Neither leftists nor rightists can come up with a coherent strategy to deal with this. Drug production and distribution remain the only viable source of income for peasant farmers and the urban poor, and the only solution offered up by the rich is to kill the lot of them.

In consequence, Latin American politics is like a centrifuge with each election spitting out new presidents from either side with monotonous regularity. The temptation to hold on to power is difficult to resist, hence the phenomenon of Daniel Ortega in Nicaragua (president since 2007) and of Nicholás Maduro in Venezuela (president since 2013). Liberal democracy cannot be imposed from above; it requires the painful process of welding disparate communities together towards a common goal. I suggest that equality of opportunity and a reasonable social safety net could create the conditions for breaking this impasse. It has not been impossible in Chile and Uruguay, despite, or perhaps because of, their turbulent pasts.

For all these reasons, history in Latin America seems circular rather than progressive. It gyrates inconclusively from market reforms to social programmes. Our media refer to presidential candidates as being left or right, a binary classification that reflects an anachronistic view still rooted in Cold War concepts. The latest election in Colombia (at time of writing) featured an ex-FARC commandant versus a septuagenarian billionaire akin to Donald Trump. Latin America needs better than this: governments that are in service of the entire electorate and with the know-how to create a unified nation out of all the disparate parts.

PART 4
THE SOVIET UNION AND ITS AFTERMATH

CHAPTER 17
Russia: 1993 to 1998
Collapse and its Consequences

'Russia has seen many things during the one thousand years of its history. There is only one thing that Russia has not seen in one thousand years—freedom.'
Vasily Grossman

I first went to Russia in 1992 and left for the last time in 2008. I discovered there a nation of cultural depth, high educational standards and strongly held common values.

I had arrived with evangelical intent as a starry-eyed apostle of Western values and the ability to convert this utterly defeated nation into a fully integrated player in the world's economy and values. A 1984 visit to Bulgaria had convinced me that the politico-economic model of Soviet Marxism was doomed to failure; my initial impressions of post-Soviet Russia confirmed it. I left thirteen years later, disillusioned but recognising that this was the consequence of my binary thinking: one problem, one solution. What I had failed to appreciate fully was what history had done to the psyche of the Russian people. One day Russia had been a superpower, the next it was on life support. This cataclysmic change and the legacies of history provide the rationale for why Russia is as it is.

Moscow in February 1992 was a frightening place. Sheremetyevo Airport, a gloomy cavern of concrete, linoleum and dismal lighting, was my point of arrival. The customs form was lengthy, requiring declaration of all foreign currency and anything else of value that would be re-exported. Immigration control involved long queues, with booths staffed by uniformed men and women, all wearing those peculiar wide-brimmed peaked hats that hark back to Soviet May Day parades. The paperwork was done in silence. There was never any hurry. When checking one's passport photograph, the immigration official would scan one's face with the air of someone examining an unwanted and unattractive life form. That was the only eye contact.

Outside it was minus something or other, snowing out of a black sky in a strong breeze. Pools of lamplight dotted the carpark in a palette of white, grey, brown and black. The ground was frozen, and previous snowfalls were heaped up in mini mountain ranges. All the vehicles were encrusted with dogshit-coloured ice on the undersides and around the wheel arches. This was how it was in winter. The drive into the city was rapid and uneventful until we got stuck in traffic in the centre of Moscow, when the driver mounted the pavement to get to the head of the queue. This was my first lesson in the fundamentals of Russia. If you have a car you are, by definition, more important than those who do not. Mounting the pavement is your right. No need to apologise.

My hotel, like Sheremetyevo airport, was a legacy of the 1980 Olympic games: a featureless block with Western-style facilities but Soviet-style staff. It overlooked a now-abandoned stadium. There were a few streetlights but the city felt empty.

My opposite number was the general manager of the Coca-Cola Company (TCCC) in Russia. Michael O'Neill had been the commercial counsellor for the Irish Embassy in Moscow, spoke fluent if accented Russian, knew the country, was a born optimist and became a good friend. He outlined what was on offer: a franchise in European Russia that excluded Moscow and St. Petersburg.

I took this back to London and received an enthusiastic reception from the board, which authorised an initial £175 million investment in the project—but I had to run it. For nearly six years, I did a weekly commute to Russia. At the end

I burned my suits, encrusted with Russian dirt, in a ceremonial bonfire. It had been the most difficult period in my professional life up to then.

I arrived less than two years after the Soviet Union had collapsed. What survived was a monolithic bureaucracy but without the command-and-control system that characterised the USSR in its heyday. It took me a while to recognise that the new reality would entail interminable negotiations with local and regional administrators whose motive was personal gain rather than regulatory control. But who could blame them? The central power structures were eroding and they were no longer being paid.

One normally thinks of Hitler's Germany as the exemplar of modern totalitarianism, but it was Stalin's Soviet Union that first established the ground rules of autocratic tyranny. Robert Conquest's *The Great Terror* sets out the excruciating narrative in detail.[1] Promoted as the requirement of Marxist orthodoxy, the real purpose of totalitarianism was to eliminate anybody who posed a threat to Stalin's absolute authority and deploy fear to create a climate of loyalty. Any historical association with Trotsky or the Mensheviks made one automatically a traitor. If there was no evidence of either, corroboration would be concocted from the 'confessions' of colleagues or friends, obtained under torture and assisted by the threat of dire penalties for their families.

Failure to achieve centrally generated production targets was therefore the fault of those tasked to execute them; and then they were executed on the grounds of economic sabotage, unless someone else was found to blame. Conquest estimates that, in the 1930s, over 300,000 people were executed and 3 million sent to labour camps, where death rates exceeded 20 per cent each year. This does not include the

---

[1] Robert Conquest, *The Great Terror: Stalin's Purge*, Vintage (1968).

5 million starved to death, mainly in Ukraine, in the anti-kulak programme. The scale of this beggars belief and only ended when the purge extended to the NKVD (precursor of the KGB), at which point the system came close to collapse under its own weight.

The result was in one sense what Stalin had intended: it put him beyond challenge but also stripped the Soviet Union of professionals in every field. Nobody dared to compete and loyalty became more important than competence.

Autocratic rule was characteristic of government at all levels in Russia but also extended into the household. To understand what it was like to live in such a society, there is no better witness than Vasily Grossman, who has described how lives were ruined by the petty politics of centralised control.[2] His novel, based on personal experience, is as powerful as Tolstoy's *War and Peace* but more relevant to our times. At 853 pages it is even longer but leaves a lasting and disquieting impression. When submitted for publication to the Soviet authorities, they told Grossman that it could not be published for at least 300 years. As he stated at the time, his book had been taken prisoner, though he remained free.

Everything was censored, everything was proscribed from above. *Gostandart*, written in the 1930s, gave detailed technical requirements for every building and every project, which is why the old Soviet Union is still architecturally unified by drab concrete blocks of factories and houses, all constructed to the same shoddy standards. And everybody was employed by a state that did not trust them and was watched over by neighbourhood committees, often zealous in pursuit of infractions, fictional or not. Fear of the state then became a fact of life for every Soviet citizen for over seventy years. With that fear came

---

[2] Vasily Grossman, *Life and Fate*, trans. Richard Chandler, Vintage-Random House (2006).

a culture of dissimilation, toadying and betrayal.

The Soviet Union crumbled because the monumental edifice of central control, while endeavouring to maintain its position as a superpower, was inefficient and incapable of meeting the basic needs of its citizens. The same thing happened in China, and then Vietnam and Laos, which had unquestioningly followed the Moscow orthodoxy.

The collapse of the Soviet Union began with the failure of its own will. The economic realities against the (possibly imaginary) threat of Reagan's Star Wars programme were stark. Gorbachev, who recognised that the economy was rapidly becoming a dead end, became general secretary of the Communist Party from 1986 to 1991 and instigated a series of reforms designed to revive Soviet society—*glasnost* (openness), *perestroika* (restructuring) and alcohol rationing (not as daft as it seems).

In a Russian joke from that period, Sasha meets Kostya struggling to the Metro station with two heavy suitcases. 'Kostya! Where you go with those two big suitcases?' 'Never mind that; I want you see my new watch.' 'Very nice, but are you leaving town?' 'No, but look at watch. Tell time in any city in world.' 'Wonderful, but where you go?' 'Sasha, is not just watch but also radio, with AM and FM.' 'Is no FM in Russia.' 'But soon will be. And watch is also calculator.' 'Impressive, but where you go?' 'Is also telephone: you pull this out here and is receiver and you speak back to watch.' 'Amazing. Is Americanski watch?' 'Nyet.' 'Is Japanski watch?' 'Nyet.' 'Is Svistky watch?' 'Nyet. Is Sovietskiy watch.' 'Incredible. Finally, Soviet state is at leading edge of innovation. Our future is golden.' 'Da, but is small problem. The batteries are so heavy.'

Gorbachev is now blamed for the collapse of the Soviet Union but the USSR was a seventy-year-old monolith that even Lenin would have been embarrassed by. It was falling apart. Gorbachev had little choice in letting the Comecon countries go their own way. The break-up of the Soviet Union itself was precipitated by Boris Yeltsin, first president of the Russian Federation, and Leonid Kravchuk, first president of the newly created Ukraine who refused to join what Gorbachev had proposed as a post-Soviet equivalent of the EU (thereby ending his political career as general secretary of nothing). As soon became apparent, this had little to do with self-determination and much more with preserving the power bases of the next level down: mini-soviets in all but name.

Meanwhile Russian citizens remained mute. It is illuminating that Gorbachev is reviled for being weak, for being an American patsy and for being willing to give up the Soviet empire. In subsequent presidential elections, he received less than 2 per cent of the vote. The Russian people feel that they did not vote for the monumental change that came over them, it just happened. But nor did they protest much, except through the anonymity of the ballot paper. The fact is, they didn't know what was best for them.

This potted history provides a clue as to where Russia stands now. This was a massive state and one that had survived and scared the rest of the world. The legacy of that would take generations to expunge—yet I and other foreign investors thought we could fix it in three years. Like medieval crusaders, every foreigner charged into the new Russia, determined to convert them to the true way of democracy and free-market principles (and make a buck on the side). Like the crusaders, we were naïve in our assumptions, putting too much trust in our own values to recognise how little they were shared by our hosts. The remainder of this story attempts to explain why it all went wrong.

As TCCC manager for Russia, Michael O'Neill's strategy was to recommend a joint venture approach with local breweries in the key strategic points of our franchise area. My second visit involved visiting all these.

We went first to what had been the capital of the Tatar Autonomous Soviet Socialist Republic, now Tatarstan. At the time it was in no recognisable sense autonomous, nor did it have any chance of becoming so. Nominally the home of the Tatars, it was in fact a thousand miles from their ancestral beginnings as part of the invading Mongol hordes. History was made more complicated by the forced relocation of these recalcitrant warriors in the Soviet era. There were a lot of them in Kazan, recognisable by a slightly oriental cast to the eyes and their high cheekbones, but they all spoke Russian, had intermarried with Russians and regarded themselves as Russian. And they were surrounded by Russian oblasts.

As is perhaps usual in times of social and economic upheaval, new local power structures had emerged and these made tortuous progress towards what seemed like sensible inward-investment plans, but I had not yet realised that the concept of win/win had no traction in Russia. Their win meant that everybody else had to lose.

Along with the rest of provincial Russia, each visit to Kazan entailed a banquet where copious vodka toasts had to be raised. Apart from that, the city offered few of even the most basic creature comforts to Western visitors. Almost invariably we stayed in government rest houses as the only hotels were little better than barracks. Not long after another visit, our host was assassinated in one of those murky local-government power plays. Nobody was charged, but it was enough to put an end to our Kazan project.

Next stop was Sterlitamak, a town on the edge of the Urals in another 'autonomous republic'—that of the Bashkirs, another component of the Mongol hordes, though there seemed few of them about. The director general of this establishment was an ex-armed-forces wrestling champion. Again we stayed in a government guest house, again we had a banquet. However, the DG was friendly and seemed willing to cooperate.

On a subsequent visit to Sterlitamak, I took a charter flight which was unable to land because of the snow and we ended up instead in Ufa. The wrestling champion sent a car for us and although Sterlitamak was normally two hours' drive to the south, it was midnight before we got there. No matter, another banquet was awaiting us. Then I realised I had left my briefcase at Ufa airport. I always carried $5,000 with me in case of emergencies and I doubted whether I would ever see it again. The following morning the case turned up, with the money. As theft was a means of survival in the Soviet Union, I have often wondered how this miracle occurred. The generous interpretation is that Russians only steal from the state, not their fellow citizens. The other way of looking at it is that you do not touch the property of those protected by people who can harm you.

Progress was slow. With no internet coverage, a labyrinthine bureaucracy, the absence of a common language, and mutual incomprehension of each other's culture, the only way forward was to meet face to face. Another visit to Sterlitamak was memorable for the worst hotel I had ever experienced. Together with a recently recruited colleague, we were greeted by an old concierge with Jaws-like metal teeth.[3] At three o'clock in the afternoon she was already drunk; her companion had fallen asleep with his head on the reception desk. Our room proved to have no heating, no toilet seat, no hot water, no toilet paper, and no towels. It did have two Soviet standard single beds, rammed into alcoves, but I am 185 cms tall and the Soviet bed was 160 cms long. The manageress explained in wobbly sign language that nothing could be done but would be more than happy to make love. The offer was refused. A week later my new colleague

---

[3] Jaws was a professional assassin in the James Bond novels, *The Spy Who Love Me* and *Moonraker*.

resigned.

Another visit, thankfully staying in the government guest house again, started at 11:00 am with a breakfast and the inevitable vodka toasts, before moving on to a picnic of *shashlik* and more vodka beside the Ural river. At this point my finance manager fell asleep. Lucky him. My day continued with a *banya* (sauna) and two more meals, incidental accessories to more vodka toasts. Somewhere in all of this I realised the significance of vodka toasting: you raise your glass with your right hand so you cannot grasp your sword (or today, I suppose, your gun) and drinking to the bottom of the glass means that everyone is equally inebriated.

There is a Russian proverb about only being able to trust someone you have got drunk with. The result of this mammoth drinking session was three days of alcohol poisoning in which reality became increasingly remote, but playing by their rules was indispensable to making this project work, and it wasn't the alcohol that put paid to the project but something more prosaic. Bizyarkin lost his job and that was the end of that.

Gorbachev's attempts to stop Russians drinking are now regarded as risible, although people got around the official suppression of vodka by making their own home-distilled hooch called *samogon*. Only recently have I realised the extent to which the problem that Gorbachev was trying to address continues to bedevil Russia today. Heavy drinking is common in many countries in northern latitudes; what else could make the long winter nights tolerable? But nowhere else than Russia is the acceptability of drunkenness so engrained in a nation's culture, at least for men (although Vladimir Putin is said to be teetotal). From Tsarist times it is a constant in the accounts of foreign visitors. Vodka plays a major role in Grossman's novel *Life and Fate* in providing Dutch courage. Histories of the Russian Revolution (1917–1923) and of the

Great Patriotic War (1941–1945) reference endless examples of soldiers raiding liquor stores, becoming insensibly drunk and going out of control.

Much more so than the Orthodox Church, vodka offers Russian men a temporary refuge from the restrictions of autocracy (and sometimes not so temporary). As a depressant it removes their behavioural inhibitions, allowing them to become tyrants, on the political stage and in the home. From the Revolution to the Second World War to Chechnya to Syria to Ukraine today, the evidence is that Russia respects neither the Geneva Convention nor its adversaries. Perhaps vodka is the only way that its soldiers can reconcile their inhumanity with their need for self-respect. It wasn't their fault; they were drunk at the time.

Yekaterinburg was another TCCC prospect. It would involve exactly the same procedure and another series of hangovers but the general manager, Oskolkov, did not inspire trust, a fact validated later by the contact we had retained, an FSB[4] colonel, formerly of the KGB, and it never got beyond talks about talks.

The background is that another company, Sun Brewing, owned by the Indian Khemka family, had used blocked rouble funds to buy up shares in breweries and now had enough to take management control of Yekaterinburg.

The Russian method of privatising state enterprises was through a voucher programme. All employees were given vouchers, or shares, in the companies they worked for so that those who understood their inner workings best could buy them up. It sounded very idealistic although I doubt that this scheme had any lofty ideals: it was just a way of getting now defunct enterprises off the state's books. Unfortunately, the collapse of the Soviet economy at the start of the 1990s was so

---

[4] Federal Security Bureau, successor to the KGB.

dramatic that over 90 per cent of companies ceased operations through lack of markets and working capital. Employees lost their jobs and found they owned nothing but outdated, mothballed, rust-bucket factories. As times got harder the temptation to sell these shares grew, even for a few roubles. Sun Brewing identified beer as a basic commodity—rightly so, as Russia's breweries and distilleries continued to operate, after a fashion. The same logic had led Michael to assume that these same facilities could provide a jump start for Coca-Cola.

Elsewhere, some Russians, savvier than us Western new arrivals, had recognised that control of Russia's formidable natural resources could be bought for a pittance. They also knew how to manipulate Russian bureaucracy, which remained Soviet in principle and amenable in practice. It was here that the oligarchs were born. In the wake of what they thought of as the USSR's capitulation to liberal-democratic capitalism, they saw that Western investors had underestimated the power of the Soviet bureaucratic legacy, and this caused untold problems—a lesson I was to learn the hard way.

Sun Brewing's experience in Yekaterinburg provided an early warning. They installed a management team which was ignored by Oskolkov. Attempts to obtain legal redress were dismissed out of hand. When physical threats against their staff began, the team quietly withdrew. Oskolkov was in cahoots with the *oblast* governor, this was to be their path to riches. It did not work out as they had planned. Oskolkov died in a 'traffic accident'.

Finally to Volgograd. The director general seemed enthusiastic about our plans but wary. He insisted on giving me a tour of the local sights. Volgograd, previously known as Stalingrad, is on the west bank of the Volga River and is a ribbon development that extends several miles from north to south.

It is also the site of what Russians regard as the most important battle of the Second World War.

There are many personal and historical narratives about this battle but it was brutal beyond comprehension.[5] Stalin ordered that anybody, military or civilian, who retreated across the river without permission should be shot. After weeks of hand-to-hand combat in freezing temperatures, with Soviet redoubts restricted to a couple of hundred yards and food rations exhausted, the Russians won. There had been over a million casualties.

There is a hill to the west of Volgograd called Murmaev Kurgan, an old Tatar burial site, atop which stands a gigantic statue of Mother Russia, posed defiantly to the West to fend off invaders, a sword brandished high over her head. It is claimed that on every square metre of this hill, a soldier died. It was here that the director general told me that he still had his father's last letter from the battle of Kursk, describing bullets 'falling like rain'. That was my first inkling of what it meant to be Russian: intensely patriotic, highly suspicious of foreigners, resilient in the most appalling of circumstances, nostalgic, and simultaneously brutal and sentimental.

Russia is a monotonous country. Its landscape is either flat or gently undulating, except at its extremes. The steppes go on forever. It is also sparsely populated. Arriving in a town always feels like a relief from the featurelessness of the surroundings. But it is also a reminder that the lack of any geographical features to provide barriers to troop movements creates a sense of being permanently under threat: there is no topographic protection.

The legacy of an economy that cared nothing for environmental damage remained. The Volga empties at Astrakhan into the Caspian Sea, which is home to the sturgeon from

---

[5] Antony Beevor, *Stalingrad*, Viking (1998)

which comes caviar, a major Russian export. But the Volga dam between Volgograd and the Volzhskiy brewery spewed out bilious green water producing waves of chemical bubbles. It did not seem to bother them—but at least this envrionmental threat was visible; others were not. An ex-USAID employee told me that his Geiger counter had gone off the scale on the road between Chelyabinsk and Yekaterinburg. This may well have been the site of Russia's first nuclear accident at Ozersk.[6]

In theory the basic state protection of Russian citizens remained in place. They had places to live and now 'owned' them, having been given tenure in a parallel process to the privatisation coupon programme. They had communal heating, electricity and water supply, though the latter was usually rust brown, and if all three occasionally failed, so had they in Soviet times. They also had free education and healthcare, and everybody had a job—but nobody was being paid. One of our first Russian recruits, an English teacher, told me that he was now responsible for an extended family of forty-five and that he was the only wage earner. His wife was a teacher but had not been paid for nine months. The same was true of those in the medical profession and all those who had worked in the shut-down factories of the planned economy. Russia's biggest tractor plant in Volgograd, Rotor (also the name of their football team), did nothing but lay on buses to take now-unpaid employees to their allotments.

The dislocation brought about by market economy principles left the vast majority destitute. The first decade of post-Soviet Russia saw male life expectancy drop 10 per cent from sixty-seven to fifty-nine years. Statisticians put this down to excessive drinking and smoking, both cheap forms of escape.

---

[6] Serhii Plokhy, *Chernobyl: History of a Tragedy*, Allen Lane (2018), pp. 173–5.

The collapse of the health system may also have contributed; if you wanted proper treatment you had to pay or—even costlier—go abroad. I believe something deeper lay behind this. The Soviet Union had at least had some potential to improve one's life if you were prepared to play its game. New Russia provided nothing. I was trying to provide some sort of solution by creating a viable business but those in authority were obstructive, more concerned with their own livelihoods than the people they were supposed to serve.

The hardship of getting by could be found in Moscow too. *Babushkas* (old women) stood outside Metro stations, at bus stops and on street corners trying to sell their wares, even in the most extreme weather. This was not entrepreneurship but desperation—only if you buy something can I eat—because there was nothing else they could do.

A population that had survived the risk of death-by-politics for so long now found itself at risk from death-by-impoverishment. The USSR had disappeared into history with nothing to replace it. In Latin America or Africa, people would have taken to the streets. In Russia, perhaps because of years of enforced passivity, nothing much happened. In consequence, its subsequent history has focused on its leadership. Russians have looked to powerful figures to determine their future for them, a role performed today by Vladimir Putin.

It took a long time to understand the complex genealogy of what it means to be Russian but it was a rewarding journey. It also involved a personal awakening: the glib assumptions I had made earlier in life about the universality of my values proved to be false.

To describe Russians as little better than lumpish peasants with no manners and a predilection for alcoholic oblivion is a gross caricature, for it is counterbalanced by the obvious fact that Russian culture is rich—or has been rich in the past; it hasn't produced much of importance in recent times—and is deeply embedded in society, especially in the big cities. Around the corner from our first office was the concert hall of the Moscow Music Academy, where entry cost twenty pence. The performances were of a high standard, and were listened to attentively by audiences who would bedeck the performers with flower garlands at the end of the concert, not as some ersatz social obligation but in genuine appreciation. Flowers play an important social role in Russia and the people are, or were, literate: on the Metro, over half the passengers would be reading books. (Today, as anywhere else, they focus on their mobile phones instead.)

The Soviet system treated pre-revolutionary Russian culture, suitably censored, as a means of embedding a sense of nationhood. However, the cultural values of the revolutionary élite were conservative, paranoid and highly attuned to anything that implied criticism, so that anything that diverted from 'socialist realism', probably the dullest form of art imaginable, was suspect. In the absence of much else to focus on, Russians immersed themselves in their cultural history, reinforcing their sense of nationality. The nuances of this are well summed up by Orlando Figes's comprehensive history of Russian culture up to the collapse of Communism.[7]

In the days of the USSR, the education system was élitist and classical in structure. It concentrated on two things: individual capability and technical competence. Soviet Russia was not antipathetic to social mobility; indeed, the frequent despatching of high-ranking 'comrades' in the Stalin era made mobility essential; shoes had to be filled. Even now, a large proportion of Russians are better educated and more culturally aware than those in the West. The status of technical and classical education has survived in post-Soviet

---

[7] Orlando Figes, *Natasha's Dance: A Cultural History of Russia*, Allen Lane (2018).

Russia and still ranks high in international league tables, though Putin's curricular restrictions now reflect the era of Stalin and today's China. Perhaps it has changed since I was there but Russians, like the French, have always seemed to have a sense of intellectual enquiry that one searches for in vain in much of the Western world.

The enigma of Russia resides in the mores that lie behind its cultural sophistication. There is superb musical artistry, astonishing IT skills, but neither is a synonym for wisdom. And living in an autocratic state, be it Tsarist or Soviet or Putinesque, means that one's choice of direction is limited. Nineenth-century English and French novelists—Dickens, Trollope, Hardy, Hugo, Zola, Flaubert—lived in the fluidity of democratic progress and wrote in the knowledge that social change was possible. In Russia writers were limited to the narrow ground between autocracy and what it meant to be Russian. In Tsarist Russia, all land was owned by the Crown; the vast estates of the aristocracy were thus a gift from above and could be rescinded on a whim. This 500-year dependency of the people on their rulers cemented a hierarchy which the Soviet régime took over for its own ends.

From this engrained absolutism, Russian literary titans created, by accident or design, a sort of pastoral that papered over the divisions between nobles and serfs, a sense that Russians were different from their European counterparts but united by a shared history and a common religion. Figes makes this case better than I can and emphasises that this was an aristocratic exercise in which the illiterate serfs played no meaningful part, and that in doing so they created a romantic myth that was, again, exploited by the Soviets.

I tried to read the whole of Dostoyevsky's *The Brothers Karamazov* but gave up after it meandered into a hundred pages of folk-psychology of a generally spiritual but specifically Russian Orthodox bent. What I found distatasteful was its fundamental passivity: the idea that there is nothing one can do about one's station in life. Living in a rigid hierarchy, I suppose that one had no choice but to descend into mystical debates about how things would work out. The state had no interest in such matters; that meant that resolution must come from higher forces, which in Russia meant the Orthodox Church, which was in turn one of the determinants of being Russian. The route to salvation came through internal reflection rather than external change. The values it espoused were those of acceptance, the inevitability of suffering and the expectation that relief was only possible in another world. This doctrine was rejected by the Soviets but has been resurrected, for socio-political reasons, to support the regime of today. I see it as close to masochism.

On those odd occasions when I had a weekend to spend in Moscow, I would go to the park surrounding the Dom Artista (the Artists' House). Here one could find paintings on display and for sale. Ninety-nine per cent of it was rubbish, either poorly executed or derivative—a self-conscious repudiation, perhaps, of Russia's culture of technical mastery referred to above—or maybe just lazy nihilism. The problem for artists was the country's seventy-five years of Communism. Officially sanctioned art—socialist realism—consisted of endless portrayals of tractor drivers celebrating the success of another Five-Year Plan: wall decorations with a message. As no new designs had been developed—a chair was still what Gostandart had said a chair should be, a table was still what Gostandart had said a table should be—taste had become frozen.

Freed from Soviet restrictions, the artist did not know what to produce, nor the customer what to buy. In the absence of any guidance, the few who could afford to simply bought what they assumed was acceptable in the West or what had been regarded as fashionable in Tsarist times; these were their only reference points. Most popular were green naked ladies

—versions of Vladimir Tretchikoff's commercially popular print from 1952—and anything that indicated that the buyer was richer than the hoi polloi. Another Russian joke: 'How much did that suit cost you?' '$20,000.' 'You fool, I know where you can buy the same suit for $30,000.'

In this way, trappings of wealth formed an unspoken suit of armour. This was exemplified by a character whom I will return to later, who invited me to his new home in the most prestigious new development in Moscow. My host proudly explained that even the bricks were imported, which seemed an odd extravagance as domestic bricks were entirely serviceable. It was one of the worst examples of modern domestic architecture that I have seen, over-elaborate and with neither functionality nor grace. There were other candidates for ugliness nearby. I did not have the chance to see inside but, externally, all attempted to cover as much of the available land as possible. The visual effect was like a distorted Disneyland with every feature fighting for space and attention.

I did go into my host's house. It was the last word in bad taste. The sofas were over-stuffed variations on a baroque theme, there were chandeliers in the toilets, all the taps were gold, the paintings were all original but bereft of talent. The master bathroom was the size of a tennis court. Nothing matched. I was asked if I approved. The only possible answer was, 'This must have cost you a fortune.' Luckily, it was what he wanted to hear.

In my wanderings around the art markets, however, there were gems. Some were simple landscapes, executed with skill; others were more ambitious: a *faux-naïve* family portrait or a tightly compressed, claustrophobic picture of a figure trying to mend his jeans. Both are now in our home and both say something important about what it meant to be Russian. The formality of the first, the constriction of the second. Both have a melancholy about them.

What fashioned these thoughts was a visit to an artist's studio in Nizhny Novgorod. Alexander lived in a top-floor, purpose-built apartment with large north-facing windows. His earliest memory was of the day when Stalin's death was announced. Mourning was required of all. His older sister, aged seven, was at school and remarked to her best friend, sitting next to her, 'Why are we crying? What did Stalin ever do for us?' Her best friend reported this to the teacher. His sister was sent out of the class and taken home. Their mother was panic-stricken. 'I must get her away from here,' she thought, and took his sister to stay with relatives. When their father came home, Alexander (then aged five) had had to explain what had happened. His father sighed, put his work boots back on, and went downstairs to await the arrival of the KGB.

I asked Alexander whether he welcomed his new artistic freedom. 'Of course I do. But there is a problem. In the past, if somebody criticised my art, I knew I was on the right track. Now nobody criticises and I'm lost.' He showed me his portfolio. The Soviet-era work was identifiable as socialist realism but the poses were less heroic. Buildings and the ground they stood on were painted to emphasise the rust, decay and dirt, not the triumph of socialism.

He escorted us to his next-door neighbours' apartment. They were a younger couple. In one room was an out-of-school art class, where nine- to eleven-year-olds showed a technical proficiency far in advance of their age. They were fascinated to be introduced to a foreigner and keen to show me what they were doing. I understood less than half of what they explained but their confidence and openness as much as their skill left me with the feeling that the future of Russia was in good hands.

The conversation that followed left me nonplussed. On the face of it, the young couple had done well by using their art and teaching skills to create a living for themselves—a lifeline in a crisis. 'Russians,' the wife argued, 'are not interested in politics or the material world. We are spiritual people. What matters is not what you have but who you are. All our fairy tales reward the kind and gentle. The rich come to a bad end.' She said this with conviction. Her work reminded me of Beatrix Potter illustrations: soft and fluffy with scary moments which will be come right in the end.

This pastoral had a particular resonance in Russia, much as Hello Kitty had in Japan: an escape from the rigidity of society. In Japan it was an expression of the subservience of women, in Russia that of everybody outside the élite.

In conversation, the *dacha* (summer house) was spoken of warmly. *Dachas* are usually little more than sheds in the countryside, without electricity or running water and with an outside privy. In view of how monotone and decrepit Russia's urban environments are, these bolt holes provided a welcome opportunity to enjoy a simpler life close to nature. But beyond that, they were outside the jurisdiction of the state and prying eyes, and you could say what you wanted with people you trusted. It was only in your *dacha* that you were in control.

For Russians, having no political influence was a state of being, not a cause for revolt. Yet Russians remained nationalists. This too was partly explained by their history. Russia has no natural borders and Russians were constantly looking for a mountain range or sea coast to provide protection from attack. Conquest of the east was achieved by virtue of there being nobody there and Siberia became a convenient place to dump dissidents. (Internal exile, in other words, was not a Soviet invention.) By the early eighteenth century, Russia was already the largest country in the world, and yet subsequent rulers continued to feel they needed to expand its borders, particularly in Central Asia and the Caucasus, in the nineteenth century.

Expansion to the south was more problematic because it infringed on an alien culture that was Muslim, tribal-based and hostile to infidel overlords. Russia's military power was sufficiently organised, however, to gain control of the land mass and probably brought stability to the indigenous people, who had suffered constant wars with Turks, Persians and many other preceding empires and dynasties. Catherine the Great's chief adviser (and lover) Grigory Potemkin led a successful campaign against the Cossacks and Tatars (remnants of Genghis Khan's westward invasion centuries earlier) which gave Russia access to the Black and Caspian seas. By the time the empress was ready to cruise down the Volga River to review her new conquests, the population had either fled or been massacred, and so, according to some, Potemkin instructed artisans to build fake villages along the route of Catherine's travels to reassure her that this invasion had been well received by local inhabitants. This gave rise to the phrase 'Potemkin Villages', meaning illusory displays intended to give the appearance of peace and tranquility when the opposite was the case.

Three times, invading armies from the West have invaded Russia: those of Charles XII of Sweden in 1709, Napoleon's in 1810 and Hitler's in 1941. All were defeated by a scorched-earth policy, with incalculable loss of life, all justified by the paramount objective of preserving the Russian state. While the expansionism following the Second World War was ideologically driven, I suggest there was an underlying insecurity about the Russian nation that underpinned it; the Iron Curtain, after all, had removed the border much further away from Moscow than any previous Russian régime had managed to do.

Regarding borders and landmarks, my supervisor at Cambridge, the eminent historian Norman Stone, asked me to explain an unusual kink in the railway line between

Moscow and Minsk. I offered various possible explanations to do with topography and population centres. 'These are not plausible,' explained Norman; 'the most convincing explanation is that the Tsar's ruler slipped.'

The sense of powerlessness in the face of autocracy bred a culture of opportunism: 'what can I get away with?' As living standards were eroded by the cost of maintaining the military and its conquests, petty larceny became a common means of making ends meet. I first became aware of this in a visit to Tolyatti, the home of the Lada car plant, named after the Italian Communist, Togliatti, and funded by the Fiat Group in return for Soviet steel which, perhaps predictably, turned out to be of very poor quality. The lamentable result was that Fiat Group vehicles manufactured in Europe developed a reputation for rusting rapidly.

The factory was nearly four kilometres long and when we walked the length of the production line, it was at a standstill. Meanwhile private kiosks stationed every 500 metres were doing excellent trade selling cigarettes, snacks, beer and vodka. The reason for the halt in production only became evident at the end of the line. The drivers employed to take the finished product into the huge carparks had failed to show up. My guess is that there was a rota system and that as there was only one production line, any group could bring it to a halt. But nobody did anything about it because nobody had any interest in the profitability of the business; they just assumed that life would continue as before. That was another Soviet characteristic: getting by on the bare minimum; making the least possible effort to fulfil one's duties.

I heard that another Western investor had decided to show its commitment to the new Russia by buying a significant quantity of Ladas for their sales reps. On delivery, only one of them was driveable but was missing a spare wheel. The rest had been stripped of alternators, batteries, wing mirrors, passenger seats, distributor caps, windscreen wipers, exhausts, carburettors and so on. Everything of value that could be removed easily was gone. The manufacturer admitted no liability and the opaque nature of the Russian law courts allowed no possible legal redress. Besides which, all the missing components were easily available in the aftermarket. My informant reckoned that, on average, each car cost 30 per cent more than the purchase price to get it on the road.

On one of my weekly returns home I had forgotten my $5,000 emergency fund, unused and untouched in an inside pocket of my briefcase for months, and so had forgotten to declare it. The customs officer found it and beckoned me to follow him. We arrived in a subterranean room. He proceeded to take the dollars out, count them and pocket $1,500 for himself. 'Or would you prefer to follow official channels?' he enquired. I knew that this was not a choice and so I demurred. He then offered me his hand, which I shook, and he escorted me up to the departure hall as if I was a favoured guest. I was furious because I knew there was nothing I could do about it. This was what it was like in Russia.

I have to talk also about the end of a friendship. Early on, I employed a Russian who had no qualifications, other than the ability to speak English. I made the mistake of assuming that a good salary and a strong personal relationship would be enough to convince him to abide by Western business rules. For a time I disengaged from direct control of our Russian operations, having promoted a new GM. When that did not work out, I returned to find that my Russian 'friend' had been fired for taking kick-backs from an advertising agency. As he then had a salary that put him in the top 5 per cent of Russian wage earners, I took this as a personal betrayal. And in my second stint in Russia, I discovered that he had gone on to work for my new employer as national sales manager and been fired for the same reason.

It was another indication that Western values had little to do with Russian behaviour, which could probably be best described as looking after oneself before helping anyone else. Too late did I learn from American auditors that a safer approach was 'Trust but verify.' With such a different set of values swirling around, it was a cautionary lesson that took me far too long to learn.

Corruption is a synonym for theft, and the impulse to steal is institutionally engrained in Russian society. Everything from a traffic infraction to a law suit could bring the 'right' result with a bribe. Free health care only became available to those who could afford it; everyone else sat in corridors for days until somebody took pity on them. Civil servants were either paid a pittance or not at all; to survive, they'd use their official positions for personal profit. The death of Communism simply lifted the lid on embedded practices that had been survival mechanisms. Russia was and remains a kleptocracy.

This has been a long diversion from my story but provides a context to understanding the very different mores of Russia and the failure of Western free-market and liberal-democratic principles to gain any traction. The Volzhskiy brewery shows why joint ventures became impossible in Russia. At an extraordinary general meeting, the director general voted against a proposition that would have given management control of the brewery to Sun Brewing and of the soft drinks operations to us, at Inchcape. Every possible concession had been given to him and his management team, allowing them to continue in post or accept very lucrative retirement packages. His employees, likewise, had been guaranteed continuing employment at improved labour rates, which would be paid from Day One—a rarity at the time. Under (new) Russian company law, changes to the articles of association required the agreement of more than 75 per cent of shareholders. The DG controlled 25.1 per cent of the shares and did not trust us.

We had committed too much to want to walk away from this, however, and eventually managed to engineer a lease agreement for a bottling hall and related facilities. The DG put up every conceivable obstacle to make this a failure, aided, in part, by his political connections in the *oblast* government. The building project took twice as long and cost twice as much as we had budgeted, despite the valiant efforts of our Turkish contractors. Had we contracted Russians, it would never have been finished.

The boiler room then failed inspection because it did not have the blast protection required by *Gostandart* regulations, which had been written in the 1930s and not revised since. It was encased in the equivalent of a nuclear-bomb shelter. Then, when all was complete and only a couple of weeks away from the official opening, another problem emerged. We were required to install 784 sprinkler heads in the bottling hall to minimise the risk of fire. It is incredibly difficult to set fire to Coca-Cola. But rules were rules. Some discrete conversations with local authorities established that they were 'concerned that they did not have the capability for emergency fire response', but that a 'donation' to the officials involved would resolve the matter. We gave them a second-hand fire engine from Germany and got the news plastered all over the local press. All parties were satisfied.

Michael's boss was not impressed with the facilities at the opening, however, and took the first opportunity to fly back home to Oslo in his chartered (American) jet. It was a shame he missed the party we gave in the centre of Volgograd to celebrate the opening. We had flown in several Russian pop stars to lip-synch their songs while branded delivery trucks supplied free drinks to the audience, though these ran out in an hour. The local police estimated that a quarter of the city's one million population had turned up to this free concert in an open amphitheatre on the banks of the Volga. It was a successful launch and the 250,000 people who turned up for it drank a great deal of Coca-Cola.

Once we were up and running, there were new problems. Russian accounting rules have little in common with those in the West. We worked on Western standards, because that was the only way to run a business, and then translated them back into Russian statutory accounting format. The brief of the local tax office was to make sure that we abided by Russian accounting rules. That these were incompatible with Western accounting principles was of no concern to them but gave them an excuse to ask obstructive questions.

Our response was counter-intuitive. We gave the tax officials an office and access to our canteen; they may still not have been paid but at least they had somewhere comfortable to work and free lunches. They continued to raise queries to justify their presence, but these were always resolved. And we never paid a fine or a bribe.

It was a start, but the cost of moving a high-volume, low-value product across the vastness of Russia meant we needed more production sites. It took me too long to realise that now that Turkish construction companies were available, new-build would be quicker and cheaper than brown-field conversions: new-build would not only not need Russian partners but not need Russian facilities or contractors. But none of this did away with the need to get official sanction at every level.

In Yekaterinburg and Samara, permissions took a long time. By now we were savvy enough through our FSB and other consultancies to navigate this with some certainty of outcome but the delays became an irritant to our bosses in London and to Michael in Moscow.

The exception was Nizhny Novgorod: not the perfect location logistically but Kazan had been abandoned for political reasons. The governor of the *oblast* was Boris Nemtsov. In a one-hour meeting, he promised to deliver all the required permits within a fortnight, and he did. He was subsequently promoted to deputy prime minister under Boris Yeltsin and then became an implacable opponent of Yeltsin's successor, Vladimir Putin, until assassinated within sight of the Kremlin in 2015. A very small part of his legacy was this bottling plant. By 1996, our infrastructure was largely in place and we began to run a business that employed 1,750 people across four bottling plants and twenty-eight distribution depots.

In the absence of any other employment opportunities, it proved easy to attract staff. They were well-educated, technically proficient and keen to learn. The bottling lines ran as well as they did in Europe, which was in stark contrast to those in the Russian breweries I visited—a function of clapped-out technology and a work environment in which nobody cared.

Bottling tended to be men's work, though women occupied ancillary positions. In the office, it was the other way around. The chief accountant was invariably a woman and the proportion of women in senior management positions was around 50 per cent, much higher than in the West at the time. This had nothing to do with revolutionary equality and everything to do with competence. Behind every Russian general director there was a female chief accountant who did the work. While he ranted and raved, she got on with what needed to be done.

As I spent more time in the company of these women, I learned what a low opinion they had of the opposite sex: that too many men were drunkards, had too high an opinion of themselves, knew nothing of loyalty to their families, and considered it their birthright to behave however they wanted. The women seethed but kept quiet. Why? Because everybody with real power was a man. Though this is not a universal condemnation of the Russian male, I found that compacts between equals of the opposite sex were extremely rare.

I began by appreciating what I took to be the women's old-fashioned femininity and charm: they would listen with attention to what I said, attend to my possible needs and flirt mildly with me, in spite of the age gap, but then realised I was reading the wrong page. I had twenty-six expatriates (all men) working in Russia. Six of them were married; the rest were single on arrival. When they left, all twenty-six were married or intended to become so. This included three who had decided to swap wives. At the time, I regarded the women's behaviour as unpardonably mercenary. Now I am not so sure. In a misogynistic society, a good-enough partner beats none at all, and an understandable pragmatism trumps Western posturing about love matches.

Newly rich Russian men were inevitably accompanied by an entourage of thick-set men in suits, either *vory* (literally *thieves*—though *gangsters* might be a better translation) or FSB, though often it was difficult to tell the difference, assuming there was one. What applied to both was that the henchmen were armed. In the centre of this circle was the businessman who, on social occasions, was escorted by a much younger woman on his arm, six-foot-tall, beautiful but inscrutable.

After three years there were indications, in Moscow at least, that economic growth was beginning to pick up and—the engine of growth—the fact that Russia was starting to become more open to the outside world. In the early days, the only Western-friendly hospitality venues were Irish bars like Sally O'Grady's. It has passed into history that the first McDonald's in Pushkinskaya took more money on its opening day than any other outlet worldwide. Two years later the choice was wider. Round the corner from the new hotel where I had set up home was a pizza-and-pasta restaurant. Next left, a Tex-Mex bar. Up Tverskaya, a Scandinavian restaurant.

This tiny bubble of free markets and consumer choice catered for an equally small elite who had money to spend. It was made up mostly of expatriates like me, working for multinationals; financial-services experts who found a ready market for their skills among the emerging Russian oligarchs; and brave entrepreneurs who found a highly profitable niche for their products in sectors where there was no domestic competition.

There were far too few of them to support more than a handful of expensive restaurants and luxury-brand stores, but there was a rapidly expanding middle class. My English teacher from Volgograd was an example of this. Employed for his language skills and engaging personality, he began on a salary of $500 a month but such was the demand for anybody with rudimental management skills that in three years he was pulling in $3,000 a month—quite a fortune for a country where the basic cost of living was low. Add to this that income taxes had high thresholds and low rates, that there was nobody to enforce them, and that employers were under no obligation to reveal who was paid what. That left around $2,500 a month to spend on having a good time. A further incentive to spend was the corollary of Russian fatalism: spend what you've got while you've got it; you may not have it tomorrow. The events of 2008 proved the wisdom of that.

Foreigners also benefited from the economic dislocation. For $4 each, I could buy 125-gram jars of vacuum-sealed caviar from the official supplier at the Gastronom up the road. As an accompaniment, premium vodka was available at $6 a litre. (The $1 version was used as windscreen wash or anti-freeze.)

Moscow became a better place to live in. I was confident about wandering around the city without a bodyguard and used the Metro frequently. It was part of developing a sense of belonging. I did not need my own *krysha*—a word that translates as 'roof' but was used to mean 'protection'. Our business was low-margin, we were not in hock to any local interests and we had not attracted any power players. In addition, our profitability depended on getting product to consumers in the most cost-efficient way. It was far easier for Russians to make money out of natural resources, telecoms, construction, and the media. Westerners involved in these sectors would have had a very hard time but we were of no interest to them and I was free to go wherever I wanted. And so, as a curious foreigner, I was able to enjoy the experience of blending in, unobserved. It was a delight.

By my sixth year in Russia, I began to believe that all our efforts had been worthwhile. In June 1998, we had got all our business infrastructure in place and become cash positive. Moscow's bubble economy was beginning to develop clones in the provincial cities where we operated. We had arrived at a modus vivendi with local authorities, who left us alone to continue a business that worked within our rules of corporate governance. I was optimistic, as was Pulitzer Prize-winning author David Remnick, who ended a book in February of the same year with the words, 'if Yeltsin fades away in a peaceful transition of power, then Russia will move farther down the road toward becoming what so many have hoped for for so long: to be part of the world, to be a normal country.'[8] With the advantage of hindsight, this is the mirror image of the Fukuyama hypothesis that economic growth and democracy go hand in hand. Got that one wrong.

The only downside was that we had fired our GM and I was back in charge of the day-to-day running of the business. In addition, a change of corporate strategy required the sale of our our business to the Coca-Cola Company (TCCC) and I was responsible for that too. The indicative TCCC price for acquisition had been agreed and although there would be a loss on the investment, it was not so significant that it warranted an announcement to the stock market. Relationships were good

---

[8] David Remnick, *Resurrection: The Struggle for a New Russia*, Macmillan (1998), p.382.

and staff had been reassured that their posts were secure.

What I had failed to pay attention to, simply because it had little impact on what we did, was the incompetence of the Yeltsin government. It was common knowledge that Yeltsin was an alcoholic, manipulated by the oligarchs on whom he depended for his support. His drunken displays at global events had become a source of derision. He was a clown.

What I also failed to recognise was that the bubble economies that I had taken to be a sign of resuscitation were built on sand. The banking crisis of August 1998 brought things to an abrupt halt.

In retrospect it was not surprising. Russian entrepreneurs built their businesses on debt financing, and all of it was in dollars, but few, if any of them, understood at the time what that entailed. Many obtained loans based on relationships and influence rather than on critical analysis of business plans. In this unregulated banking sector, balance sheets were dependent on unrealisable assets. This papered over Russia's cracks until the system got challenged. The moment that the average Russian citizen was unable to withdraw cash from their ATM machines, the bubble burst. Suddenly the rouble was worthless. No transaction in any other currency was legal in Russia. In a matter of hours the Russian economy came to a complete standstill. All banks closed and the value of the rouble was anybody's guess.

I was lucky enough to find an Italian restaurant where the owner was willing to feed me, on tick, and we commiserated with each other about this unforeseen disaster. Later, I found a couple of bars that were still open and accepting roubles at pre-crash exchange rates. It was there that I overheard a conversation between two foreign-investment bankers. 'What the hell are we going to do now?' said one. The other raised his eyebrows and said, 'Cabbage futures?' At the time it seemed like a good title.

The impact of Russia's financial collapse on me was negligible but on others I had grown close to, it was immense. My driver (whose salary had grown from $150 to $1,000 a month in the three years he had been employed) had recently bought a new Skoda Felicia, probably on credit. Why he had done so, I had no idea, as he had access to the company's Audi twenty-four hours a day. Maybe, as an ex-taxi driver, he wanted to show his friends and neighbours that he had made it. I was happy to go along with this, and let him ferry me about in the Skoda rather than the company car. It was during this crisis that he commented, 'Just when you think it getting better, they fuck you up.' 'They' were the élite. He made the remark in resignation, not anger.

There were many like him who had borrowed to improve their lives and now found themselves at the mercy of what had proved an unreliable banking system. What is ironic is that the Russian failure was dismissed by the global banking world as just a local glitch; the same principle of lending against unrealisable assets caused the global banking crisis that broke ten years later. In Russia, it took over a week to sort things out. The result was a devaluation of the rouble by over 60 per cent against the dollar. In the interim, the Russian Coca-Cola bottlers were the only ones in history to record negative sales, as wholesalers and distributors returned product on the grounds that they could not pay for it. More importantly, people in the emerging middle class were decimated by bank loans they could no longer afford to repay.

It is here that the first part of my Russia story ends. The consequence of the 2008 banking crisis is that the sale price of the business I had spent over four years building up was reduced by over 50 per cent. The aftermath was the closure of two of the bottling plants, the departure of all but a couple of the expatriate staff and the dismissal of a high proportion of Russian employees. I understand that our bottling operations did not return to profit for another ten years.

It was a relief to go home. Russia had proved to be unreformable. As a Russian dissident said in the 1980s, 'Perhaps the secret to understanding Russian history lies in its grammar: it lacks a pluperfect tense. In Latin, English and German, the pluperfect describes actions completely completed at a definite point in the past. .... Russian history never becomes history. Like a stubborn page in a new book, it refuses to turn over.'[9]

---

[9] Igor Pomerantsev, quoted by his son Peter in *The Spectator*, 29 May 2021.

CHAPTER 18
Russia: 2003 to 2008
'Krysha'

I returned to Russia in 2003 as Region Director, Eastern Europe, for Imperial Tobacco. Comecon had become Central Europe and I was left with what had been the Soviet Union and the Balkans, still outside the EU. At the time, the new post-Communist world order was regarded as settled. Minor wars and military interventions by Russia were seen as inconsequential and simply the detritus of a now-discredited political orthodoxy.

The West forgot that a wounded bear is not expected by its cubs to lie down and die: it must fight on. With no appreciation that outcomes might be beneficial for all, the Russians felt belittled and humiliated and, since nationalism was their only common denominator of unity—the only source of pride in a social system dogged by fatalism—they looked for a brave champion to restore their dignity. Putin stepped forward to cater for—and amplify—this need and, within the limited means at his disposal and ignoring the rules of the international community, has challenged what Russians see as the West's desire for supremacy. The implications of this require examination.

What had Russia become since I left it in 1998? On the surface, the roots of economic growth in Moscow appeared to have grown sturdier in the intervening years, and the banking crisis seemed nothing more than an unfortunate blip. Cranes hovered over new developments everywhere and the city was stuffed with luxury stores, expensive restaurants and top-of-the-range cars. Prices had soared, too: the *gastronoms* and other Soviet style stores had disappeared, to be replaced by supermarket chains. There were no *babushkas* any longer at the main stations. Traffic jams were longer.

Visits to outlying cities suggested that this was not a one-off. All now had decent hotels and restaurants. Competition among new airlines meant you could get where you wanted reasonably safely and on time. The number of Russian managers employed by Western enterprises had increased and they were now earning as much as they would in the UK.

All this disguised a fundamental shift in the management of the Russian economy. Yeltsin had been in thrall to the early oligarchs. On acceding to the presidency, Putin's first move was to reverse the balance of power: oligarchs would now be beholden to him, not the other way round.

Under other circumstances, this might have indicated a virtuous wish for a more accountable system of government; it actually proved to be the opposite and, with the benefit of hindsight, one consistent with Russian history. There is no discernable difference between Tsarism, Communism and Putin in their actions. *Putin's People* provides detail on the process on how a new élite—the ex-KGB *siloviki*—took control.[1] Aided by compliant courts and politically motivated extortion, friends of Putin were able to acquire controlling stakes in all Russia's major natural-resource producers, media and telecoms. Unwittingly or not, this was facilitated by Western bankers, who were able to convert unreliable Russian roubles into dollars in offshore banks though a labyrinth of accounts in tax havens. Russia remained a kleptocracy but with one difference: the oligarchy was now controlled by one man.

Those who opposed Putin's régime, whether economically or politically, were imprisoned or fled into exile. Some were assassinated, at home or abroad, to demonstrate that nobody was beyond Putin's reach, no matter where they might be or how rich or important. The poisoning of Sergei Skripal is a case in point. Skripal was arrested in 2004, charged with high

---

[1] Catherine Belton, *Putin's People*, Harper Collins (2020).

treason for sharing state secrets with MI6 and sentenced to thirteen years in prison. In 2010, he was part of a prisoner swap and allowed to move to the UK, where he settled in the city of Salisbury. In March 2018, he and his daughter, Yulia, were poisoned with a nerve agent. Against the odds, both survived. What is interesting is that when Russia offered to 'help' Britain investigate the poisoning, the daughter thanked them for their interest but politely declined. That says to me: 'I have no axe to grind so please leave me alone.'

Putin's bid for exclusive state power does not exclude foreign investors, as the case of Bill Crowder suggests.[2] Browder, an American financier and former hedge fund manager, had at one time been one of the largest foreign investors in Russia and was bullish about the country's prospects but became disillusioned with the rampant corruption and lawlessness he encountered. After he began speaking out against Russian human-rights abuses, he was targetted by Russia with multiple 'red notices'—international alerts for his arrest and extradition—and accused of tax fraud and other trumped-up crimes.

Companies were also targetted. BP's shareholding in TNK-BP was emasculated to 20 per cent (below the 25 per cent threshold for minority protection), in spite of its claim that TNK-BP was a successful partnership in a strategic market. For the majority shareholders, BP provided a veneer of respectability, but the reality was that joint ventures could not work in Russia, as I had found out several years before.

Putin's propaganda has the support of the Russian Orthodox church, which is socially conservative, Slavic and not averse to exploiting its position for its own financial interest. In this way, religion has become central, once again, to the idea of Russian identity. Those professing any other identity

---

[2] Bill Browder, *Red Notice: How I Became Putin's No 1 Enemy*, Bantam Press (2015).

are not to be trusted: Jews, Muslims, liberals, gays, foreigners and citizens of other ethnic backgrounds. Unlike Stalin, who mostly purged domestic dissenters, Putin targets two groups: those who oppose him at home and those overseas who have 'betrayed' him. Both are then held up to show Russians what the consequences are of any kind of opposition. All others are tolerated merely to the extent that they toe the line and provide value to the state. Such a version of Russian nationalism is fascist in all but name.

Putin has played on another myth that remains incomprehensible to Western eyes: that of the strong man. Homoerotic photos of him bare-chested, wrestling with alarming fauna, are designed to reassure the hapless electorate that he is on their side and has the willpower to achieve what they want. Near-total control of the media, the judiciary, parliamentary elections and the economy, coupled with the threat to anybody who opposes him is as close to Stalin as one can get. To be a strong man has a fundamental weakness, however. Because of the dangers in challenging the dictator, toadying is again central to Russian politics, as it has been for centuries, so that putting the best possible gloss on events becomes a well-rehearsed habit for presidential advisors. The result is that the dictator loses touch with reality.

Our interpretation of that is deeply critical; the rationale within the Kremlin is that Putin is doing nothing that Western states have not done in the past when it suited them. I do not say this to exculpate Russia, merely to insist that we fully understand its motives, before judging it. In Russia, truth is an opaque and not politically useful concept.

Putin's régime initially oversaw strong GNP growth. As I watched broadcasts from the 2018 World Cup, which Russia hosted, in cities that I had got to know well in former times, I was amazed that nobody mentioned how shoddy everything was: things must have improved, I assumed. At the same time

Russian life expectancy was growing again, which was a sign of optimism or of the success of the measures to control tobacco and alcohol consumption. Superficially, all seemed well with the Russia world. The cost may have been that Putin has enriched himself, though there is no proof of this, but so did the Tsars, who owned everything.

That is the macro picture. The rest of this chapter deals with the internal contradictions of the Russian economy and its fractious relationships with the ex-Soviet territories, and ends with some thoughts on why our 'engagement' with Russia produces no tangible results. My punchline is that we have to resist trying to teach the Russians a lesson; what they want—ardently—is to be recognised as more important than they are. That's not a bad rule for dealing with others at whatever level.

SELLING TOBACCO IN Russia was not the same as selling Coca-Cola. Smoking was an integral part of Russian daily life; carbonated soft drinks were a novelty and a luxury. Tobacco was compact and easy to transport, and the margins on it far exceeded those of soft drinks. The collapse of the Soviet Union left a domestic tobacco industry incapable of producing anything but plain cigarettes of questionable quality—assuming their cash-flow crisis allowed them to produce anything at all. And then there was the problem of criminal gangs, attracted by the tax breaks on imports given to the Orthodox Church and the Afghan Veterans Association, both of which got very rich on the proceeds.

When the authorities made it harder to import foreign goods, the logical solution for Western companies was to buy Russian factories and upgrade them. One by one they did so, as did Imperial Tobacco, but in our case, there was a legacy from the free-for-all days that proved impossible to escape.

In 1991 two young Russians turned up in Hamburg in an

ancient Volkswagen, wanting distribution rights for cigarette brands made by Reemtsma, which was the world's fourth largest tobacco company (and which we bought in 2002). One of them was suffering from acute toothache. Reemstma arranged for him to be treated and was assured, in exchange, that they could trust him, for 'being forever in your debt.'

The consequence was that I now had a national distributor linking us to the market we wanted to control. To convince me that he was doing a professional job on our behalf, Sergei took me on a tour. In both Krasnodar and Volgograd, I met his local managers, both recruited from the FSB, probably because they were reliable and worked on the command-and-control principle of management. In Tomsk, in Siberia, it was different: a local distributor was resisting Sergei's attempts to buy him out. I understood enough Russian to recognise this as a standoff. When I asked about the distributor a couple of weeks later, all Sergei replied was, 'It's been resolved.' The man had been removed.

Under our noses, Sergei had consolidated his position as the national distributor. But his ambition did not end there. He already had national distribution rights for Gallagher. When Gallagher was acquired by Japan Tobacco, he managed to bring their portfolio under his wing too. Always reasonable and protesting that he had his principals' best interest at heart, he was dealing with Western managers whose rules of engagement were more tolerant and trusting.

Finally, the endgame was revealed. The sage and unflustered general manager of our Russian business, the late Peter Quittenbaum, had always assumed that the two Hamburg visitors in the old VW had remained connected. He was right. The other had become CEO of Mercury, the Philip Morris distributor. Between them, they controlled 70 per cent of the Russian tobacco market.

I was to become the conduit for the aspirations of Sergei

and his companion. I should meet Igor, his partner, Sergei said. He would pick me up from our offices in a small cul-de-sac off Tverskaya.

The first problem was that there was not enough room to turn his enormous Mercedes-Maybach around; oligarchs tend not to be driven backwards. The process of extricating ourselves took some time. It would have been quicker to take the Metro but that is also something oligarchs do not do.

We eventually pulled up outside the 15-metre-high gates of what looked like an industrial compound. Cameras identified us as friendly and the gates rolled back to reveal a large yard and a two-storey factory, crisply painted and restored. There was an escalator to the first floor; we were escorted up it. At the top, glass doors opened silently and we found ourselves in the reception area, greeted by two young women, six-foot-tall in their high heels, who smiled warmly but asked me, politely, if I could show them my passport.

I was then escorted along an elevated walkway, one of the greeters ahead to show me the way, the other at my elbow in case I should slip. On my left was a multi-purpose sports hall, complete with a climbing wall. On my right was a swimming pool of about half the dimensions of an Olympic pool. At the end was a seating area of leather armchairs and sofas, wood panelling and thick carpet.

Igor entered. He was in his early forties, with a physique that supported the rumour that he had a black belt in one of the Eastern martial arts. He had piercing blue eyes and used them to suggest that I was the only person of any importance in the room. Sergei was uncharacteristically silent.

Igor was the personification of hospitality. It was lunchtime and he asked what I would like to eat. 'Whatever you've got.' 'No,' he insisted; 'name your preferences. We have everything here.' We settled on caviar and steak. Sergei again said nothing.

'And what would you like to drink with it? We have everything, all stored at the right temperature.' He gestured at the wine coolers in the dining room.

The luncheon followed a familiar pattern when strangers meet: tentative questions about family and circumstances, as the first stages of building trust. Igor remained charming, finding parallels in his own life that resonated with mine. Finding my answers satisfactory, he slowly moved to the nub of the matter. 'Of course, as you know, Sergei and I are partners.' I nodded, although a partner who says nothing is more like a direct report. Though Igor controlled 70 per cent of the Russian tobacco market, his ambitions were greater than that. He wanted to become a Western Europe distributor as well—and Imperial, having acquired Altadis (the combination of the French and Spanish tobacco monopolies) had exclusive distribution rights for tobacco products in both these countries, as well as in Italy. To make that happen, he needed a meeting with Imperial's CEO. I could arrange that.

He gave me his mobile number and we spoke at least once a week. We also dined together when I was in Moscow. Thus did I began to learn what it meant to be a Russian oligarch. His protection—his *krysha*—was the minister of finance. I suspect that, like Sergei, he kept silent when with him unless explicitly asked for his opinion. His master was beholden in turn to Putin and the same rule applied. The top man hears what he wants to hear, assuming he wants to hear anything.

Oligarchs operated at several levels, rather like judo belts. Everybody had a roof above them, because there was no law. However powerful they might be at their own level, all were compliant, complicit and compromised.

Igor had all the trappings of what it takes to be recognised as important. I arranged for him to meet the Group CEO. Igor called to explain he would be late. His passport with the UK visa was in Moscow but he was in Nice. No matter, he would take his Falcon executive jet to pick it up and would only be delayed by four hours. He turned up at the London hotel in his Rolls-Royce, kept only for his infrequent visits to the UK.

Too late for a formal meeting, we had to set off for the highpoint of the invitation, an international football qualifier between Russia and England at Wembley. I explained that the best way to get there was by train from Marylebone. This was greeted with incredulity at first but our guests allowed me to persuade them that it was indeed the most practical option. No traffic jams.

Igor arrived with his wife, another six-footer: charming but more mature than the usual arm candy. The CEO had gone on ahead, so there were four of us: Igor and his wife, Sergei and me. The Rolls-Royce pulled up at the hotel. Despite its enormous dimensions, it had only three spare seats; the rest was filled up with cocktail cabinets. Igor told Sergei to take a taxi. He turned up eventually, at Marylebone, breathing heavily and implying his lateness was all my fault.

Mr and Mrs Igor, however, loved it. The chance of mixing with real football fans on a real train without feeling threatened seemed to free them from their guardedness. I discovered that Mrs Igor was actively involved in Moscow's modern art world and that we had opinions in common. At the end of the match, Igor threw his arms around me and said to the CEO, 'This is wonderful,' though Russia had lost 2–0.

It struck me afterwards that all the flash, all the conspicuous display of wealth, was nothing but a carapace. Beneath it were people who were deeply scared about the consequences of their decisions. To find not only that foreigners were not a threat but that they were fun to be with allowed their masks to drop—for a moment. Both Igor and Sergei now have an estimated net worth of $5 and $1 billion respectively, and both have had sanctions imposed on them, following Russia's attempt to take over Ukraine. From the photographs I have seen, Igor now looks more like a spectre than an oligarch; I would like to meet him again and find out how he's feeling.

I had changed jobs by the time this part of my story came to an end but was told by my successor that when Igor's proposal was finally rejected by the new CEO, he pleaded like a child denied sweets. Another small step in mutual disillusionment.

And what is the moral of the story? It is a microcosm of what it takes to be successful in the Russian economy. In the eighteenth century, Adam Smith talked about 'the community of markets'. No such thing exists in Russia because it is an economy of patronage. The argument that a centrally planned *dirigiste* economy was a core element in the advancement of emerging economies overlooks the fact that such economies were designed to leverage core assets for the benefit of all; in Russia's case, *dirigisme* was applied for the benefit of the few.

That beneficial narrowness is mirrored in other conceptual narrownesses, notably its failure to develop its economic base beyond its reliance on oil, gas and raw materials. Royalties from the first two still account for over 50 per cent of the state budget. Despite being the largest country in the world, with a population of 146 million, Russia's economy is still smaller than Italy's. It has significantly fewer small- and medium-sized enterprises (SMEs) than anywhere in the EU. As one commentator said, 'If you know you are going to be shaken down by the authorities at some time or other, why bother?'[3]

THE WORLD CUP was the high point of Russian resurgence; the country has since reverted to sclerotic economic growth. Whether this is due to Ukraine-related sanctions is a moot point, but a more important factor is probably capital flight.

---

[3] BBC documentary on Russia (2016).

In such a corrupt and untrustworthy régime, anybody with roubles to spare exported them to their rainy-day piggy banks offshore. The World Cup itself was something of a *mise en scène*, with host cities decked out like Potemkin villages to prove their progress. I admit to having been hoodwinked by this until I read Colin Thubron's latest book.[4] The life he describes as he descends the Amur River is indistinguishable from what I experienced over twenty-five years ago. Only if you live in cities are living standards better, probably because there is no political benefit in spending money on the rural peasantry. On the Chinese side of the border, however, lives are improving.

It is perhaps not too fantastical to suggest that the combination of the Kremlin's promise of better living standards for all and its pact with a fabulously wealthy élite was never going to come good. Its customary 'solution' was to blame its failures on outside aggressors. As one opposition journalist said, 'Putin is first and foremost a KGB officer. The KGB recognises no rules. Its one objective is to ensure stability; that is what Russians crave.'[5] Russia has still a weak economy but it has two strengths that are highly dangerous to all: it controls much of the energy supplied to the West and it can blow the world to smithereens.

Serhii Plokhy, the Ukrainian historian, sums it up like this: 'Russia went through a huge crisis: loss of identity, loss of territory, loss of its status as a great power. It found itself in that place sooner than other countries. But there is a lot in Russia history that helped Putin and those around him to make the choices they did'.[6]

I hope there are enough clues in this narrative to explain

---

[4] Colin Thubron, *The Amur*, Vintage (2022).
[5] BBC documentary (ibid).
[6] Interview in the *Observer*, 28 September 2019.

what made Putin think that his 2022 invasion of Ukraine was a good move for Russia. Putin was never the amenable technocrat that the Western media had portrayed him as on his accession to power. For a time, a certain amount of charm disguised his sociopathic instincts; his untouchability, and the manner in which he has prosecuted his Ukraine offensive, has now revealed them for what they are. He cares no more for the lives of other people—his own or other countries'— than did Stalin. His sole objective is geopolitical strength. How his time in office will end is difficult to predict.

What worries me is the absence of a Western strategy to deal with Russia, in the short term and once Ukraine's future has been settled. One thing we have learned is that the country is not amenable to liberal democracy: everything in its history is against it. For that reason, it is dangerous and while it cannot be invaded, it needs to be constrained. But how?

CHAPTER 19
The Imperium

THE LEGACY OF THE USSR IN FIFTEEN NEW STATES
I have presumed to borrow the title of this chapter from Ryszard Kapuśińsky's compendium of experiences in the Soviet Union from 1937 to 1993, in which he highlights the failed attempt of its political orthodoxy to extinguish different cultures and beliefs, particularly at its fringes.[1]

Russia has not forgotten its geographical history. Like the imperialist nations of the West, it carved out its empire by force. Western states then abandoned theirs through a combination of economics, local opposition, public opinion and sheer exhaustion. Once the Comecon states had declared independence, the final collapse of the Soviet Union was engineered by three people—Boris Yeltsin, Ukraine's Leonid Kravchuk and Belarus's Stanislav Shushkevich—thereby ridding themselves of Gorbachev as president of an entity that no longer existed.

As with all major decisions from the Romanovs onwards, this realignment was made by a tiny coterie. Over thirty years later it is denounced by Putin as illegal—illogically, in view of his professed commitment to Russian tradition—and disputed by force rather than diplomacy, just as his predecessors did. Defence of Russian (Slavic) minorities in these newly independent states is also contradictory because the USSR, which he venerates, officially recognised differences of cultures and religion in the fifteen autonomous republics that made up the Soviet empire, even if in practice it suppressed them.

One source of conflict was promoted by Russia as a purely internal matter. Chechnya lay within the Russian Federation but had a predominantly Muslim population and a history of

---

[1] Ryszard Kapuściński, *The Imperium*, Granta (1994).

rebelling against its overlords. The First Chechen War (1994–96), botched by Yeltsin, was an early attempt to keep the Russian Federation together, but was ignored in the West. The Second Chechen War (1999–2009) should have made the West take more notice but was again dismissed as a domestic affair, although there was international outrage at Russia's disregard of humanitarian law. To capture Chechnya, the Russians laid siege to its capital, Grozny, in the winter of 1999–2000, having previously carpet-bombed it in the First Chechen War and then lured its fighters to their deaths. In 2003 the United Nations called Grozny the most destroyed city on earth. This brutality together with the appointment of a compliant warlord as governor nonetheless achieved its objective. Revolt in Chechnya and neighbouring 'republics' was suppressed and Russia temporarily felt safe from insurgency, although it left disaffected rebels to become a mainstay of the jihadist movements that were becoming a problem everywhere else in the world.

EASTERN EUROPE 2003 to 2008
Simultaneously, extra-territorial interventions began in places nobody in the West could even identify on the map. Russia was judge and jury in the settlement of a 1992 armed conflict in Moldova between Romanians on the right bank of the Dniestra river and a majority Russian population on the other side. The Russian solution was to divide the country in two, creating the new state of Transnistria. Only the UN took much notice.

In 2007 I transited Transnistria on a journey from Ukraine to Chisinau. Three impressions of it remain: the border guards and military were all Russian, it looked and felt like a Russian provincial outpost of the 1990s, and the country was effectively a monopoly of Sheriff, a company said to control most of Transnistria's businesses and most of its government ministers too. Its owner, originally a Ford car dealer, had expanded into drug and sex trafficking, assisted by the fact that as a breakaway state, Transnistria was not subject to any international law. Sheriff now owns a chain of petrol stations and of supermarkets, a television channel, a publishing house, a construction company, a Mercedes-Benz dealership, an advertising agency, a spirits factory, two bread factories and a mobile phone network. It also owns FC Sheriff Tiraspol, a football club which consistently wins the Moldovan football league (the only remaining fragment of united Moldova) and manages to get to the qualifying stages of the European Cup, by only recruiting international players.

Other than Russia, Transnistria is only recognised by Abkhazia, South Ossetia and Artsakh. All are themselves the outcome of Yeltsin's military interventions, all with their origins in inter-ethnic conflicts and all resolved by cementing ethnic partitions by shifting large minorities across borders, a traditional Soviet recourse deployed also on Poles in Western Ukraine, Germans in the Volga basin and Tatars and Cossacks in Crimea.

Abkhazia and South Ossetia are territories that Russia helped carve out of Georgia in the chaos following the Soviet collapse. Artsakh was better known as Nagorno-Karabakh, until absorbed by Azerbaijan. These faux-states have no international legitimacy and could not evolve into independent nations because they are tiny and isolated; two are landlocked. When conflict arises, as it did in Georgia in 2008 and between Armenia and Azerbaijan in 2020, Russia determines the outcome. They survive only as Russian client territories.

Putin inherited Yeltsin's assumption of authority over the ex-Soviet states, reinforcing Russia's claims over them with the same myths that had justified the expansion of the Romanov empire and its Communist successor. Appointing itself the guarantor of the freedom of all Slavs enabled Russia to argue that its own interests in the region were paramount, though this made little sense in the Caucasus and in Central Asia, neither of which is ethnically Slavic. It played well at home, however, as it recalled a time when Russia was important even to regions that were far away. The reformation of the armed forces into what was heralded as an effective fighting machine also gave Putin the military resources to defend his claim. Similar tactics have been employed in Ukraine.

The path from small engagements in places nobody much knew about to the 2022 invasion of Ukraine—Europe's second largest country after Russia—is a logical extension of Russia's 'near abroad policy', but with the ambition not just of securing its borders but re-establishing Russia as a superpower.

Putin had set out his manifesto as far back as 2014, when he first annexed Crimea from Ukraine and supported pro-Russian separatists fighting the Ukrainian military in Ukraine's Donbas region. His core argument was that the Russian state had an inalienable tight to rule Ukraine because it had done so before 1991. This was accompanied by a disavowal of those countries that had 'illegally' broken up the Soviet Union, a lot of strident rhetoric about Ukraine being ruled by fascists, and a mash-up of distorted propaganda about NATO being at the gate and intent on world conquest. Putin's case was highly selective and open to interpretation. In particular, there was no suggestion that citizens had the right to elect their own governments.

So lacking in confidence was Moscow about its own rhetoric that it had to ban and punish all dissent. After all, the USSR had fought the Great Patriotic War against Hitler, at massive personal cost, meaning that no one was better qualified to recognise fascism than Russians. They recognised it in Ukraine, because factions in Ukraine had eighty years earlier assisted the Nazis (after their country had been raped by Moscow in the mid 1930s), and they recognised it in the West, because the USA and Europe had been ideologically opposed to the USSR throughout its existence.

What was absent in Russia was any notion that citizens should have a say in how they are governed, and by whom. Instead, its invasion of Ukraine was a show of power and national purpose; no other considerations had any currency— not human rights, not free speech, not democracy, not the right to protest, not adherence to the rules-based order. As in Afghanistan and Syria, Russia behaved in flagrant defiance of the UN conventions it was signed up to.

At the same time, its much-vaunted new military capability proved to be a mirage, with an old-fashioned, cumbersome command structure mirroring that of the Russian state itself: control from the top, imposed on top of hierarchies of distrust. In spite of Putin's constant appeals to history, nothing had been learned from the past except how to emulate it.

After Europe's seventy-five years of fraught but ultimately peaceful coexistence, Russia now poses an existential threat to the continent's stability. The conundrum is how to resolve this threat and, in the case of Ukraine, how to ensure that any peace treaty holds.

PUTIN IS AN effective tyrant. He has solidified his position internally by stoking Russia's traditional xenophobia and promoting the need for his own authoritarian rule. Opinion polls suggest that he is still supported by the majority of Russians, and this does not surprise me, in spite of the apparent sophistication of Russian education; what has surprised me is the difficulty that Western observers have in accepting the fact.

What strikes me is that the Russians have grown up in a

culture that demands compliance and subservience, and which is shaped by media censorship and Kremlin propaganda. The few who cannot accommodate themselves to this —largely the urban intelligentsia—have left. I have Russian friends who are now in Sweden, Germany, Türkiye, Georgia and Armenia. This is also nothing new: those under threat usually choose exile. Jews fled in the face of state-sanctioned pogroms in the late 1800s and early 1900s; aristocrats fled after the 1917 revolution; then those described as 'class enemies' and 'enemies of the state' in Soviet times. Recently oligarchs who have fallen out of favour have fled, as have dissidents and entrepreneurs who want their families to grow up in a safer environment (many of whom now reside in the UK).

The Ukraine War—Putin's 'Special Military Operation'— has damaged our economy and our living standards. Utility bills have skyrocketed; food is short in the Sahel. But what has hurt us most, perhaps, is the realisation that Russia has many more allies—or, at least, uncritical beneficiaries—than we had imagined. The wake-up call for the West was not just the invasion itself but the UN resolution condemning it. Two thirds of the world's population were represented by member states that either abstained or opposed it. It turns out that Russia is far less alone in the world than the West had imagined. Our much vaunted respect for territorial integrity and self-determination is belied by the invasions of Iraq and Afghanistan (and a long history of doing the same elsewhere). Pot calling the kettle black.

Those who opposed or abstained may have regarded this as just another Cold War stand-off of no direct concern to themselves, or more proactively, recognised the political and economic opportunities it presented. But the lesson for the West is clear: we no longer own the global moral high ground (if we ever did) and our influence on the Rest is much reduced.

UKRAINE 2003 to 2010

What is Ukraine? It is not a name that appears on any old maps. Plokhy offers a tortuous history which provides ample ammunition to all those, past and present, who have laid claim to it.[2] The details are particularly hard to navigate if one comes from a settled state, like Britain, with a relatively simple national narrative. Over the centuries Ukraine, or parts of it, have been ruled by Poles, Lithuanians, Swedes, Austrians, Nazis, Hungarians, Tatars, Cossacks, Ottomans and Russians. They have been referred to as Ruthenians, Galicians, Cossacks, Bessarabians and a lot more besides. Ukraine was often divided between different polities and had no recognised permanent borders until Soviet times. (The same could also be said for most of Central Europe, however.)

What Ukraine does have is a truly horrific twentieth-century history. We talk about the suffering of soldiers in the trench warfare of the First World War and of the tribulations of being alone in Europe against the Nazis but this was as nothing compared to what Ukraine suffered. After the Russian Revolution, it became the battleground between the Red and White armies, both of which regarded the local population as no more than a source of provisions, and had a shared disregard of human rights. The Ukrainian nationalist leader, Symon Petlyura, was also an antisemite, as were the Cossacks, the backbone of the White armies. Jews made up around thirty per cent of the population, indispensable as traders, craftsmen and financiers but regarded as undesirable aliens by much of Ukraine's population and forced to live in a 'Pale of Settlement' that went back to Catherine the Great in the 1790s. Attacks on Jews, as referred to above, were known

---

[2] Serhii Plokhy, *The Gates of Europe: A History of Ukraine*, Basic Books (2015).

as *pogroms*: a borrowed Russian word which has no synonyms for other racist massacres. The Jews had more enemies than most, but the entire population, both rich and poor, was subject to a reign of terror. The Second World War built on Russian and Polish (and Ukrainian) hostility but the most ruthless Jew-killers were now German Nazis, with a industrialised, systematic, extermination campaign.

It is arguable whether the Germans were as bestial as the Russians, the former regarding Slavic speakers as sub-human and beneath contempt, the latter believing that a people's revolution required absolute loyalty, on pain of death. In between, millions (irrespective of religion) died of starvation in the forced Soviet collectivisation of agriculture. That Ukraine has emerged as a genuine nation state in the twenty-first century is partly a determination never to let it happen again.

Reconciling the opposing narratives of Moscow and Kiev, or Kyiv, requires examination but provides few clear-cut answers. Language provides one possible approach. Ukraininan sounds very much like Russian but has in recent years played up the difference in its spellings and in the use of Cyrillic script, for which there are now modified Latin letters with additional diacritic marks. But is it really Russian and are the people really Russian? Under the tsars, publications in Ukrainian were restricted and even banned in order to suppress Ukrainian identity, then tolerated somewhat in the late nineteenth century before being banned again by the Soviets, along with the speaking and teaching of the language. Yet Russian Soviet officials argued that it would take only twenty minutes for a Ukrainian and a Russian to understand each other fully. A parallel lies in the difference between Czech and Slovak; only after the Velvet Divorce in 1993 did 'Teach yourself Slovak' publications start to appear.

This leads to another debate. If Russian was the native

language of Ukraine, albeit corrupted by peasants, and Ukrainians were referred to as 'Little Russians', albeit patronisingly, then Ukrainians should embrace Russia as their natural home. No, no, say Ukrainian nationalists: Russia is the upstart nation; Kievan Rus emerged in the ninth century and was ruled by a dynasty of Vikings. Its capital was Kiev (hence the name Kievan Rus); Russia was merely a later offshoot.

Ukraine's current borders, though not the territory it currently controls, were only fixed (by Moscow) after the Second World War and Crimea was only added to it in 1954 by Khrushchev—apparently drunk at the time, according to the Putin narrative. The core question is thus: what is Ukraine geographically?

A quick look at the map of its vast territory identifies a geographical feature that divides the country in two: the Dnieper River that flows through Kiev and today makes up most of the frontline between Russian and Ukrainian forces. That has been the case for centuries and represented, until recently, the border between Russian and Ukrainian speakers.

West of the Dnieper, other regimes have been in control. The Lithuanian-Polish Federation (which nobody but historians has ever heard of) was in ascendency for nearly 200 years, before it became part of the Austro-Hungarian Empire between 1772 and 1918, and then reverted to Polish sovereignty until 1940. While none of these were benign rulers, they did not reflect the authoritarianism of the Russian state.

The notion of separatism from Russia is complicated further by another Ukrainian nationalist myth: that of the Cossack Hetmanate of the eighteenth century, which was part of Russia but which Ukraine likes to portray as a proto-democratic state. The problem here is that it was ruled by Cossacks, which rather undermines the Ukrainian claim.

About the only conclusion one can draw from this is that Ukrainians, unlike Russians, had some experience of a more open society, or like to say that they had, and this plays an important part in understanding more recent history.

Ukraine's religion is also contentious. Nominally Orthodox Christian (although with Jews as a prominent minority), the state Church was originally Byzantine, then Greek, then Russian but it also had a Polish-generated Uniate (Greek Catholic) church from the sixteenth century. The denominations' inability to reach a consensus created another political schism to be exploited, a situation repeated today in the break of Ukrainian Orthodoxy from Russian Orthodoxy in response to Russia's invasion (though some Ukrainian Orthodox priests have been accused of a privately remaining loyal to the Moscow Patriarchate).

The seeds of the current dispute between Russia and Ukraine were sown by the process that led to Ukraine's independence. In the final months of the USSR, as mentioned above, Gorbachev granted independence to the autonomous republics but tried to tie them into a new union. Had he succeeded, Ukraine would have lost Crimea and its entire Black Sea coastline, leaving it landlocked. He was however sidelined by Yeltsin who, as elected head of the Russian Federation, was more powerful than Gorbachev (who had only been appointed, not elected), and by Leonid Kravchuk, speaker of the Ukraine parliament and leader of its still-Communist majority of MPs. Briefly united with Yeltsin in seeking the dissolution of the USSR, Kravchuk delivered (on the strength of a referendum with a turnout of over 80 per cent) a majority of 92 per cent in favour of an independent state with its borders intact and guaranteed by a bilateral treaty. This was 'due process' but it was driven by a carve-up between two politicians. For Yeltsin, it opened the path to his becoming undisputed leader of the Russian Federation.

As by far the most important of the autonomous republics, the loss of Ukraine rankled Moscow. The Russian argument today is that it was opportunist, illegal and without historical precedent, and that it trampled on the rights of minorities—in particular, Russians. Russia was prepared to overlook this if Ukrainians elected presidential candidates who supported Moscow, and every possible form of political pressure was put on the electorate to achieve this, most visibly the supply of gas on which Ukraine depends.3

But with independence, Ukraine started to turn away from the embrace of Russia to explore the idea of Western-style freedoms, and hundreds of thousands took to the streets of Kiev every time they felt such moves were threatened—first in 2004 and then again in 2014, a demonstration of self-determination unthinkable in Moscow.

Ukrainian independence had been intended by Kravchuk to be a 'civilized divorce,' rather than accepting what the Russian politician and diplomat Yevgeny Primakov called the 'near-abroad' policy of Russia towards its former Soviet partners, which offered friendship on the condition of Russia's being *primus inter pares*. Plokhy argues that Russia's 2014 annexation of Crimea was a failure in that its objective was to create a new state of Novorossiya (New Russia) that would have cut Ukraine off from the Black Sea and left it less than half its current size. That interpretation needs to be put in context, for Plokhy is a Ukrainian with strong nationalist leanings. It was much more complicated than that, as Tim Judah's book reveals.4 At the time, loyalties were divided. Russian speakers' allegiance was to Moscow as the lesser of two evils, as both governments were more concerned with self-enrichment than improving their living standards. In addition, every new regulation that relegated Russian to a

---

3 Serghii Plokhy, *The Last Empire: The Final Days of the Soviet Revolution*, Oneworld Publications (2015), pp. xxi–xxii.
4 Tim Judah, *In Wartime: Stories from Ukraine*, Allen Lane (2015).

subsidiary language was interpreted as an attack on their sense of belonging. Presidential elections reflected the Dnieper split: west of it they voted for Western-leaning candidates, east of it for those favoured by the Kremlin.

But all of this is just semantics. Since February 2022 the majority of Ukrainians have been implacably opposed to Russian domination and their numbers have only grown. One reason for this was that the 2014 annexation of Crimea suggested that living under the control of Moscow was worse than putting up with a corrupt and incompetent government in Kiev. That in turn led to the election victory of Zelensky with his vision of a clean administration in the service of his citizens. Putin may have thought that electing a professional comedian was a joke—a common trope among Ukraine's enemies—but Zelensky's leadership and his intransigence have solidified Ukrainians in their attachment to their homeland and their belief in self-rule. Ironically this would not have happened had Putin's two military interventions forced Ukrainians to take sides. Putin's fixation with geopolitical objectives and contempt for ordinary people left him blind-sided.

Kiev always seemed a nicer place than Moscow, somehow softer, more open, less intimidating and monumental, and certainly less drunk. Those I met there were more thoughtful, individualistic and less constrained in their opinions. In our Moscow office, all were determined to demonstrate their capacity to achieve the company's goals; in Kiev, they dared to suggest alternatives that their bosses had not considered. Ukraine in my time there was no model for liberal democracy. It held regular and reasonably fair elections but had all the vices of its larger neighbour, if on a smaller scale. But unlike in Russia, the authorities left us to get on with our business. Our local management team was mainly under forty, the first generation not to have been brought up under Soviet rule, and had a natural antipathy to command-and-control.

Driving south from Kiev to Odessa, one enters the miles upon miles of flat wheatfields. The remnants of collectivisation are still visible in the vast fields and isolated villages. After 300 miles we got to Odessa, still a late nineteenth-century city of impressive grandeur—'the Paris of the East'—at least in its centre. Here one had a glimpse of how life used to be lived, before the arrival of the Communists.

Sergey (or should I call him Serhii?), our general manager, told me that his hometown of Lviv was surrounded by hills and forests. He also recommended Crimea as a holiday destination, dotted with the villas of the Tsarist nobility. His enthusiasm impressed me with the idea that nationalism is partly a function of shared and common memories of landscape. There is a sense of place in Ukraine, be it the home or family, that seems distinct from the Russian *dacha*. It is where one belongs, not a place of escape.

BELARUS: 2007
Whereas Ukraine has gone on to follow a democratic path, Belarus remains wedded to the idea of ruthless autocracy. President Alexander Lukashenko, an ice-hockey enthusiast who allegedly rewarded those who won the Miss Belarus title by making them his mistresses, has been in sole charge of this newly independent state since 1991. Lukashenko decided that the collapse of the Soviet Union was a mistake (whether for ideological or personal reasons remains unclear) and acted as if it had never happened.

His country is monotonously dull. It is also broke. Its sole claim to fame is that it suffered more damage than any other country in the Second World War. It is however geo-politically important, as its position provides the easiest route for invasion, whether eastwards or westwards. Hence Russia has a strategic interest in ensuring it remains a client state.

In consequence, all industry in Belarus remains state

controlled, the currency is not convertible, there is no foreign investment and private enterprise is stifled. Imports are subject to quotas and high tariffs. The state owns all media and appoints its own judges. Its former bureaucratic edifice remains intact. This was Soviet Communism preserved in aspic—until 2020. Until then, this quiescent society put up with the restrictions and privations that it had got used to over the decades of the Soviet Union. Then, suddenly, it seemed, the people of Belarus woke up to the fact that they were living in an anachronism. It had taken nearly thirty years for popular revolt to take root.

The absence of dissent may have something to do with the fact that Belarus had never been independent before and that its population was almost entirely ethnic Russia. Did it really have any reason to be independent at all? Plokhy thinks it does and claims that 80 per cent of its population spoke the native language at the time of the break-up of the Soviet Union,[5] a higher proportion than any other of the European Soviet autonomous republics. As parts of Belarus were included in the Hetmanate and Kievan Rus, this maybe more sentiment than fact: I have been unable to find a secondary source that backs it up.

Indeed, the history of Belarus is even more convoluted than that of Plokhy's Ukraine. I have thrown doubt on the linguistic differences between Ukrainian and Russian; in Belarus, they are even smaller—a question of little more than accent and perhaps some local dialect.

Belarus's alternative trajectory from Ukraine is a function of its autocratic president, who has suppressed any attempt to create a genuine sense of national identity that might operate in opposition to him. As far as Putin is concerned, that means that Belarus is in safe hands. Political squabbles have been

---

[5] Serhii Plokhy, *The Last Empire* (ibid.) p.xxvi.

about gas supplies and the constant demands for subsidies, as Belarus has little in the way of resources of its own.

Minsk in 2007 was indistinguishable from any Russian provincial city in 1993. The same Soviet buildings, *babushkas* on street corners hawking anything that might sell, wide boulevards with little traffic, the only lick of paint in the centre of town, not a construction crane in sight, weary people in cheap, drab clothes, state-run shops with close to nothing in them, my hotel room in mahogany brown and nicotine yellow paint with a giant Bakelite radio that did not work. Even the countryside was drab: just forest and marshes, and a fabricated culture of supposedly contented peasants handcrafting useless souvenirs. It was a depressing place because of its politics and its geography.

Belarus has two problems: its dictator and its geopolitical position on the North European plain—the invasion route to Russia. The *vox populi* revolt of 2021 was bound to fail for both reasons. Russia and its legacy is just too much of a presence.

But all these states and statelets have suffered in the same way. All have been defined by Russia. None, even Ukraine, has been allowed to determine its own way. That is why they are in the mess they are. Left to themselves, all could have found a way out of their frozen wars. Russian intervention has only made their bad situation worse.

CHAPTER 20
Central Asia

THE LEGACY OF THE SOVIET IMPERIUM Part 2
On the map, there are magical places with names that suggest unknown civilisations, antiquity, mystery, intrigue—Tashkent, Bukhara, Osh, Almaty, Ashgabat, Samarkand, Dushanbe, Bishkek, Baku—peopled with Uzbeks, Kazakhs, Turkmen, Tajiks, Kyrgyz, Uighurs, Azeris and other exotic-sounding ethnicities. These names and these peoples are as romantic as the Silk Road, which ran through their territories. In the West we still know little of them, which is why they still send an anticipatory thrill through anyone thinking of visiting them for the first time. I went there on business and only once felt overwhelmed by the other-worldly drama of the place. Most of my time was spent in cities which entirely failed to live up to my glamorous expectations.

Kapuściński's vignettes of most of these states in the 1960s were still recognisable fifty years later.[1] They did not conform to the drab uniformity of the European and Siberian Soviet Union, but exotic they were not. Attempts to impose Communist orthodoxy by decree and by the mass introduction of ethnic Russians achieved little more than passive obedience but could not change a history that considerably predates Russia's foundation. These Central Asian states found Communism as incomprehensible a concept then as liberal democracy is now.

If they did not conform to Communist imposition, they also did not conform to Communist boundaries. Borders are built for order and to combat disorder. When Stalin partitioned up Central Asia to respect racial boundaries, this was an

---

[1] Ryszard Kapuśiński, *Imperium*, Granta Books (2019 reprint), pp. 37–94.

administrative and temporary nicety, since borders would become irrelevant after the inevitable victory of Communism. The foisting of divisions on nomadic ethnic groups who had either lived in peace or torn each other to shreds, depending on the economic and climatic conditions of the time, remains an irritant to people who were accustomed to going where they wanted. As Rory Stewart[2] and Gillian Tett[3] respectively experienced in Afghanistan and Tajikistan, long-held antipathies between rival clans of the same ethnicity were addressed by blood feuds that lasted for generations, which explains why these theoretically ethnically homogenous regions remain essentially ungovernable.

Soviet insistence on a cotton-growing monoculture has been destructive in other ways and the Aral Sea is now disappearing as massive quantities of water are diverted into cultivation. Like all such grandiose projects, it is an ecological disaster. Over millions of years, snowmelt from the high mountains created rivers that shifted and disappeared in the sands of the deserts, in the rain shadow behind the massifs of the Himalayan mountains and in other ranges that separate Central Asia from India and Persia. Water plays a profound part in Central Asian history; civilisation could only survive around oases, and deserts engulfed the capitals of many ancient civilisation when rivers changed their course.

Colin Thubron, in 1994, suggested that Central Asia's mountain ranges acted as barriers to the influence of Persian Islamic thought.[4] Islam is the dominant religion in the region but is practised here without the extremist and fundament-

---

[2] Rory Stewart, *The Places in Between*, Picador (2004).
[3] Gillian Tett, *Anthro-Vision: A New Way to See in Business and Life*, Penguin Random House (2021).
[4] Colin Thubron, *The Lost Heart of Asia*, Harper Perennial (1994), pp. 341–2.

alist elements that can be found in strands of Shia and Sunni religious ideologies. Islam's touch in Central Asia is light, infused with Sufism and Shamanism. Here are tribes and peoples who until recently could recite an oral history of their forebears going back for centuries. Empires rose and fell for thousands of years. The riches of the Silk Road made this territory worth fighting over. Hence Islam here is not a code of behaviour but one of mixed beliefs incorporating elements of long-dead religions, mythical and mystical saints, and sagas that held peoples together on their incessant wanderings across an inhospitable land, all spoken in a shared language. All except Tajiks speak variants of the Turkic language group and can understand each other, even if they come from places a thousand miles apart.

This linguistic, geographic and ethnic interplay came to an end with the stasis of the Soviet régime. As Kapuściński suggests, the Imperium never did more than impose rules of behaviour. Underneath the currents of history, values and religion continued to operate in a clandestine manner. In its inability to change the hearts and minds of native subjects, the Politburo sent out Slavic Russians to put the people in their place and manage the society the way that Moscow thought fit. In response, religion and everything else that was alien to Soviet culture went underground.

In the first years of independence there were still no hard borders, in spite of Stalin's maps, and it was still possible to move from one state to another without visas but just a few roubles, as Thubron discovered for himself. This porosity made ethnic sense, for the reality was that Kazakhs, Uzbeks, Tajiks, Kyrgyz, Uighurs and Turkomans were inextricably mixed up. Thubron claims that the Uzbekistan cities of Bukhara and Samarkand were majority Tajik with the physiognomy of Persians, which Uzbeks shared, while Uighurs and Kyrgyz were of a more Mongol appearance.

Attempting to identify ethnicity by physiognomy, however, had become increasingly difficult after centuries of intermarriage.

The collapse of the Soviet Union had nothing to do with the Central Asia states but affected them profoundly. The certainty of something instinctively disliked was replaced by chaos. Workers were not paid because their output was worthless, and whatever money they already had was devalued by rampant inflation. The resulting problem, in the absence of any unifying political creed, was that there was no obvious alternative to the system that had just died around them.

In consequence, five of the seven states continued operating under their old Communist masters, who declared that they were now nationalists, rather than Communists, but ran their fiefdoms just as they had done before. Only Kyrgyzstan ejected the old elite in favour of a physics professor as their new president but he soon adopted the repressive tendencies of his predecessors. As for Tajikistan, it descended into civil war in an unlikely coalition between democrats and Islamists versus the status quo, all irretrievably confused by clan grievances.

There are three value systems that could theoretically convert these proto-states into nations, but none of them works. The first is Communism, which is often looked at with nostalgia by those who cannot understand how it fell apart. The second is Islam, the dominant religion, in theory if not in practice. Those in favour of Islamicist politics have tended to adopt an uncompromising attitude towards the behaviour of others and thus threatened both the state itself and those of the population with more moderate views. This lens is important in considering the massacre at Anjiran in Uzbekistan, where Islamic fundamentalism had the greatest impact and posed, it is assumed, a threat to the authoritarian régime in Tashkent.

The third political system is nationalism, which all these régimes have chosen to emphasise but which has problems of its own. Nationalism makes sense for a state that has some kind of unity but none of these states is unified, whether ethnically or in other ways. About the only thing that holds them together is the borders, defined a century ago by their Soviet overlords and requiring force and authority to give them any meaning, and modern Russia, which continues to act as their guarantor against régime change. Traditional ethnic squabbles dominate, so the opportunity to create a common economic bloc, the only way to create added value, remains moribund. Liberal democratic values play no part in any of this so Moscow has nothing much to fear from the 'Stans'. I have visited five of the seven states but have restricted my commentary to only two.

KYRGYZSTAN: 2004 to 2008

I first arrived in Kyrgyzstan by road from Almaty. The journey to the border in late winter was dull, though Thubron was able to furnish it with the poetic prose that only he can manage. Brown hills, grey sky, grey snow in north-facing clefts and nothing to catch the eye. We were through the border in less than twenty minutes. Borders were permeable if you had the connections. Our Austrian GM knew how to handle them. The drive to Bishkek, the capital, was equally monotonous but ended at a Four Seasons hotel, an oasis of well-ordered tranquillity but half empty.

The following morning we drove to the factory, the only one operating in the allocated industrial sector. It was surrounded by silence, gates closed with padlocks, muddy streets with no sign of a vehicle passing, rusting structures of no obvious value or function. Nobody, not even stray dogs. Not even a For Sale sign. This was archaeology.

The factory functioned, after a fashion, and its employees

seemed a happy lot, Asiatic faces smiling and explaining their tasks with enthusiasm. What made it slightly strange was that they had to explain what they did in Russian, which most of them spoke fluently. My Russian language skills remained at shop-floor level but at least I could understand some of it, which kept the translator honest.

As we were one of only two major foreign investors, our activities were subjected to often hostile scrutiny in the press when there was nothing else to write about. Our general manager dealt with it in his customary manner, which was that of a patriarchal colonial officer. He regarded all his staff and stakeholders, expatriate or local, as his children. He was working in an environment where nobody understood even the basics of a market economy. He was treated with respect because he demanded to be, in a society that had only the vaguest idea of what he was trying to achieve but admired his conviction.

Over the course of four years and several visits, it became clear to me that this country had no interest in becoming a Western state. An eruption of ostensibly political but essentially tribal hostility between the north and the south (Kyrgyz vs. Uzbek; animists vs. Islam—who knows?) resulted in a change of government, hailed by the West as another flower revolution (I can't remember which one—tulip? crocus?), after which nothing changed. Investment, whether Soviet or Western, had been nothing more than an irrelevance.

Bishkek, a Russian invention, was now just an administrative centre. Any commerce of significance was run by foreigners, Turks predominantly but leavened by aid workers and other expatriates. Bishkek was however a city with the heart torn out of it, surviving on the scraps provided by government and relief agencies. Why this was so was revealed by a day out.

Driving south out of the city on a dual carriageway were various government ministries on the right. Facing them, on the undeveloped left side, was a series of encampments with protest signs. I was told that the protests had to do with the absence of land rights, following the collapse of the *kholkhoz* (collectivised farms), but that the two sides of the road had peacefully ignored each other for years.

Very soon after this the road became a single track and was no longer tarmacked. It took a further ten minutes before we turned off up a valley, using the stream bed as the highway in our 4x4 vehicles. Out of the Central Asian plain rose the Tian Shan (the celestial mountains) to over 5,000 metres. This was not a gradual accumulation of height but an explosive upthrust that left one feeling dwarfed and astonished.

We stopped in a grove of silver birch by an ice-cold stream. With the engines turned off, there was only the sound of water and of a soft wind. The midday sun highlighted every feature. I could see for miles but had lost all sense of scale. The mountain peaks soared around us to unimaginable elevations. It was beautiful, and the air was so clear that I could make out tiny details at huge distances.

Down one of the side valleys came horsemen, unhurriedly picking their way through the scree. Their horses carried heavy loads, their masters' only possessions, for these were nomads who moved their flocks up and down the precipitous defiles according to the seasons. They were self-sufficient and comfortable living as their forebears had for generations. To them, government was at best inconsequential and at worst an irritant. They wore strange felt hats, rather like pixie hats, but upturned at each of its four corners, like the roof of a Chinese house. Their homes, which I had seen on my way out of town, were not houses but tents, known as 'gers', which provide relief from heat and from cold, with a hole in the centre of the roof that serves as a ventilator in the summer and as a chimney for fire smoke in the winter. Furniture was made up of bedding and carpets, plus a couple of ancient boxes for holding more treasured possessions.

We were the only others in this mountain valley of the Ala Archa national park, conspicuous foreigners with our Toyota Landcruisers. The horsemen rode by in silence. This reminded me of Laos—a people who were baffled by what was going on in their country and clung stubbornly to their old ways and rituals. This nomadic lifestyle and culture went back centuries and showed no sign of withering. Some 80 per cent of Kyrgyzstan is made up of rural dwellers and the various population censuses suggest that the compilers had great difficulty counting them. This is unsurprising. Mountain fastnesses account for over 40 per cent of the land mass but are populated, in the summer months, by these nomads and their families. There are only two roads that connect the north and the south of the country. If you don't know where they are, or you can't even get there if you do, a census is an impossibility.

There is another story about census data. In 1959, 30 per cent of those who were counted were ethnic Russians. This is an extraordinarily high percentage for an imperialist power, even one that shifted populations all over the place as a means of diffusing opposition. Even at the height of the Vietnam war, Americans made up less than 5 per cent of the population. As Kyrgyzstan was unlikely to be a destination of choice for most Russians, given its isolation and lack of development, what explains the large numbers? My suspicion is that the Kyrgyz proved uninterested and therefore inept at the roles the Soviet Union required; Soviet expertise had to be shipped in. Or maybe the Kyrgyz simply ducked when the census people looked in their direction, while the ethnic Russians stood up to be counted.

That has another legacy. Capitalism has its own requirements, equally alien to the Kyrgyz. Our factory workers were happy and engaged but that was because they had been trained to do their jobs and were grateful for wages that secured their modest lifestyles. At lower levels of management, enthusiasm to learn overcame ignorance, particularly for the younger generation, who were in the majority women. After the Austrian GM retired, my successor appointed a Kyrgyz. I approved at the time because he seemed intelligent and spoke 'our' language. It was a disaster. While very good at forming relationships with local stakeholders, he had no idea what it meant to run a company and resorted to a dictatorial style that failed to produce results and alienated him from his workforce. His predecessor was paternalistic to an extent I found difficult to accept, but his heart was in the right place.

The wider reality for Kyrgyzstan was that independence led to a flight of expertise. Remittances from Kyrgyz abroad now make up 40 per cent of the country's GNP.[5] Most of them work in Russia, where they share the language, but suffer from the xenophobia and disdain of their hosts, while doing the most menial jobs and at lower wages than Russians are prepared to accept. We complain about the treatment of workers from the Indian sub-continent in the Middle East but forget that the same economic imperatives lie behind the migration of workers from Central Asia to Russia. In Tajikistan, foreign remittances make up close to 50 per cent of official GNP[6] (I say 'official' because the figures do not record how much income is generated by the heroin trade) and money sent back home is significant in all the Stans, save for Kazakhstan. There is an irony in this too for while Russian nationalism is essentially ethnic, it relies on foreign labour.

AZERBAIJAN: 2004 to 2008
Azerbaijan sits somewhere between Central Asia and the Caucasus depending on how you look at it. Geographically it is separated from the Stans by the Caspian Sea but its culture,

---

[5] Wikipedia.
[6] Wikipedia.

religion and politics are closer to those on the far shore than its immediate Caucasus neighbours. In 1918, albeit for less than a year, it became the first secular democratic state in the Muslim and Eurasian worlds but is now an authoritarian presidential republic—a corrupt dictatorship, in other words—with limited civil rights and unreliable elections, much like its Muslim neighbours to the east. I offer it up as a bridge to understand how culture clashes continue to bedevil any rapprochement between the region's now-independent states.

Everywhere I went to in Azerbaijan had to do with business and all of it was in the central plains, which were dull and bereft of interest. I had been told that 40 per cent of Azerbaijan is mountainous but the map tells a different story. It included Nagorno-Karabakh, then under the control of Armenia.

Our distributor there deserves a biography of his own. He was an Azeri, born and brought up in Tehran, with a father who had been a major civil contractor in the Shah's Iran. After the revolution the family fled to Britain to their 'shopping flat' in Kensington and had to survive on the modest amount of money left in their UK bank account. The father was forced to remain until he had completed all the projects he had won in Tehran, but was not paid for any of them. Javad, meanwhile, got jobs at Angus Steak Bars and other establishments to fund himself through a degree at the London School of Economics, emerging as a very competent business manager and going on to control over 80 per cent of the Azeri market with his two tobacco principles. This small country, one that most people couldn't identify on a map, became an Imperial Tobacco success story.

Javad was the ideal distributor. His upbringing enabled him to bridge the gap between Western business procedures and the rather different approach of the Azeris. Of his homeland, Iran, he once told me, in private, 'I can't see the mullahs ever giving up. The trouble is that the educated middle class who like partying and shopping have nothing in common with the peasants who make up 70 per cent of the population. The promise of a place in Paradise if they do what the mullahs tell them is enough to keep them quiet, no matter how shitty it all is. If you went to northern Tehran, it looks like the European city it once aspired to be. But it isn't, and never will be.' He was almost as dismissive of the country he made his living from and I think I understand why. Although I went to Azerbaijan several times I felt disconnected from it and still do. President Aliyev, son of his predecessor, is the beneficiary of a dynastic approach to government that resembles that of Iran's Pahlavi family before the arrival of the Ayatollah. Inevitably the new airport at Baku is named after his father. It is far too big for the number of flights but is, as it was designed to be, an impressive point of entry.[7]

Baku is an extraordinary place. Situated on the west bank of the Caspian Sea, it must be the only capital city perched on an oil field. The sea is covered with a chaotic assemblage of tottering oil wells, nodding donkey pumps and pipelines. Most of these seem to be over a hundred years old, rusting hulks leaking black ooze into a giant oil slick. Are they still

---

[7] I woke up one morning recently to hear on the Today programme on Radio 4 that a certain Javad Marandi had lost his legal case for anonymity in proceedings in which he was a key witness, concerning a money-laundering scheme to move over one billion dollars out of Azerbaijan—the so-called Laundromat Scheme. His star had continued to rise and, as a British citizen, he had donated a considerable sum to the Conservative Party. His sister had once told me over lunch that she was worried he was flying too high. Nothing has appeared in the press since then, so this parallel with Icarus remains unproven. I think I am more upset about his political donations in the UK than his involvement, innocent or not, in the dubious financial schemes that infest his own part of the world.

working? Could nobody be bothered to clear the mess up? Javad remarked that the Caspian was three parts chemicals, five parts oil and two parts water. It makes up such a bizarre seascape that it was featured in a Bond movie.

Oil may not be great for the environment but it brought wealth. There are remnants of that wealth along the corniche, not in sight of the oil wells, which indicate how rich this city was at the start of the twentieth century. At the centre is something older, the castle and its surrounding neighbourhood of desert coloured stone, winding alleys and several storied residencies where the best restaurants are. Elsewhere there are recent constructions of prestige apartment blocks and a pedestrian mall in the city's old main street, along which groups of head-scarved girls wander as they peek into the emporiums to buy an ice-cream as relief from the heat or to check out the latest fashions. Though there are boys about, this is entirely innocent. There is safety in numbers and their chaperones are not far away. As girls from good families, their future will be assured by the marriage arrangements their parents make for them.

It seems their president is keen to make Azerbaijan's good life more rewarding. He sponsored the European Song Contest despite being as far to the east of Istanbul as London is to the west. Now there is a Formula 1 Grand Prix round the streets of Baku. His desire to make a name for his country is understandable, and oil revenues allow him to do it. Good relations are maintained with everybody, except Armenia.

Away from this economy of imported prestige cars, rising real-estate prices and brand-name boutiques, the rest of the country seems stuck. In dusty towns and suburbs, making a living seems as difficult today as it was centuries ago. Meeting shopkeepers in these places left me with the same impression that their fortunes were in the hands of others. The system did not help them. I questioned why the nation's oil wealth was lavished only on the few and not the many. Then it occurred to me that raising the expectations of the masses and being unable to fulfil them was a much greater threat than maintaining the status quo.

Like many Central Asian states, Azerbaijan's de-facto dictatorship relies on a self-sustaining system of graft to keep the wheels turning. Javad said that it cost $500 a month to be a policeman. The inducement was that you only had to hand over 50 per cent of the bribes you received to your superior, who did the same to his. That was how things were.

At important meetings another Azeri was always present. Who he worked for was unclear but he acted as the intermediary between us and government. Probably he worked for both. I was advised to treat him with respect. Despite this being a Muslim country, alcohol is available in all grocery stores and this gentleman was a frequent customer, the hints being in his bloodshot and rheumy eyes, and appearing and then disappearing without explanation.

Quite how he managed to hold on to his position, whatever it was, was also opaque but it seems to subscribe to the general principle of these countries that who you know is more important than what you can do.

As my time in this role ended, our distributor's star continued to rise. He was the guy who could get things done. His business diversified into the management of the president's pet projects. He had become indispensable.

Since my time there, observers tell me, nothing much has changed save a sense that their ruler is described as insecure, issuing laws that ban clothing and beards associated with Islamic extremism and using the conflict with Armenia as the means of creating a sense of national identity.

In regional terms, Azerbaijan's oil revenue is on a par with that of Kazakhstan and, further afield, Malaysia, Norway and Colombia, making it a relatively minor player in world supply, compared with the Arab states, Russia and the USA, for example. When the price is high, however, vanity projects prevail; when it is low, panic sets in. In either case, the country's ruling elite is said to plunder the nation's oil wealth and to have operated a secret $2.8bn slush fund to pay off European politicians and make luxury purchases.[8] It seems so normal as barely to warrant a mention.

---

[8] BBC News, 'Azerbaijan "operated secret $3bn secret slush fund"' (5 September 2017): https://www.bbc.co.uk/news/world-europe- 41156933

Chapter 21
The Caucasus

SURROUNDED STATES
The location of the Caucasus continues to be something that geographers cannot quite decide: Europe or Asia? Not that it matters much, but the main Caucasus mountain range is spectacular and way higher than anything in Europe proper. Three countries are described as making up the majority of it: Georgia, Armenia and Azerbaijan; another three—Russia, Türkiye and Iran—overlap parts of it. All have a profound influence on it, Russia more than the others, but only two are entirely Caucasian as defined by geographers: Armenia and Georgia, the first two states in history to adopt Christianity as their official religion. Both are culturally aligned with Europe, and my wife and I travelled to see them in a small group led by an expert guide. Unlike our visit to Cambodia, this was an immersive experience, as the guide had been a regular visitor for many years and his two local guides wanted to make the most of this opportunity to tell us everything. In Georgia in particular, everybody we met shared the same keen desire to engage.

Despite isolation and invasion, these two countries seem to have moved in step with Western thought—anchored in concepts of freedom and self-determination, not dissimilar from Ukraine, but in an even more complicated geopolitical situation. Both have convoluted politics but benefit from a free press and an independent judiciary. In simple terms, they are safe and pleasant places to be—for the moment. What makes this extraordinary is that they are surrounded and beset by states with very different precepts.

The history of the region is fiendishly tangled with interludes of independence followed by much longer periods under foreign domination. Each country has been invaded, going back to the ancient dynasties and empires of the Assyrians, Greeks, Romans, Persians, Byzantines, Arabs, Mongols, Turks and Russians. Yet Georgia and Armenia remain genuine nations defined by their mountainous geography, their history as the first Christian states, and their languages, which use unique alphabets and bear no relation to each other. These are far from being primitive societies; their ecclesiastical architecture pre-dates the Gothic European school by 500 years.

Russia invaded in 1801; it only achieved territorial dominance in 1864. Its imperial empire then ended up in Soviet control until 1991. Georgia and Armenia were there before Russia arrived; they are still there, now that it has gone.

Georgians and Armenians are intensely proud of their heritage and relish their freedom and independence in a very personal sense, despite having little room for manoeuvre and being hemmed in by more powerful states less enamoured of national self-determination.

What handicaps them is that their sense of nationhood is essentially ethnic, and interregional feuds continue to dominate their internal and external politics, not helped by having leaders whose passions have sometimes ignored political reality. In a region with only 9 million inhabitants, there are reportedly over fifty languages.

GEORGIA: 2022
Over 20 per cent of Georgia's land mass is off-limits as it is controlled by Russia. The once autonomous South Ossetia region, landlocked in the mountains between the Black Sea and the Caspian, was the first to break away in 1990, leading to wars of independence in 1991–92, 2004 and 2008, all backed by Russia and ending with South Ossetia's becoming a Russian military enclave.

Abkhazia, on the eastern coast of the Black Sea, had also

been an autonomous region within Georgia in the Soviet era but simmering tensions were aggravated when Georgia's first post-Soviet president declared Georgia to be a country of ethnic singularity. A war followed in 1992–93, after which UN and Russian peace-keepers moved in until a bungled attempt to reassert national control by Georgia's President Saakashvili in 2008 ended in a humiliating defeat after only five days and, like South Ossetia, left the territory under Russian control.

Georgia currently has no diplomatic relations with Russia but has an open border and allows Russians to enter visa free. Russians can even buy Georgian property if they want. The arrangement is not reciprocal, however: Georgians need a visa to enter Russia and evidently despise their bullying northern neighbour, as their pro-Ukrainian banners, flags and graffiti have recently attested. Although the Russian threat rumbles like a storm over the mountains, the situation is not currently inflamed. A catastrophe might happen at any time—it would be no great surprise; it has happened before—but seems not to be an immediate worry.

Despite all its trials and tribulations Georgia is a delightful place to be. It is a fertile land and the people are largely self-sufficient: smallholders outside the cities grow quantities of fruit and nuts, and raise cows, pigs, sheep and goats on their abundant pasturage. Of greater economic significance is wine, made everywhere in *kvevri*, conical-bottomed terracotta urns that are buried in the ground. The sediment sinks to the bottom and grape stems rise to the top, where it is distilled into *chacha*, indistinguishable from Italian *grappa*.

Some say that wine-making originated in Georgia, as *kvevri* have been found in archaeological digs dating back to some millennia before Christ, and wine is as much a part of their history as Christianity. Any social occasion becomes a feast with, on important occasions, a *tamada* as official toast-master. I suspect that as a small country with so many different languages, drinking became a way of resolving differences —and a potent one, in both senses of the word. In a country that has always welcomed strangers, the role of social drinking has not much changed: better to get to know outsiders than fight them. It is a welcoming nation.

Cars are prominent status symbols; old highly polished Mercedes sit proudly outside modest houses. We were told that driving standards had improved but a lot of cars that we saw had no front or rear bumpers, a consequence of their cheekily overtaking whatever line of vehicles might lie ahead of them and then trying to squeeze into small gaps to avoid oncoming traffic.

Georgia has become a transparent society in a physical sense. As a manager of foreign affairs Mikheil Saakashvili may have been incompetent but his reforms to the civil service created a belief that his government was on the side of the people. The police headquarters in Tbilisi are glass-walled, so that everybody can see what goes on inside. Every town has a similar building where permits, registrations, authorisations and so on can be obtained in one place. Physical transparency creates trust.

Georgia has moved on from its ultra-nationalist first president, Zviad Gamsakhurdia, who generated immense hostility in western Abkhazia. As far as I can tell, acceptance of the country as a multi-ethnic or even multi-tribal population is far advanced. Overall, Muslim Azeris make up 10 per cent of the population and seem to rub along well enough. Is this politics or self-determination? Difficult to tell.

HM Queen Elizabeth II died when we were in Georgia, in late 2022. People offered condolences to us as soon as they knew we were British, not as a formality but as an expression of real grief, which contrasted with my own feelings of mere sadness. The same happened in Armenia and I was left wondering why people were so upset. My wife came up with a credible explanation: the Queen had been a symbol of continuity and stability, something they had little experience of.

ARMENIA: 2022
Armenia looks different—less verdant, more reminiscent of the steppe lands of southern Russia, though at more elevated altitudes. Whereas Georgia is a land of deep valleys and high mountain ranges, Armenia is predominately high plateaux. The image that sticks in the mind is of ancient tractors tilling fields without boundaries, dark-hued land that sets off the bleached autumn grasses that cover both valleys and hill tops. Farming here seems hard work.

Each farm, each village, has its own junkyard of redundant and defunct machinery; perhaps they are kept in the hope that they will be useful again someday, or maybe they serve as a source of spare parts. As the most industrialised of the Caucasus states during Soviet times, Armenia's empty factories and mines are also derelict, slowly collapsing into the land, with trees growing on roofs, smashed windows, crumbling concrete and rusting steel—many of them no more than ruins. I wonder why they don't sell their scrap iron, as Vietnam did as a means of generating foreign exchange in the early years of *Do Moi*. Probably not worth it, as Armenia has only two open borders and these account for only a small percentage of its frontier. It is blockaded by Türkiye and Azerbaijan.

As with the rest of this region, relations between different ethnic groups have an unhappy history. The ruins of villages destroyed by the conflict between Azeris and Armenians that began in 1998 are clearly visible as our bus passes close to the eastern frontier. Our local guide does not mention the conflict or the ruins, both of which are obvious. A little further on she points out a reservoir over the border which provides water to both countries. No explanation is offered.

Armenians have been referred to as Christian Jews because

they were and are successful manufacturers, merchants and financiers. In consequence, they were despised—not for having the wrong religion but for being more successful. The history of these people has been one of perpetual repression. The Turkish holocaust from 1915 to 1921 killed a reputed 1.5 million of them but is just one in a long list of massacres, purges and deportations by other invaders from north, west and south. Türkiye denies responsibility for the genocide, arguing that atrocities were committed by both sides, but the Holocaust Memorial in Yerevan, the Armenian capital, is a powerful experience in its austere simplicity, and the neighbouring museum provides proof enough of the barbarity.

Armenia now occupies less than a quarter of the land it governed in the nineteenth century. In 1921, Lenin ceded northeast Anatolia to the Turks, a parcel of 27,000 square miles that included the symbol of Armenia, Mount Ararat. Because of their dispute, the border with Türkiye has been closed since the early 1990s, which means that Mount Ararat, the physical symbol of the Armenian nation and the Biblical location where Noah reached dry ground, is now inaccessible to those on the Armenian side of the border, though visible from the capital, Yerevan, on a clear day.

A one-hundred year problem of territorial ownership has further reduced Armenian territory. Nagorno-Karabakh, which called itself the Republic of Artsakh and had a flag that resembles that of Armenia, was unrecognised by any other state (but, as a sop to Russian pressure, itself recognises Transnistria—the Pridnestrovian Moldavian Republic—which no other country recognises). Until the start of the Soviet era, Nagorno-Karabakh was part of Armenia but was populated also by Azeris who made up the majority in summer, when the herdsmen moved their flocks into the highlands, becoming the minority again in winter. But not any more. With the end of World War One and the birth of the USSR, inter-ethnic (and perhaps religious) rivalry drove Armenians out of Azerbaijan and back to the highlands of Nagorno-Karabakh.

Moscow then allocated Nagorno-Karabakh to Azerbaijan, probably a trivial decision at the time for the Politburo but with long-lasting consequences. Azeris and Armenians, living in separate villages, still hated each other but could do nothing about it. Then in 1988, just before the Soviet Union collapsed, hostilities resumed. The Azeris invaded.

This meant that Armenia now had three potential enemies: Türkiye, Azerbaijan and Russia. Since the only one that could protect them was Russia, Armenia sued for peace, very much as a supplicant, and signed a mutual security pact, the implications of which were its accommodation of two Russian military bases and an implicit understanding that it was not to rock the Moscow boat.

At first this expedient seemed to work. An Armenian offensive recovered all its lost territory. But then in 2020 an offensive by Azerbaijan, supported by its ally, Türkiye, left the highlands as an exclave with only one access road, and Russia did not intervene.

That a mutual security pact could be discarded so easily suggests that this was not, and never had been, a partnership of equals. Then came the war in Ukraine, which changed the balance of power completely. Challenged by the West, Russia sought new arrangements with powers that had remained on the sidelines. Türkiye, which was allied to Azerbaijan, was one of them. Add to that the unavailability of Russian soldiers to enforce the Armenian security pact, and quietly dropping Artsakh would keep Türkiye on side—or so I speculate.

On our final night in Yerevan fighter jets flew low over the city. The following morning our guide's stoicism had evaporated. She was in tears as she explained that a hundred Armenians had been killed in a major skirmish. Less than six months later Artsakh had been consigned to history, overrun by Azeris while Russian soldiers stood on the side-lines. 120,000 Armenians fled to what remained of their homeland.

I found Yerevan very different from Tbilisi: much quieter, more reserved. Its centre is the only example I have come across in the ex-USSR of a successful fusion of local and Soviet architecture. It was designed by an Armenian; like his ancestors, he had evidently learned how to accommodate conflicting interests. Armenians are used to compromise, so no Ukrainian flags are flown here except on the Polish Embassy, and the second language is Russian, not English. But Armenians are also used to betrayal and the Azeri recapture of territory in 2020 crystallised such fears.

Little wars in little places: not enough to interest world media even on a slow news day; not enough to bother the great powers either, but nonetheless devastating for those in the firing line. Perhaps there are more important matters to attend to. But even small events leave a legacy of resentment. In Armenia this is important.

Underlying all this is a diffidence, an undercurrent of despair, and a fatalism that things are unlikely to get better. The people feel besieged. The Christian Jews analogy could be replaced by another: the Armenians are the new Palestinians.

THE POLITICS OF THE CAUCASUS
Complicated. Even an expert historian would have difficulty explaining, let alone understanding, the complex genesis of not just Georgia and Armenia but all the other lands that abut them. There is a national narrative of struggle against adversity, to which Russia's abandonment of Armenian interests adds another chapter. There is an equally long a history of pragmatism, and multiple instances of alliances with more powerful states, of switching sides at opportune moments and of the provision of mercenary armies to support one side or another.

Compromise is also a well-developed capability. National

narratives take precedence but behind them lies another story of accommodation and acceptance of whatever the wind may bring. In contrast to Central Asia, where the collapse of the USSR has resulted in autocratic fiefdoms built on shaky assumptions, both Georgia and Armenia walk in step with Western concepts of democracy, egalitarianism and freedom of speech. What I wanted to explore was whether independence and, on the other hand, the shadow of the Russian bear, had blunted mutual antagonisms and created the possibility of a more unified future.

Appeasing, let alone provoking, Russia seems sensible but while Russia's resources are taken up in Ukraine, there would appear to be a little more room for manoeuvre than in the past. Practical examples of cooperation include the reservoir that Armenia shares with Azerbaijan, and visa-free access to Georgia for Russians, in spite of their having no diplomatic relations.

There is also evidence that previously warring ethnicities and clans are assimilating, even while 10 per cent of Georgia's population is Muslim. A statue of Heydar Aliyev, father of the current Azerbaijan president, was given to Georgia and has thoughtfully been placed near the ancient *hamams*—the public bathhouses—in the centre of Tbilisi because, 'He would feel at home there.'

There is also a sense that previously hostile minorities within the country have got to know each other. Some 98.1 per cent of residents identify as Armenian but Armenia reserves five seats in its 105-seat parliament for ethnic minorities. And Georgia and Armenia get along well enough, despite their very different attitudes to Russia.

Those proto-states that form part of the Russian Federation but adjoin the Caucasus would probably like to be part of this. Georgia proved a welcome source of refuge for Chechens fleeing their civil war; the carved-out territories of

Abkhazia and South Ossetia remain Russian rubbish dumps with no prospect of a better life. Some form of transition away from the Russian sphere of influence and towards greater and more independent regional harmony may not be easy to achieve but does seem a reasonable and logical ambition.

Is it possible? Perhaps. Moscow's obsession with regaining superpower status partly depends on the idea of Slavic unity, but that does not apply here, however much Putin may wish it so. How long could he resist it? Russia cannot fight on every front and we in the West may well overestimate the capabilities of a nation with a smaller GNP than Italy and twice the population; Russia has only limited resources and it needs to concentrate these on its priorities. The Caucasus is not one of them.

The Azeris offered a generous peace deal. Armenian land rights in Nagorno-Karabakh would be respected and returnees would have full rights as citizens. An opportunity to turn the page of a hundred years of conflict? Perhaps, but there is no evidence of returning refugees at present.

PART 5
THE MIDDLE EAST

CHAPTER 22
Arabia and the Arabs: 1992 to 2016

After twenty-four years of intermittent travel to the Middle East, I remain as befuddled as on my first visit. I had come across a long list of unresolved grievances, without quite understanding where they stemmed from. On the surface it seemed clear: rapacious and repressive rulers, perfidious regional powers, anger at the interventions of the West, the dream of secular and socialist redemption, the appeal of Islam and its divisions, Israel and the Palestinians. Only now do I think I am beginning to understand why things are as they are.

The West likens Arab and Arabic. The scope of each is very different. Arabs were nomads in the Arabian Peninsula, Bedouin tribes who had survived on banditry and the protection of the fertile and settled communities of Saba (Sheba) in Yemen and Mesopotamia in the north for at least 1,500 years before the Prophet Mohammed. Their origins explain much of today's Gulf politics and they are largely homogenous.[1]

Today, there are about 460 million Arabs (there are no exact figures) and Arabic is the official language in twenty-six states. By contrast, Arabic is the language of liturgy for 1.8 billion Muslims, whose domain extends far beyond Arabia. This linguistic penetration resulted from the extraordinary growth of Islam into an empire in the century following Mohammed's death, thanks to military expansion and the proselytising mission of there being only one God and his word having been revealed by the Prophet.

Arabic as a language is not homogenous. In addition to being fiendishly complex, it is divided into 'high' and vernac-

---

[1] This and much of the following is based on Tim Mackintosh-Smith, *Arabs: A 3,000-Year History of Peoples, Tribes and Empires*, Yale (2019).

ular versions. Most Arabic speakers from different countries find it difficult to understand each other's dialects. The Koran is 'high' but understandably little concerned with everyday life. Its origins lie in the ancient history of poetry, which has little bearing on the need to describe things as they are for the edification of common people.

But Arabic is not the sole language of the Islamic world. In the Middle East there are two languages that have had an impact on politics and culture: Farsi (or Persian) and Turkic, the family of languages spoken right across Central Asia. Today's fight for political supremacy are split on linguistic lines defined centuries ago.

Underpinning this is Islam, the only religion to have had an explicitly political agenda from the outset and which was immediately successful. Its development after Mohammed's death was as much to do with temporal power as spiritual, not least in the Shia/Sunni schism. In contrast to the pope and Catholicism, Islam remains open to interpretation as it has no recognised hierarchy of imams among either its Sunni or Shia adherents. Therein lies another root of conflict within and without the region.

Taking all that into consideration, I now think that the Middle East is not as baffling as I had once imagined. Appreciating its historic roots makes understanding it an easier task. To explain further, I separate my comments on the Arab world from those on the Islamic Middle East, to identify a division that is not sufficiently apparent.

THE ARAB STATES

Mohammed and his successors were the driving force in the creation of the Arab Empire. Their triumph saw the expansion of Islam as the state religion into much of Africa, Central Asia and as far east as Indonesia. The further it spread, the more diverse its practice; and the absence of a recognised temporal theocracy made space for various strands of interpretation that still apply today, as well as long-lasting rifts. High Arabic became a language of devotion on the grounds that the words of the Prophet were those of God and could only be understood in the original; translations into other languages continue to be treated with suspicion. My English copy of the Koran is the official Saudi version; there are many others, with only relative degrees of correspondence between them.

I make a distinction between Arabs and Arabic speakers for this reason. For citizens of the Arabian peninsula, Islam is part and parcel of their collective history and has been irretrievably mixed up with the values that predate it, to produce the misogynistic, conservative and hierarchical assumptions that dominate their thinking. This did not matter much to the rest of us as long as there was nothing there of interest.

As for Mecca, it was established long before Mohammed's birth, served as a pilgrimage site for the worship of a variety of deities, and had a very big stone—the Kaaba. The Arabist scholar Tim Mackintosh-Smith refers to stone worship by Bedouin tribes: if prayers were not answered, the worshipers would kick the stone away and move on to another. The Prophet clearly had political skills: he made Mecca the centre of a new religion, smoothing the path to conversion.

The discovery of oil changed everything. My godmother's son has photographs of Abu Dhabi in the 1960s. The only solid building is the British Consulate, the only car that of its resident. Today there is money—masses of it.

It would be easy to assume that oil wealth was the sole driver transforming tribal statelets into the collection of massively wealthy emirates and kingdoms that make up the Arabian Peninsula today. Their transformation is limited, though. They may seem to have embraced modernity, especially in their courting of tourism and Western approval, but they still reflect much more ancient customs, values and beliefs. Radical Islam or Jihadism originated in Saudi Arabia, and is, in its novelty, something of a bridgehead between these older local values and newer alien ones, for its radical agenda embraces ideas recognisable from Marxism-Leninism and only emerged in response to capitalist imperialism and the new wealth of consumerism, both of which threatened tradition, identity and autonomy. Radical Islam, which conflates Satanism with Westernisation, now pops up all over the place, offering an idyllic afterlife for martyrs that tempts those who consider themselves life's victims and who blame the outside world for their misery. The rulers of the Arabian Peninsula have a tough time navigating the conflicting desires of a better life or a better death.

In an earlier draft of this book, I wrote at length about why I have always found Arabia an artificial construct, with supporting anecdotes taken from Bahrain, Dubai and Abu Dhabi. I can now distil this into a few paragraphs, as these states are essentially the same. All are ruled by families that trace their lineage back to Mohammed, assume the divine right of kings and behave with more licence than they allow their subjects. All in addition depend on expatriates to run their countries, with Westerners at the top, Middle-Eastern or educated Indians at middle-management level and indentured labour from all of Asia to do the actual physical work (and face expulsion if they complain about conditions).

The rulers are preoccupied with kitschy vanity projects that they hope will draw admiring stares from tourists. They have built the first 'six-star' hotel and the highest buildings in the world. In the face of their massive dependence on energy to counter the heat of the sun and the absence of naturally occurring drinking water, they have nurtured fantasies of creating role-model twenty-first-century high-tech eco-cities, with little idea of what they could be used for, other than attracting awestruck but compliant visitors. At the same time they remain feudalistic, misogynistic and authoritarian. They educate their young but provide no jobs for them, and are too pampered to take on the roles that foreigners perform for them. Alcohol is available for those who want it (even in states that ban it) as well as the barely discrete services of Eastern European sex workers. No, I have not been charmed. Having said that, I should add that I feel exactly the same way about Westerners who take their privileges for granted.

Admittedly, my opinion did not warm with the discovery of a significant corporate fraud by our regional manager in Dubai, which necessitated an acceleration in the frequency of my visits. The problem I inherited was to determine who was complicit in these arrangements. It was soon obvious that most members of the management team were equally guilty and had to be escorted off the premises.

That left a question that I never resolved: who among our local distributors was also implicated? Solving this became an exercise in probabilities rather than facts, not helped by the distributors' assumption that it was my company's fault that fraud had been allowed to happen and that it was their money that had been stolen, not ours. A reasonable point, though their payments were rightfully ours. What was implicit was an acceptance that dodgy deals were commonplace and nothing to get excited about.

We fired one distributor on circumstantial evidence; he will reappear in the pages that follow. It was only because another had complained about the regional manager earlier that I was convinced he was beyond reproach. He too comes back in the story. But we in the West work on the assumption of certainty and that does not exist in the Arab world. It is a common trope but a true one that where we expect solidity there is sand.

SAUDI ARABIA: 2012–2013
Sand filled the streets of Jeddah and contributed to my feelings of surprise at how shabby it all was when I first visited. The buildings also gave the appearance of have once been nice but then neglected.

Sheikh Yasar was a congenial host, 'sheikh' being an honorific for a man of integrity and standing. He and his brother presided over a commercial empire that distributed not just tobacco but pharmaceuticals and healthcare, as well as operating several automobile franchises. He also owned a house near Henley, on the River Thames, where he would spend the summer with his large family. He knew enough about Britain to act as a conduit between his culture and ours. He reminded me of a grown-up Billy Bunter, with his large girth and pebble glasses. Fortunately he was nowhere near as petulant.

I think he liked me as much as I liked him. By now I had learned to listen and not interrupt. He was garrulous. His interpretation of Saudi Arabia was of two conflicting forces. The Sauds were the ruling tribe, having in the 1930s displaced the Hashemites, who now rule Jordan. This is consequently the only country in the world named after its rulers.

The Sauds were determined to modernise but were obstructed by their people and by the Wahabi imams who were intensely conservative in their beliefs. Women were (and still are) treated equally with men in terms of education up to degree level, with the government paying their tuition fees, but were not allowed out on their own, let alone drive. Depending on which prince controlled home affairs, the religious police, an informal organisation beholden to the imams, were given greater or lesser freedom to decide on what was *haram* (forbidden). Sheikh Yasar said it was impossible to get rid of the imamate; all one could do was retreat.

The citizenry took comfort in the fact that a Saudi's home

is his castle; what happens within it is of no concern to anybody else. This offered a lot more freedom but only out of sight.

Yasar knew nothing about our fraud case but I would not have expected him to: it was his Palestinian general manager who ran the day-to-day business. Whether the general manager knew more than he would say, I cannot tell.

I had learned to work effectively in whatever culture I had found myself in, but felt frustrated here by the provisionality of everything. I had enough sense to realise that any progress I made in business depended on whether I was thought trustworthy, since trust was not an absolute but a matter of degree. Truth was also a relative concept, as was transparency. Would I listen and try to understand? I would try.

These considerations made me think of desert tribes, struggling over scarce resources. The alternative to bloodshed was conversation, conducted on the rules of chess, with the proviso that you could always go back a few moves and restart. Whatever proposition was put on the table had to be negotiable, and an intrinsic part of any discussion was the preamble, which was invariably exhausting.

My frustration had nothing to do with the people I met. All were charming and hospitable but never got to the point. I once met a man in a long airport queue, whose appearance corresponded to the archetype of an Islamic fundamentalist: long brown *dish-dash* (robe), full beard and skull cap. He turned to me and said, 'They are bloody useless, these immigration people,' before asking me where I was going. 'Dubai,' I said. 'Me too,' he replied, 'with my family', pointing to his wife in full black *burqa*, trying to corral an errant toddler. 'You've got to get away from time to time, or you'd go mad.' We stayed together until it was time to embark. Apart from his appearance, there seemed no real difference between us.

OMAN (1993–2010)

Among all the states of the Arabian Peninsula, Oman is an exception—a pleasant surprise, after the cities in the sand of Bahrain, the United Arab Emirates and Saudi. It has a sense of continuity and evolution that contrasts with its neighbours, and it gets little revenue from oil, which requires it to engage with the world more realistically. It is mountainous and usually catches the tail end of the eastern monsoon in Spring when the desert bursts into flower. Historically it was part of the southern Fertile Crescent.

Oman has a large indigenous population and is the only territory in the region deserving of the title of nation. Its people have jobs and ambitions; they do not rely on immigrant labour to get things done.

Our partner in Oman, probably in his sixties and always in Omani dress, invited us to his house. He sat at the head and centre of the reception room, on a more elaborate cushion than the others that were scattered around the walls, on a floor that was covered with an enormous Iranian carpet. Low chairs had been made available for Western guests.

We were a large party and he had his own retinue. Much time was spent exchanging business cards and introductions. There was a purpose to this: to establish the correct seating precedence. While this was going on, the host smiled beneficently, making eye contact with all his visitors. My boss was seated on his right. When all was arranged to his satisfaction, he clicked his fingers and servants arrived with tea and orange juice, dates and nuts. Only when all had been served did he begin to speak in Arabic, pausing to let a son translate. 'Salaam Aleikum,' he beamed, again catching everybody in the eye.

We were truly welcome. 'It is an honour and a pleasure to have everybody here in my humble home. Though it does not need saying, we have been friends and partners for many years and have together overcome difficulties to achieve many successes. You are all truly my brothers. Brothers may argue from time to time, but the bond of the family is strongest.' He continued in this manner for several minutes before addressing a complimentary remark directly to my boss, who, having more experience of this part of the world than I did at the time, reacted to the cue with aplomb. He too spent several minutes praising the partner for the knowledge, understanding, forbearance and above all sage advice that had allowed our company to prosper.

He then went on to honour the presence of each one of the host's retinue and somehow found a story or anecdote with which to flatter them all. He ended with heartfelt thanks to the partner, on behalf of all of us, for the privilege of being invited to his wonderful home.

The partner then said, 'We are not here to talk business but to get to know each other. I have a few matters to discuss with my esteemed friend and brother, if he will do me the goodness of allowing me to call him that. Please feel free to get to know each other a little better.'

I had been placed between two Omanis who both spoke good English and immediately engaged me in conversation. They were witty and self-deprecating, and I had the sense to adopt a similar approach, while being careful to avoid giving offence. Soon soft laughter could be heard around the room. The servants kept coming round to refill drinks or top up the food trays. Finally, in a lull of conversation, the partner brought the meeting to an end. 'Thank you for coming. It is an honour and a privilege to have you here. I am pleased that this modest get-together has cemented even further our mutual understanding.'

I came away from the evening having enjoyed the conversation with my neighbouring Omanis but feeling that it had all been pointless. I had wanted to get down to business and the evening had seemed like a diversion. Only later did I appreciate that our coming together had not been the social event it purported to be, nor an exercise in cultural engagement, nor even an opportunity to soften us up for the hard bargaining that lay ahead, which is what I first assumed: it was in fact the necessary precursor for discussions in a world without dependable formal channels for seeking redress should anything go wrong. Once I understood that, it all made a lot more sense and I felt more comfortable; it also showed that however different the details, the Omanis were demonstrating a serious wish to trade.

Oman is a seafaring nation and accrued its wealth transporting slaves from East Africa and goods from India. This mercantile background, not unlike England's in its seafaring years, seems to have given Omanis a confidence in themselves. In talking to Omani managers, I felt we were on level terms, albeit with different perspectives. As one of them said, unexpectedly, 'It takes two hands to clap'—a cliché but true.

Oman is also a relatively recent state. Like all Middle Eastern sultanates, its fortunes ebbed and flowed but with the mid-nineteenth-century outlawing of slave-trading by Western powers, and with increased competition from steamships, its triangular trade, depending on monsoon winds between East Africa and India, became marginal.

Internal ructions prevented the creation of a coherent polity well into the twentieth century. Jan Morris's *Sultan in Oman* provides an exuberant account of the chaos in which it was brought together.[2] In the age of imperialism and the grab for Africa, Britain had become the Western power with most influence, occupying Aden on the other side of the Red Sea. Now, in 1970, the British became instrumental in the removal

---

[2] See Eland, new edition (2008).

of the sultan, whom they found too conservative, installing his son in his place. A wise move, as it turned out.

The son, Sultan Qaboos bin Said, had graduated from the Royal Military Academy Sandhurst and served briefly in the British Army. He went on to rule the newly proclaimed Sultanate of Oman for fifty years until his death in 2020, and was revered for being far less autocratic than his father. He opened up an insular and intensely conservative régime to outside influence. He remained an autocratic ruler and, rather oddly, had plastic replicas of local wildlife positioned on roundabouts at the junctions of Muscat's roads. On the other hand, he kept the old centre of Muscat largely intact. His instinct was that harmony was a necessary precursor to progress.

There was, however, a problem: Sultan Qaboos was homosexual. His habit of giving temporary lovers an Audi car left the Audi franchise with no other buyers. The issue—to quote a joke at his expense—was that he had none. He therefore proposed a plan for his succession from a selection of the best-qualified of his cousins and nephews. He stated his preference in a sealed envelope, to be confirmed or rejected by a council of senior elders. It was a very Middle Eastern solution that fitted the concept of benign autocracy.

Homosexuality was no big deal in the Arab or even the Muslim world, despite the ruckus about it when Qatar hosted the World Cup in 2022. Arab history is peppered with gay rulers who were judged on the quality of their leadership, not their sexual preferences. Islamic marriage is primarily to do with protecting material interests and catering for male lust; mutual attraction comes third—or so things were—hence the Ottoman preoccupation with harems and the search for pleasure elsewhere. Homosexuality is still *haram* but prosecutions are exceedingly rare because the home is beyond the reach of the state.

What I did not know until recently is that Sultan Qaboos

was a skilled and internationally respected diplomat, as are members of his family. He maintained friendly relations with all in the Middle East and acted as an unofficial intermediary between Sunnis and Shiites, Muslims and Jews, Christians and Arabs. Israel's Benjamin Netanyahu has been a visitor.

THE POLITICAL SYSTEMS OF THE ARABS
Arab political structures seem to have operated largely unchanged until oil wealth started to transform their status and influence in the first half of the twentieth century. The first major oil discovery in the Middle East occurred in Iran (not an Arab country) in 1908, followed by Iraq in 1927 and in Saudi Arabia in 1938 but large-scale oil production in the Middle East didn't really take off until after the Second World War. At the time, Kuwait imported water supplies from the Shatt Al-Arab river and distributed it around the country in goatskins on the backs of donkeys. Oman only had 10 kms of metalled roads. Much of Abu Dhabi's housing was made of earth or palm leaves. Egypt's capital, Cairo, was one of the few major cities in the region with a sewage system.

Saudi oil exports in Dammam did not start until 1946 and then only on a very modest scale. Production began in Abu Dhabi in 1962, in Dubai in 1969, in Sharjah in 1974, and in Oman in 1967, with each expansion making capital available to fund further expansion and broader economic progress.[3]

The status of the oil-producing states was further enhanced in the early 1970s by the impact of the OPEC oil-producing cartel, which effectively rebalanced the relationship between the West and the providers of its most treasured commodity. The money this brought in created an economic

---

[3] A.A. Kubursi, 'Oil, Influence, and Development: The Gulf States and the International Economy', *Southwest Asia*, Vol. 41, No. 2, pp. 362-382 ((Spring, 1986).

revolution and the opportunity for traditional feudal hierarchies to entrench themselves further.

Dispute resolution relies on quiet diplomacy, a skill developed millennia ago in which grievances may be alluded to but without ever giving offence. Whoever is sitting opposite is always 'my brother'. One might kill one's enemy; one does not insult him.

The unspoken compact between the Arab states was not to rock the boat. Exactly what fuelled their ire in 2017 is hard to explain but Saudi Arabia, the United Arab Emirates, Bahrain and Egypt imposed a sea, land and air blockade on Qatar and cut diplomatic and trade ties with its emir in Doha, claiming that it supported 'terrorism' and was too close to Iran.[4] Perhaps *Al-Jazeera*—the most popular news channel in the Arabic-speaking world and owned by the Qatari state—ran an editorial that they found objectionable. Or maybe it was felt that Tamim bin Hamad Al Thani, Qatar's leader, had a less impressive bloodline back to the Prophet Mohammed than King Salman bin Abdulaziz Al Saud of Saudi Arabia, or King Abdullah II of Jordan, or King Mohammed VI of Morocco, or Sheikh Mohammed bin Rashid Al Maktoum of Dubai, or Emir Sabah Al-Ahmad Al-Jaber Al-Sabah of Kuwait, or King Hamad bin Isa Al Khalifa of Bahrain, or Sultan Haitham bin Tariq of Oman, or President Beji Caid Essebsi of Tunisia, all of whom claim lineage to the Prophet. Sometimes an upstart needs to be put in his place.

The legacy of the Arabian peninsula is the Arabic language and Islam, but there is a little more to it than that, and a little less.

---

[4] *Al Jazeera* (5 June, 2020): https://www.aljazeera.com/news/2020/6/5/qatar-blockade-five-things-to-know-about-the-gulf-crisis

CHAPTER 23
Other Islamic States

JORDAN: 2010 to 2015
I am sitting in my usual armchair, which is heavily upholstered in leather on its seat, back and arms, and framed in thick mahogany in the same style as the round table in front of me, the distributor's desk and the bookcases that line the walls. Though of imported design, this furniture is more pleasing to me than the garish expressions of wealth to be found in the Gulf—or in nouveau-riche Russia, for that matter.

The barred windows of this ground-floor office in Amman are open and there is a view across the quiet street to ochre houses behind privacy walls that descend into the valley below. It is a warm day and the sky is blue, but in this room it is cool and sombre.

Occasionally the distributor discretely summons somebody. A servant appears to offer more coffee or tea, bring fruit or local snacks, or empty the overflowing ashtrays. Every so often, one of the other managers enters to discuss a particular point or bring some necessary paperwork. By now I know them all and I greet all but the serving boys with the embrace and three kisses on cheeks, as is the custom here.

There are four of us at the table: the distributor, his partner, the manager of his *shisha* business, and me. I am here to talk about cigarettes, not shisha. The partner is Syrian, Tarek Iraqi and Nisreen Jordanian. Other managers are Palestinian or Lebanese. When I question this, they laugh. 'We are all brothers and sisters; we marry who we want. The passport does not matter.' Jordan's majority population is Palestinian, mostly refugees from Israel. They worry that extreme elements in the refugee camps might cause trouble.

Nisreen speaks English and is relied upon to translate, but she is also an intermediary with a greater understanding of the West than Tarek, the distributor, or Suheil, his partner. I think she calls me Yanni when translating back to Tarek. I find this disconcerting until discovering it is Arabic for 'but'.

Like me, she chain-smokes while Tarek smiles benignly and his partner looks glum until he suddenly flares up, denouncing in bad English the injustices they have suffered. His rage is not directed at me—not personally, except by implication—but what am I going to do about it?

These meetings last all day and into the night. They are interrupted by lunch which happens anytime between midday and 4:00 pm. We drive to the restaurant on a route that passes in front of the National Assembly. In the middle of the roundabout, a few dozen protesters are watched by the police. I am told that their complaints are local: housing, education, electricity prices, the lack of water. A bomb, of which there have been a few, though never during my residency, is regarded as an outrage and then forgotten.

The restaurant is hidden down a side street in this upper part of town—difficult to find, if you are new to the area. The place is full, without a tourist in sight, but there is always a table for us. It is a fine mansion, with a large terrace overlooking rooftops that tumble down the valley. In winter and high summer we sit inside, otherwise we take the balcony. By now I am known to the management and greeted with a two-handed shake and a formal bow. Tarek is treated with greater deference, maybe because he always pays the bill, despite my protests.

(I am reminded of Mackintosh-Smith's trilogy,[1] following in the footsteps of Ibn Battuta, a thirteenth-century traveller from Tangiers, who traversed those then-known parts of the world where Islam had made its mark. A traveller was rewar-

---

[1] *Travels with a Tangerine* (2001), *The Hall of a Thousand Columns* (2005), *Land Falls: On the Edge of Islam* (2010).

ded for his presence in a foreign land. For Tarek, that was still how it was.)

The conversation turns to personal things. Tarek talks about his son and his fixation with video games. My children are older and I say that they have grown up fine. He thanks me for reassuring him and says he will not get so angry in future.

I look around while Nisreen is translating. Some of the diners are in traditional Arab dress, probably visitors like me. Elsewhere there are tables of women talking animatedly, dressed in Western style. This could be London on a warm day, as could the demonstrations. Tarek does not drink alcohol so neither do I, but there is always an ashtray handy, unlike London.

This is not a Western meal. A plate arrives and is shared among us. Then another and another, until the table is filled with dishes you might want to go back to if you want. At a certain point something more substantial is served, effectively the summit of the meal, though introduced with such delicacy that it seems more like a step up than preparation for a step down. Eating together in this world is more of a ritual than a necessity. It is a time to step back and connect with the company you are in. In that frame of mind it becomes memorable, no matter how many times you experience it.

Eventually we go back to the office and stay until well after dark. All the business options we need to resolve have been rehearsed so many times by now that I am losing my ability to think straight. My fatigue shows and it is time to call it a day but instead of going back to my hotel, we go out for dinner. Tarek's favourite restaurant is a fusion of Oriental and Western cuisine. We sit on sofas with a low table between us and eat chili-coated edamame beans. When a day has been particularly arduous, I allow myself a beer and Tarek does not object. We eat again, often in a comfortable silence. Our day has been satisfactory.

Tarek drives me back to the Four Seasons. There is a complex of concrete barriers to prevent a ram-raid bombing. The boot is searched and the underside of the car inspected with mirrors, though Tarek is well known here. I walk through the metal detector, and forget to remove my mobile from my top pocket. The alarm goes off and I place the phone with my briefcase on the conveyor belt. At this time of night, the foyer is deserted. I go up to my room, light another cigarette and pour myself a large Scotch. They do a good breakfast at the Four Seasons, with an excellent buffet. I always order eggs benedict, which has salmon rather than bacon: I prefer it that way. It sets you up for the day ahead and the hundred-metre stroll down the hill to the office again.

This routine continues for three years. In my first months in Amman, I was taken for dinner one evening to a private house, with a landscaped oasis garden and streams, pools and shade from palms and casuarina trees. Our host was a Jordanian Christian, previously another of our distributors. I was surprised to be welcome here, as his contract was terminated after our lawyers and security staff in London interviewed him about the fraud. In addition, he took the view that our ex-manager had stolen his money, not ours. Looking back, I think the suspicions that led to our cancelling his contract could have applied to any of our distributors, as our investigations team adopted a more Western concept of corporate governance. I expected the host, therefore, to be resentful and to direct his resentment at me. He never did; on one occasion he apologised that his wife was away in Beirut and suggested we meet there too sometime; Amman was too quiet. Business was never mentioned.

A pleasant evening, the air is warm and liquid and not uncomfortable. Talk turns to political developments in the Middle East. It is the time of the Arab Spring and tired dictators are being removed by street protests. A good thing in

Western eyes, but my experience of Russia makes me less convinced that the outcome will be a happy one. How can anyone create democracy in a week?

Abu Sayeed is a thoughtful, gentle, self-deprecating and intelligent man, his round face framed by his pebble glasses. Abu means father and I think he would have done a better job as a parent than me. I cannot remember the detail of our debate, but the gist of it was that he blamed America for all the woes of the Middle East while I suggested that some were self-inflicted. There was disagreement for the only time I can recall in this part of the world. Abu Sayeed apologises the next morning and I tell him to think nothing of it—just an exchange of views. Later he is diagnosed with cancer and disappears for a year. On his return I am delighted to see him. I like him very much, the only person I met in the Middle East who had the temerity to say what he thinks.

Afterwards I explain to Tarek that I was surprised to be invited to the house of Shamoun, our recently dismissed distributor. Tarek regards Shamoun's dismissal as being of no consequence. The two of them had remained on good terms and he could see no reason why I could not also. I learned from that that friendship can survive disputes at work—or perhaps that if friends disagreed, talking might provide a solution. Later, Tarek shows me his house, more modest than where we had dinner, but does not invite me in. That made me feel as if our friendship was less certain than I had imagined.

It was complicated. Everything was complicated. Every meeting had an unspoken agenda. Or hadn't.

Tarek introduces me to Nisreen's competitor in the *shisha* business. He is charming, only in his early 40s, I guess, but has an unspecified disease which confines him to a wheelchair and is looking to sell his business. This is not an option for us but we part on good terms. A year or so afterwards we meet by chance in the business lounge in Dubai airport. He shrugs off his disability and seems more concerned about my health.

Meanwhile the Middle East is becoming more unstable. My holiday in Syria has had to be cancelled. Egypt has got rid of its fourth president, Hosni Mubarak, but now has a government dominated by the Muslim Brotherhood. In the absence of coherent government, economies are collapsing and radical Islamic groups are looking to seize power. Tourists and tourist dollars are disappearing; attitudes are hardening. The schism between Sunni and Shia Muslims is crystalizing into a power struggle between Iran and Saudi Arabia. Tarek has another outburst, this time about the insensitivity of one of the companies he represents in appointing a Shia manager to look after his affairs. Tension is high.

The real challenge is Iraq. Tarek goes there regularly and sometimes encourages me to go with him but then decides it is not a good idea, even though he assures me that Kurdish Iraq is safe; besides which, company rules do not allow me to travel there. Our problem is a Kurd who refuses to accept the termination of a contract which gave him a commission of \$5 per case of 10,000 cigarettes and who has demanded \$300m in compensation. I am told that the gentleman in question looks and behaves like an illiterate Taliban, and has embarked on a private guerrilla war to right the injury that has been done to him. Officialdom being what it is in this part of the world, it costs a lot to get goods through (backhanders are expensive) and Tarek is losing money.

Details aside, the story encapsulates the division between the West and the Middle East. On our side there is a prescriptive and legalistic approach to business dealings; on their side, an acceptance of greater laxity and an absence of any hard-and-fast rules—a situation we shrink from as conducive to corruption but which they regard as both normal and unremarkable. Aligning stringent practices in the West with the fluidity of business arrangements among the Rest can be a struggle and its resolution turns into the most difficult professional challenge I have ever faced, but a solution is eventually found within 'lines in the sand' set by a non-exec-dominated board with the assistance of an eminent QC.

Tarek goes to Iraq and secures a deal in Erbil one Sunday —a working day for him but not for me—but he cannot leave the negotiation room until I have approved the agreement and none of my senior colleagues is available to do this. I approve, knowing that the settlement is covered by a provision in the accounts. Later I discover that he will have to pay for the settlement himself, but a mountain of documents provides enough evidence to suggest that we can cover all his costs.

The story ends in Paris, where Tarek and I are to meet. The new boss, who lacks experience, thinks that my proposal to reimburse Tarek for his losses goes too far and he refuses to honour it. He imagines that a meal in a swanky restaurant will be enough to win Tarek over.

It isn't. Tarek explains that in addition to what he has already paid out, there is the question of what he has already sacrificed for the company. My boss is unimpressed. Not only has he no decent counter-offer but he fails to recognise the importance of trust in a world without formal arrangements. He does not understand that by dismissing Tarek's claims, he is stoking a resentment that will be remembered for generations. It's a disaster and it has its roots in the failure of the Western mind to appreciate the protestation of non-Western thinking.

I leave the company not long after. My successor decides that Tarek has been dishonest. He may have been but he was good at his job and I had faith in him. And that is where our paths diverge.

The Middle East is a spider's-web culture. Everybody

knows everybody else. Everybody lives in what the West would regard an ethical vacuum, where everything has to be worked out and balanced. There are moral compromises; games have to be played. Had we not played them, we could not have won. Those hundreds of hours spent in Tarek's office were not wasted; we were building a web.

I recognise all of this and look back on those times with great affection but, with my Western mindset, still regard it with incomprehension. I found it impossible to make wholly rational decisions; Western business conventions meant nothing. Everybody I worked with was decent, charming and hospitable, enormously easy to like, and doing their best by their own values, but they operated in a way that I found and still find hard to fathom. There was honour but not what we Westerners—perhaps patronisingly—would call *morality*. One had to rely on intuition. The gulf was huge.

So it wasn't just the differences in religion and language in the Arab Empire that left me feeling undermined but a feeling of fluidity: the shifting sands on which nothing is sure. And I now see that these working conditions were not unique to the Maghreb and Levant: they applied further afield too. The problems that came up in Morocco, Algeria, Lebanon, Egypt and even Türkiye were not so different from those that came up in Central Asia—in Kyrgyzstan, Azerbaijan and Uzbekistan—when my business counterpart was a native of these countries. One travels around the world with a set of Western expectations and never quite realises how little one has really penetrated other cultures—how little one has understood or been understood. There is the West and there is the Rest.

LEBANON: 1993 to 2013

After all I have said, Jordan had one thing going for it that made it stand out: when each of its neighbours was embroiled in violence, Jordan was an island of peace. Lebanon had also been peaceful, in the halcyon days of the 1960s, according to my father, a frequent visitor. It was the closest thing to a secular state that the Islamic world could offer and a playground of the few who could afford it.

I arrived in 1993 after the fifteen-year-long civil war. Beirut was a deformity, with every building in the centre wrecked. There was no public water, electricity supply or garbage collection. The streets were festooned with wires from private generators, and the detritus of war and domestic life piled up on street corners.

But its previous history was not throughly erased. I stayed at a seafront hotel that had seen better days and, on the terrace, I spotted signs that the country my father had talked about was beginning to reassert itself. Affluently dressed men and women without a headscarf drank, smoked and chatted as if they were on the French Riviera, which is what Beirut had once aspired to—or was it the other way round? The sea glistened in front of them in the setting sun, which cast into silhouette a few ships which hovered menacingly a few miles offshore. 'What are those,' I asked. 'The Israelis,' came the reply.

The following day when I made a tour of the city with my local contact, a closed gateway in a poorer suburb prompted another question. 'That's Hezbollah. We cannot enter.'

That evening, the contact took me to visit a friend of his who had an apartment downtown in a building that looked like the Beirut Holiday Inn. From the outside, every surface had been pitted or smashed. Even the lift doors had bullet marks on them. But it still worked. Arriving at the steel front door of his apartment, we were greeted effusively by the friend. 'Come in, come in, what a pleasure. Make yourself at home. Come. Meet my family. We are so happy you are here.'

It was Ramadhan and, with the sun setting, time for Iftar. My host asked what I would like to drink, confiding that the only thing he gave up for Ramadhan was Scotch whisky.

Would I like some? I diplomatically declined but then did not feel that I'd needed to: the whole family was as charming and welcoming as the host. The meal was delicious and the family so pleased to have a foreign visitor that it made me feel I was at home.

This was an immaculate apartment, expertly designed and tastefully decorated and yet it was in the middle of what had been a war zone. I asked our host how he had managed.

'When the fighting became too bad we left, to Cyprus or Europe. When it died down, we came back and repaired everything.'

'How often did this happen?'

'Four times.'

'Why did you bother to come back?'

'Simple: it is our home. We knew the madness would end some day.'

He was an importer of lighting equipment, not a rich man; this was just what you did when it got tough. I had experienced the kindness of strangers; intolerance was not part of their vocabulary.

For a short period after my 1993 trip, Lebanon attracted inward investment which saw the rebuilding of the city centre and the glossy hotels, the restaurants and the shopping malls, and these greeted my return twenty years later, though there was still no municipal electricity supply. Mutual hatred still simmered between Hezbollah and the Israeli warships though there was now a new target of distrust: the million-plus refugees who had arrived since the collapse of Syria.

Since then, Lebanon has fallen apart again, because a botched peace agreement assumed that mutually adversarial factions could be induced to unite and work together, without realising that neither Syria nor Israel could resist interfering. The government, such as it was, was reduced to providing perks to its supporters. Then came the 2020 nitrate explosion in the Port of Beirut—the result of unsafe storage but causing damage that the state has been incapable of rectifying. In short, Lebanon has run out of money; as I write, its pound is trading at 10 per cent of its value a year ago. Basic goods and pharmaceuticals are no longer available.

I wonder where my *Iftar* host is now? Enjoying life abroad, I expect, but hoping to return home as soon as possible.

EGYPT 2010 to 2012
My final story about the Middle East concerns foreign domination. Long before the concept of a nation state had even been born, the question of who ruled whom was a simple matter of military might. I knew nothing about the history of Egypt until I met Tarek Swelim (not to be confused with the Iraqi Tarek, living in Jordan). For me, as for all visitors, the attraction of visiting Egypt was the Pharaonic age, and Tarek was able to explain its evolution in six objects from the then chaotic old Cairo Museum.

Tarek's PhD thesis was on the mosque that Ahmad ibn Tulun had constructed in the ninth century. It is now considered an exemplar of Islamic architecture on account of its large size, its use of brick and stucco instead of stone, and its spiral minaret, but what interested me was Tulun himself. Tulun was brought up in Iraq, taken as a slave to Samarra, became a member of the Turkish military elite and was sent to govern Egypt by the Abbasid caliphate, which stretched from Spain to India. He soon made the country into his personal fiefdom and founded his own dynasty. It lasted only forty-three years but is revealing of the centrifugal forces that were splitting up the Islamic empire at the time.

The mosque he built was to a large extent a replica of the one he had seen in Samarra, which in turn reflected the Persian style. It reflected his origins specifically and was thus unlike any other building in Egypt at the time.

As a foreigner, Ibn Tulun was interested only in the preservation of his dynasty and reputation. That required grand designs—and what better than a mosque? His wealth came from taxing the Egyptians but not to the extent that they became rebellious, and impressive public buildings were testimony of his benevolence. Taxation and munificence were a balancing act which also required military might as the final safeguard. Tulun's praetorian guard was made up of foreign mercenaries, both costly and lacking any investment in the régimes they were paid to support. In spite of that, Ibn Tulun was successful in holding his dynasty together but his son was not. Yet his model of governance held sway over the Islamic world for over a millennium.

The subsequent rulers of Egypt were also foreigners, notably the Ikhshidids (935-969), the Fatimids (969-1171), the Ayyubids (1171-1250) and the Mamluks (1250-1517), who again built architectural gems from the wealth they acquired and remained titular heads of state until overthrown by Napoleon. But the Mamluks were never Egyptian, nor did they speak Arabic. Their language was Turkic, having been brought as slaves from Asia Minor, and they represent another example of bodyguards for foreign rulers eventually seizing power for themselves.

That protectors can become rulers is surprising. What is not surprising is that in the absence of any rooted legitimacy or interest in the people they governed, a succession of bloody conflicts took place over succession. These conflicts ended in 1517 with the arrival of yet another foreign régime, the Ottoman Empire, which survived until after the First World War when its void was filled by Britain which, under the guise of a protectorate, fulfilled its long-term dream of an imperial map stretching all the way from Cairo to the Cape. Disentangling the colonial yoke led to the establishment of a new monarchy when Ahmed Fuad Paşa—Fuad, for short—dropped his title as sultan of Egypt (and the Sudan) in favour of king in 1922. There was no historical precedent for this, nor for any other African country bordering the Mediterranean to gain a monarchy, but the United Nations required the emir of Libya to become a king after the Second World War and the last Alawi sultan of Morocco made himself into a king in 1957.

Fuad was succeeded by his son Farouk, who was toppled in 1952 by Gamal Abdel Nasser, an Arabist whose politics was based not on religion but on the fraternalism of all Arab countries. Nasser did not assume the position of the head of state until he had cauterised the power of the Islamic Brotherhood two years later, after an attempt on his life. He attempted to unify the Arab world behind the common cause of opposition to Israel, which was seen as a Western imposition on Arab territories. This was ultimately a failure both militarily and diplomatically and any aspirations to Arabic unity disappeared with his death in 1970. Since then it all has gone downhill and reverted to type.

My friend Tarek supported the demonstrations in Tahrir Square in favour of the overthrow of Hosni Mubarak in 2011 and hoped for a more pragmatic approach from Mohamed Morsi's Muslim Brotherhood, a hope in which he was disappointed. Morsi proved inflexible and politically maladroit; recreating an Islamic state was more important to him than assuaging powerful domestic stakeholders. To be fair, no other Egyptian ruler had ever done anything different about stakeholders, other than get rid of them, but Morsi lacked an army of foreign mercenaries to protect him.

Someone who did have an army was Abdel Fattah el-Sisi, whom Morsi had appointed minister of defence. On July 3, 2013, Sisi's army (with very strong vested interests in Egypt's economic sector, like their Mamluk predecessors) chose to usurp him and then imposed a régime that was even more autocratic than that of Mubarak.

Shortly after, Tarek moved to Qatar—not in protest at the new régime, as I had supposed, but simply for a better-paid job. Tarek's wife Hend, however, remained in Egypt to manage their furniture manufacturing business, an enterprise that had been close to shutting down as tourists went elsewhere, scared of the volatile political mix. So much for Western assumptions.

THE POLITICAL SYSTEMS OF ISLAMIC STATES
Throughout the Islamic world there are but two poles of authority: religion and rulers. Citizens acquiesce, having no other option, especially after the failures of the Arab spring. Religion in its most conservative form now challenges rulers, having gained a secure foothold in Iran and Afghanistan, both rigid theocracies. In such circumstances, religious rule transforms the habits of previous autocrats. With few exceptions, neither democracy nor liberal values get a look-in.

On the one hand you have the Lebanese family in Beirut, on the other you have those who blow up ancient monuments in the name of Allah, force women into marriage and behead infidels. The closest I have ever come to meeting a genuine fundamentalist Muslim was a Punjabi taxi driver who drove me to Heathrow and argued that the Koran was indisputably the word of God. This was a matter of faith for him, because, as he revealed, he could not understand high Arabic and thus relied on the opinions of the imams. Every other Muslim I have ever met on my travels has been of a liberal persuasion, relying on their conscience to interpret Islam as they saw fit.

The rise of fundamentalism, though led by self-elected imams and ferocious warlords, is predominantly fuelled by a lumpenproletariat which regards autocratic rule as natural because it has been brought up in a culture that has known nothing else for millennia. The promise of an afterlife for martyrs can be much more appealing than the struggle for earthly survival. After being marginalised and oppressed for centuries both by their own leaders and by conquering invaders, grievance becomes a permanent state of mind. And then along comes digital interconnectivity to explain it all, provide instruction on what is *haram*, and offer the comfort of social conservativism and political rage. And this too cannot be challenged, any more than autocratic leaders can be challenged. Dissent is disloyalty. Why should women not have equal rights? Because equality would run counter to the pronouncements of the Prophet. End of conversation.

This fundamentalist mindset gains considerably from casting the West as the Great Satan, a not-unreasonable point of view, considering the impact 'we' have had on the Islamic world. For more than 200 years, Western powers tried to extract everything they could find of any value, becoming increasingly compromised by opportunistically playing off one leader or faction against another, irrespective of their virtues. For my friend Abu Sayeed, however, though he remains a tolerant liberal, political islamicisation started with the creation of Israel, referred to by Palestinians as the *Nakba*, the disaster. Then came the overthrow of Shah Pahlavi, in what was then Persia, giving birth to the world's most repressive religious totalitarianism. Then Afghanistan, where the Mujaheddin were helped by the West to remove a Communist government, only to revolt—ultimately successfully—against foreign invasion. So to Iraq, where the replacement of Saddam Hussein's brutal dictatorship led to a violent schism between Shias and Sunnis, and to Libya, which fractured on tribal lines. And finally—though not really finally —to Syria, where its interventionist policy left the West ending up on the side of a hotchpotch of fanatical Islamists, secular reformists and competing clans until Russia decided to back the savagery of the Assad régime, without a moral scruple in sight, leaving the West bleating in protest.

These are the triumphs of the West's supposedly well-intentioned but ill-informed interference in the affairs of others. The result is that our actions have not only failed to generate the solutions we had hoped for but have alienated the people we were supposed to be supporting. In our wake, Islam has become a source of fracture rather than of unity, leaving its moderates peripheralised by the news headlines.

Where governance and religion compete for control, they also clash in pursuit of ambitions. Élites may be toppled but those who replace them are just as wedded to stasis. The culture remains feudal: keep the populace quiescent, by force if necessary, but never relinquish power. Avoid speaking your mind; dissimulate instead. Say what is required of you; above all, profess allegiance.

I have not used the word 'nation' about this part of the world because it seems to me inappropriate; autocracy is the better word. And in an autocracy, whether political or religious, it is understood that citizens should do what they are told. But centuries of control have led to a culture in which the strictures of government are ignored if one can get away with it, a reasonable attitude when government does nothing for you. There are about 100 million Egyptians who carry on in the same way regardless; only middle-class liberals and religious fanatics are locked up.

There is of course change in the Arabic-speaking world, the most notable examples of which, in my view, are Tunisia, Jordan, Morocco and Oman. Of these, Tunisia's was the only successful revolution of the Arab Spring, and inspired calls for democracy in other Arab countries, though when I went there, what I saw was rising fundamentalism, rampant smuggling and a crippled economy.

By contrast, Jordan, Morocco and Oman share the model of benign monarchy, with sovereigns who evidently wish to serve of their citizens. All are popular, all have been influenced by the West, all are modernisers and all are relatively safe from internal threat. King Mohammed VI of Morocco studied law at Morocco's Mohammed V University in Rabat before being awarded a PhD from the University of Nice Sophia Antipolis in France. King Hussein of Jordan trained at Sandhurst and has received honorary degrees from European and American universities. And Sultan Haitham bin Tariq Al Said, the current Sultan of Oman, studied history at Oxford University before earning a postgraduate degree in international relations at the University of Geneva. In each case, their appreciation and internalisation of Western values has helped them transform feudal states into potential nations. So it is not all bad.

But this is top-down history. My blithe presupposition was that the Arab masses were victims, or saw themselves as such. But a conversation with Tarek suggested otherwise and gave me something to ponder that I had not thought of before. I had asked him about how the people were coping with the Covid situation in Egypt. He laughed: 'They carry on as they always have and take no notice.'

I had thought I was being dispassionate in exploring the assumptions of the West towards the rest of the world; Tarek's comment made me reconsider. I had been thinking of 'the Rest' as made up of people damaged by the oppression they had suffered throughout their history. My friend's comment made me realise how much fortitude they have, how much resilience, and how much more capable they probably are than 'us' privileged denizens of the West in withstanding adversity and working out their problems their own way.

CONCLUSION

CHAPTER 24
Wrapping Up

For forty years I worked as a manager in various global companies, handling operations, integrating acquisitions, setting up activities in new markets, gently controlling local distributors and occasionally overseeing the hand-over of businesses to new ownership. Much of this time was spent overseas, in places as diverse as Nicaragua and Singapore.

My experience of overseeing new trading arrangements in countries I initially knew little about taught me a vital lesson: that where there are incompatibilities between countries, trade can oil the wheels in a way that nothing else can. In every case, although we sought to extend our global production and make profits for ourselves, we had to take a considered view of what would be of mutual benefit to the countries we were seeking to gain entry to.

It meant that the managerial side of the business needed to be backed by intelligence and research about how the country in question worked, about the nature of its politics and culture, and about how we could contribute to its legitimate long-term goals. In some cases, as I have shown, our introduction of a production facility—even in a field as controversial as tobacco—helped to stabilise the country we were seeking to operate in by bringing what had previously been a black-market product into the regulatory system, thereby making it subject to taxation and so adding a new income stream to the nation's exchequer (see my chapter on Vietnam).

The same applied in Cote d'Ivoire, where business continued despite a civil war, and in Nicaragua, where a joint venture involving leaf processing with Bulgartabac following the Sandinista revolution kept the business going, and in Chile, where the company I worked for survived the political dislocation of the economy under the Marxist Allende regime and proved to be a robust competitor to US imports. Often these things are a judgement call and based not on objective realities but on personalities. While I was at BAT in 1990 I declined the government offer to participate in the privatisation of the Lao tobacco monopoly, but Imperial Tobacco did so later, before I joined them in 2003, and the venture proved worthwhile.

Successes like these are not possible if we allow our sense of estrangement from other countries—our unfamiliarity with them, even our bewilderment at them—to act as an automatic brake on whom we approach and are prepared to deal with. In the businesses I was involved in, we had a financial incentive to make profits, and because we were working a long way from home, geographically and culturally, we had to engage with other countries constructively, establish connections and find routes to mutual understanding, all the while withholding judgement—to some extent—in cases where a country's political system was distasteful.

Admittedly, objecting on moral grounds to some of the people and nations that overseas trade has to engage with is a natural reflex in a liberal society but it can rely too much on simplistic binary assumptions about foreigners and may amount to nothing more than virtue signalling—or even cultural prejudice. Many would argue that investing in Egypt, for example, is immoral because of its dictatorship but distaste for a military regime has to be set aside against the added value that investment creates for the population at large, always assuming that the benefits ever get that far.

It doesn't always work. Investing in Eritrea's Coca-Cola bottling business, which I tried to spearhead in 1998, made huge economic sense, for example. It was after only meeting Isaias Aferwerki, Eritrea's totalitarian leader, that the project became politically impossible as we would have had no leverage at all over financial flows or even commercial operating terms. More or less the same reasons applied to the opportunity that Mr Tay brought to us in Myanmar.

We are mostly suspicious and untrusting of trade because it is driven by the profit motive—of course, otherwise there would be shareholder revolts—but all companies have to operate within trading systems that seek to balance corporate goals with other considerations. In the USA, home of Wild West capitalism in the nineteenth-century, the federal government has long sought measures to promote vigorous competition and protect consumers from anti-competitive practices. The first antitrust law, the Sherman Act, was passed in 1890 and was intended as a 'comprehensive charter of economic liberty aimed at preserving free and unfettered competition as the rule of trade'. The Clayton Act, which followed in 1914, prohibits anti-competitive mergers, predatory and discriminatory pricing, and other forms of unethical corporate behaviour. Both are in force today not just to protect the public but because the federal government recognises that it itself is ultimately harmed by bad practices.

The same is true of the World Trade Organization, which seeks to regularise trade between nations. The WTO requires nations to sign up to a system of global rules, the main function of which is to ensure that trade flows as smoothly, predictably and freely as possible. That in turn affects how nations think. Although it took them fifteen years, the governments of Vietnam and Laos eventually realised that if they were going to enjoy the benefits of international trading, it would help to throw over their incompetent and inflexible systems of central planning in favour of more malleable and responsive systems. Trade provided a reason for rigid political orthodoxy to be ousted by common sense. It is instructive that Donald Trump, while president of the USA, refused to nominate a US candidate for the WTO board, which came close to collapse in consequence. Trump's antipathy to the WTO reflected the fact that his role as the USA's chief executive was always compromised by his personal ambitions as an entrepreneur, and the WTO's regulatory framework limited the freedom that he sought for his own business empire. Other business leaders have a more balanced approach to the regulatory environment, which is why it works for the many and not just, as Trump would have it, for the Trump Organization.

Having to operate within a system of rules means that, like it or not, trade is inextricably linked to politics and social well-being. As a result, big business today has much longer planning horizons than do most governments. It also has considerable insight into the markets it operates in, and is acutely aware of reputational risk, in a way that politicians are not.

And yet our distrust remains. That is because, in the world of public morality, it is easy to be censorious, as we all know from protest movements. There are countries that are constantly targeted for condemnation by NGOs and censured by the United Nations and other governments. Typically, moral condemnation has no effect because it makes no effort to enter the mindset of countries thus accused, or to understand their motivations. Moral condemnation, moreover, is more committed to public censure than to beneficial outcomes, and there is little evidence that its tools—from public protest to economic sanctions—are necessarily effective. For all the outrage over Russia's attempted takeover of Ukraine, for example, the Russian economy, at the time of writing, is expected to grow this year by 2 per cent, compared with only 0.6 per cent in the UK, despite Western sanctions.

In reality, global trade provides an incentive for mutual understandings and mutual benefits, and while there are legitimate questions to be raised about its motives and methods, there are also some fundamental virtues about the way in which it is conducted, because agreements are based on assumptions of trust, transparency and commitment.

Those assumptions have nothing to do with public morality or pandering to domestic interest groups, because they take place behind closed doors; they are not performances constructed for the public stage. The morality that they represent is more pragmatic than idealistic.

Business also has to account for itself, and does so; government is meant to do the same but mostly doesn't. While creating the moral conditions in which businesses are required to operate, Western governments are much more lax about their own procedures. Based on a Memorandum of Understanding, Rwanda has received £140 million from the UK to house would-be migrants, some of whom may in fact be legal refugees. Similarly €1 billion has been provided by the EU to the new autocratic president of Tunisia to hold potential migrants, and informal arrangements have also been made in lawless Libya. None of these arrangements carry watertight guarantees on the decent and legal treatment of migrants and would seem therefore, on the face of it, to contravene the US Foreign and Corrupt Practices Act and the UK Bribery Act (2010). Both laws require that payments made to third parties, no matter in what jurisdiction, require the giver to ensure that funds are used entirely for the legitimate purposes, as defined by the commercial arrangement. No such protections exist in the case of Rwanda, Tunisia and Libya.

If businesses were to act in such a cavalier way, the ensuing sanctions could include hefty commercial fines and criminal charges against individual managers, bringing considerable damage to corporate reputations. The exemption that Western governments (in this case) allow themselves illustrates not just the hypocrisy of the moral framework they apply to themselves but, conversely, the rigour that they customarily hold business to. Business, in short, cannot get away with what governments get away with.

Money, of course, is power. Somewhere deep within the

George Bush Center for Intelligence in Langley, VA, beancounters spend their days working out what it would cost to buy off each of the world's most corrupt dictators and install alternates more palatable to Western tastes. They calculate how much the warring parties in the Horn of Africa or Central Africa might demand to bring their fighting to an end, for example, or those leaders in Myanmar and Cambodia who come to power only to strip their countries' national coffers for their own benefit. Acceding to extortion by the wicked and greedy is certainly one way to try and make the world a better place and there is no shortage of regions of the world where it has been attempted—especially in the supply of bribes disguised as foreign aid and relief. The execution of foreign policy in this manner is not, however, a failsafe solution, as the USA's previous record of interventions in South America demonstrates. It failed dramatically in Iraq and Afghanistan.

By contrast, trade-based initiatives provide our most likely initiative for global reforms because they tend to be motivated by rational actors rather than ideologues and showmen. An example of a beneficial intervention occurred in the Autumn of 2022 when an irrational actor, the new and populist British prime minister Liz Truss, caused tens of billions of pounds' damage to the UK economy in just a few days by her introduction of untested and eccentric financial policies, all inspired by a strange inversion of her own father's radical left-wing politics—that is to say, by her neo-Marxist-Leninist commitment to building a new reality by nuking the status quo. Once it became clear that Truss was set on bringing the established order to its knees, the banking system came riding to the rescue and shut her down, and she was ousted from office by her own party mandarins in just forty-nine days. Rarely have doubters been more grateful for the existence of a system of global finance, for it showed that, behind the edifice of sentiment and political emotion—in this case the froth of populist bluster—money is the most obvious driver of lucidity and reason.

Most of our political leaders underplay the economic consequences of their policies, or are either unaware of them or in denial about them, as Truss was. Populist leaders are the worst offenders in this respect, not only because of their indifference to economic and political structures that are the product of decades of negotiation but because of their wish to abandon such structures altogether, in favour of the unknown and untested (or, often, the tested and failed), on grounds of sentiment alone. Such sentiment is usually the same, wherever it occurs, and focuses on an exaggerated reverence for the country's national identity, the wish to defend it by controlling immigration and the fabrication that the nation can be isolated from the complexity and challenges of the wider world by the introduction of protectionism, branded by Brexit campaigners in the UK as 'taking back control'.

The fact is, though, that raising tariff barriers, protecting domestic businesses and limiting the free movement of labour all come at a high economic cost. Protectionism, for all its accompanying mythology, does not protect anybody: it does the opposite, as testcase after testcase attests. Herein lies the fundamental contradiction between populism and economic growth: protectionism makes weak countries weaker and the only arguments that make it seem desirable are those mired in the self-interest of its promoters. By contrast, the move from protectionism to free-market principles is well established, as illustrated in this book by Chile. In 1973 Chile's per capita income was $1,623; in 2022 it was $15,356,[1] close to a tenfold nominal increase. The benefits of free trade are unquestionable.

---

[1] https://www.macrotrends.net/countries/CHL/chile/gdp-gross-domestic-product#:ffi:text=Chile gdp for 2022 was,a 5.72% decline from 2018.

Those who think that that erecting trade barriers will protect domestic producers are terribly misguided: whatever goods are made in any country, the components and raw materials, to say nothing of the fuel, usually need to be sourced from abroad. Putting additional tariffs on them raises their price and the price of end products, as well as depressing wages and the prospect of wage rises, which puts more manufacturing out of reach of more consumers. Barriers can also damage relations between countries and their nationals. The theory behind all of this has been common knowledge for hundreds of years.

For much longer than that, trade across borders has been the foundation of civilisation, creatively repairing the damage caused by war (though war, for all the horrors it inflicts through death, destruction and despoliation, can also be creative, and not only in respect of the technological advances to which it gives birth). Trade, indeed, is the one thing that holds together the interconnectivity of the modern world, and so successful is it that, like many of civilisation's successes in the past, it is now at risk from being taken for granted or regarded as so well established as to be resistant to the thousand natural shocks that flesh is heir to.

It was a surprise to many, for example, that covid-19 disrupted supply chains and continues to affect price inflation and stock shortages, or that Russia's invasion of Ukraine in 2022 prompted a surge in grain prices. We are not good at recognising the importance of trade, or the good that it does, or its vulnerability to the short-termism of politics. In Britain, the prospect that Brexit would see a four-per-cent decline in GNP worried none of the Brexiteer leaders, who behaved as if 'four' was a small number, and as if new opportunities in the Commonwealth, and especially the white Commonwealth, would more than compensate. But four per cent is not a small number in economics, nor have new global opportunities

Wrapping Up

compensated—nor can they. Britain had had a healthy and well-established trading relationship with its nearest neighbours and the rest of the world, and could boast of having the world's fourth largest economy in 2016. Now, thanks to Brexit and its irrational political posturing, the UK economy has slumped to sixth because trade is now more complicated, more costly and less fluid, issues that go unobserved by the emotional fantasists who brought these conditions into being.

Things will more than likely bounce back, however; that is because one of the merits of commerce is that it is inventive and invariably finds ways of circumventing bad politics, though good politics can be thwarted too (in, for example, the exploitation of tax loopholes). In spite of the grain supply problems caused by Russia's grab for Ukraine, and the protectionist and isolationist policies of Donald Trump during his presidency, world trade started to mend itself sooner than many thought possible. As the Economist has pointed out, 'Goods made in China, or by Chinese companies, [are now being] traded via countries like Vietnam, which is already prospering as a result.'[2] The same is true for Russia, where Western efforts to shut down the Russian economy in retaliation for its military adventurism were undermined by black-market arrangements via countries friendly to the West and to the pariah state but allied to neither.

Such a warming of relations with rogue traders was certainly not what was wanted by the West but it may come to have future benefits; it certainly changes the structure of the market. A parallel, during the Second World War, was the way the Italian Mafia assisted the USA in its invasion of Sicily and the Corsican mafia sided with anti-Communists within the

---

[2] https://www.economist.com/the-world-ahead/2023/11/13/an-onslaught-of-protectionism-will-change-global-trade

French Resistance. One cannot always choose one's friends, who may well be the enemy of one's enemy, or simply disinterested neutrals. That's because trade, for better or worse, always has its own agenda: if the government of the People's Republic of China is ever brought down, for example, Chinese trade will be found to have played as active a part in its removal as it currently plays in sustaining it.

Perhaps the most encouraging thing about trade is that it requires a contract, just as democracy requires consensus. To contract with a trading partner means measuring what you can give them against what they can give you. That mutuality is finely calibrated and because of the benefits it can bring, there is always an incentive to conclude a deal.

In addition, historical problems can be worked around. In the case of Britain's colonial past—or the troublesome pasts of any prospective nations—prospective partners who have suffered injury from, say, colonialism can build the cost of reparations into new negotiations, without entering into the innumerate and emotional minefield of morality. Is there a deal to be struck? What are the terms? What can be compromised? Is the other party asking too much? What can we do to win them round?

I was lucky. At an early age, I experienced a society very different from the one I was used to. I had two choices: reject it or try to understand it. I chose the latter, and continued, in my professional life, to be more interested in learning about the societies I interacted with than in condemning them out of hand, and this became my commercial modus operandi. While the companies I worked for were always looking to extend their global reach and make profits for themselves, we had to take a considered view of what would be of mutual benefit to the countries we were seeking to gain entry to. That meant developing an in-depth appreciation of how any particular country worked, the nature of its politics and culture, and what we could contribute to its legitimate long-term goals. It required us to be on the ground, to listen and to be sensitive to what we heard. It meant recognising that the goal was always a win-win contract. It happens that I spent much of my career in tobacco—not looked on kindly, for obvious reasons—but any business set up to become a source of government revenue in a poor and unstable country ought then to prove robust in the face of disruption. It's a matter of intelligence, not imperialism.

We in the West may have lost our confidence in democracy but we should not lose our faith in trade. In a culture of trade, no one and nothing is ever off limits. That is how commerce works—and it does work, though misunderstood and undervalued by so many. It is admirably adaptable, creative, forward-looking, unprejudiced, informed and based on trust. And that is why I vest my faith in it, for the sake of all our futures.

What I would like is for the West to remember this, for what the West forgets is that it is still the most powerful economic bloc and has the ability, through diplomacy and even force, to swat away its self-declared enemies. It has the ability to confront threats to its existence with conviction and to embrace a realpolitik approach to foreign affairs. Instead, it seeks compromises and 'dispute resolution' with societies that threaten its values and that we would all hate to be citizens of. That, I think, is its fundamental weakness: its failure to use trade to bring about justice. The West needs to fight back against extremism, repression and tyranny, and the soft power of trade must be an intrinsic part of how it goes about doing so.

BIBLIOGRAPHY

This selection covers fiction, travel writing, current affairs and history—a mixture of fact and feeling.

Japan
- Christopher Harding, *Japan Story: In Search of a Nation—1850 to the Present*, Allen Lane (2018).
- Haruki Murakami, *The Wind-Up Bird Chronicle*, translated by Jay Rubin, Vintage (1997).
- Yasunari Kawabata, *Snow Country*, Vintage (1996).
- Junichiro Tanazaki, *In Praise of Shadows* (1933). English Translation, Leele's Island Books (1977). New translation, Sora Books (2017)

The three fiction writers provide a window into Japanese sensibilities.

Laos
- Edward A. Gargan, *The River's Tale: A Year on the Mekong*, Vintage (2002).
- Christopher Kremmer, *Stalking the Elephant Kings: In Search of Laos*, Flamingo (1997).
- Christopher Kremmer, *Bamboo Palace: Discovering the Lost Dynasty of Laos*, Flamingo (2003).
- Oden Meeker, *The Little World of Laos*, Charles Scribner's Sons (1959).
- Martin Stuart-Fox, *A History of Laos*, CUP (1997).
- Hugh Toye, *Laos: Buffer State or Battleground*, OUP (1968).

Vietnam
- Bernard Fall, *Street Without Joy: The French Debacle in Indochina*, Stackpole (1961).
- Frances Fitzgerald, *Fire in the Lake: The Vietnamese and Americans in Vietnam*, Backbay Books (1972).

- Christopher Goscha, *The Penguin History of Modern Vietnam*, Penguin (2016).
- Max Hastings, *Vietnam: An Epic Tragedy*, William Collins (2018).
- Duong Thu Huong, *No Man's Land—a novel*, Hyperion East (2015).
- Mark Atwood Lawrence, *The Vietnam War: A Concise International History*, OUP (2010).
- Neil Sheehan, *A Bright Shining Lie: John Paul Vann and America in Vietnam*, Random House (1998).
- Neil Sheehan, *Two Cities: Hanoi and Saigon*, Picador (1992).
- Justin Wintle, *Romancing Vietnam: Inside the Boat Country*, Penguin (1991).
- Gavin Young, *A Wavering Grace: A Vietnamese Family in War and Peace*, Viking (1997).

Many of these books are focused on the Vietnam War but provide a Western perspective and a description of its brutality which frames the narrative. Many have won important awards.

Cambodia
- Francois Bizot, *The Gate*, Vintage (2004)
- Joel Brinkley, *Cambodia's Curse: The Modern History of a Troubled Land*, PublicAffairs (2011)
- Malcolm Caldwell and Lek Tan, 'Cambodia in the Southeast Asian War', *Monthly Review Press* (1973).
- David P. Chandler, *The Tragedy of Cambodian History: Politics, War and Revolution since 1945*, Yale (2008).
- Carol Livingstone, *Gecko Tails: A Journey through Cambodia*, Weidenfeld and Nicholson (1996)—a useful source on the state of Cambodia before and after the UN-monitored elections.

Myanmar
- Christina Fink, *Living Silence in Burma*, 2nd ed., Zed Books (2009).
- Rory Maclean, *Under the Dragon: A Journey Through Burma*, Tauris (2008).
- Thant Myint-U, *The River of Lost Footsteps: A Personal History of Burma*, Faber & Faber (2007)
- George Orwell, *Burmese Days*, Harcourt Brace Jovanovich (1934)
- Benedict Rogers, *Burma: A Nation at the Crossroads*, Rider (2015)
- Pascal Khoo Thwe, *From the Land of Green Ghosts: A Burmese Odyssey*, Harper Collins (2002)

Singapore
- Dennis Bloodworth, *The Tiger and the Trojan Horse*, Times Books international—Singapore (1986).
- Paul Theroux, *Ghost Train to the Eastern Star: On the Track of the Great Railway Bazaar*, Penguin (2009).

Southeast Asia
- Charles Nicholl, *Borderlines: A Journey through Thailand*, Picador (1998)—an account of the hill tribes found in the high margins of Indochina, Myanmar and Thailand.
- John Swain, *River of Time*, Heinemann (1995).
- Alfred W. McCoy, *The Politics of Heroin in Southeast Asia*, Harper Colophon (1973).

Africa
- Chinua Achebe, *Things Fall Apart*, Heinemann (1958).
- Howard W French, *Born in Blackness: Africa, Africans and the Making of the Modern World*, Liveright (2021).
- Ryszard Kapuściński, *The Shadow of the Sun: My African Life*, Allen Lane (2001).

Latin America
- Giaconda Belli, *The Country Under my Skin: A Memoir of Love and War*, Bloomsbury (2002).
- Salman Rushdie, *The Jaguar Smile: A Nicaraguan Journey*, Vintage (2007).
- Brian Keenan and John McCarthy, *Between Extremes*, Transworld Publishers, London (1999).
- Eduardo Galleano, Open Veins of Latin America: Five Centuries of the Pillage of a Continent, Monthly Review Press (1973).
- Pamela Constable and Arturo Alenzuela, *A Nation of Enemies: Chile Under Pinochet*, Norton (1993)
- Matthew Parris, *Inca-Kola: A Traveller's Tale of Peru*, Weidenfeld & Nicholson (1990).
- Andrew Graham-Yooll, *A State of Fear: Memories of Argentina's Nightmare*, Eland (1986).
- Charles Nicholl, *The Fruit Palace*, Heinemann (1995).
- Michael Reid, *The Forgotten Continent: A History of the New Latin America*, Yale UP (2017).

The Soviet Union
- Vasily Grossman, *Life and Fate*, Vintage (2006).
- Vasily Grossman, *Everything Flows*, Vintage (2011)
- Vasily Grossman, *A Writer at War*, Pimlico (2006)—edited by Anthony Beevor.
- Robert Conquest, *The Great Terror: Stalin's Purge of the Thirties*, The Bodley Head (2008 edition).

Russia
- Antony Beevor, *Stalingrad*, Viking (1998).
- Catherine Belton, *Putin's People: How the KGB took back Russia and then took on the West*, Harper Collins (2020).
- Orlando Figes, *Natasha's Dance: A Cultural History of Russia*, Allen Lane (2002).

- Orlando Figes, *A People's Tragedy: The Russian Revolution 1891–1924*, Pimlico (1997).
- David Remnick, *Resurrection: The Struggle for a New Russia*, Random House (1997).
- Simon Sebag Montefiore, *The Romanovs: 1613–1918*, Weidenfeld & Nicolson (2016).
- Colin Thubron, *The Amur River: Between Russia and China*, Chatto & Windus (2021).
- Colin Thubron, *In Siberia*, Chatto & Windus (1999).
- Colin Thubron, *Among the Russians*, Heinemann (1983).

Ukraine
- Serhii Plokhy, *The Last Empire: The Final Days of the Soviet Union*, Basic Books (2014).
- Serhii Plokhy, *The Gates of Europe: A History of Ukraine*, Basic Books (2015).
- Philippe Sands, *East West Street*, Weidenfeld & Nicolson (2016)

Central Asia
- Peter Frankopan, *The Silk Roads: A New History of the World*, Bloomsbury (2015).
- Peter Frankopan, *The New Silk Roads: The Present and the Future of the World*, Bloomsbury (2018).
- Rory Stewart, *The Places in Between*, Picador (2005).
- Colin Thubron, *The Lost Heart of Asia*, Heinemann (1994).
- Colin Thubron, *Shadow of the Silk Road*, Chatto & Windus (2006).

The Caucasus
- Philip Marsden, *The Crossing Place: A Journey among the Armenians*, Harper Collins (1993).
- Philip Marsden, *The Spirit-Wrestlers: A Russian Journey*, Harper Collins (1998).

- Wendell Steavenson, *Stories I Stole*, Atlantic (2002).
- Colin Thubron, *Among the Russians: From the Baltic to the Caucasus*, Vintage (2004).
- Thomas de Waal, *The Caucasus: An Introduction*, OUP (2019).

Middle East
- Ryszard Kapuściński, *Travels with Herodotus*, Random House (2007).
- Jan Morris, *Sultan in Oman*, Faber & Faber (1958), reissued by Eland (2008).
- Jan Morris, *The Hashemite Kings*, Faber & Faber (1959).
- Jeremy Bowen, *The Making of the Modern Middle East*, Picador (2022).
- Tim Mackintosh-Smith, *Arabs: a 3000-year History of Peoples, Tribes and Empires*, Yale (2019).
- Tarek Swelim, *Ibn Tulun: His Lost City and Great Mosque*, American University of Cairo (2015).

ACKNOWLEDGEMENTS

This book had a very long gestation. I began to write a memoir in 2015 and was encouraged by those who read early drafts to keep it at that. As I proceeded, however, I detected patterns across experiences that resonated with my interest in history, politics and human psychology. The eventual draft was a mishmash of all both—memoir and analysis—and far too long. That might have been the end of it had I not learned the wisdom of listening to advice. Others have fashioned this into a book that still does not bore me.

My publisher Dr. Stephen Games was the first to suggest that it had to be one thing or the other. His advice led to a radical rewriting and a much shorter, more focused final version. If I was the builder, he was the architect (and sometimes the hod carrier).

Jamie (Rusty) Ross, my son, was an impartial but supportive critic whose comment that this was now a book of interest to people outside the family encouraged my change of tack.

I have relied on corroborative evidence from many people who were in the places that I describe. John Keary on Japan, Stuart Lane-Fox on Laos, Robert Gordon on Chile, Burma, Vietnam and Cambodia, David Stockley on Chile and Latin America in general, Xavier Durroux, Robert Danloux and Lassiné Diawara on French West Africa, Daniel Einhaüser on Russia and the ex-Soviet Union and Dr Tarek Swelim, whom I thank for his insights on Egypt in particular and the Arab world in general.

I have also benefited from a variety of writers—mostly Western, admittedly—who have looked at my topics through lenses of their own. These were particularly valuable in forming how I dealt with issues such as feminism and slavery but are too many to mention. Thank you all.

INDEX

Notes are indicated by the letter 'n' followed by the note number.

A
Abbasid caliphate 306
Abkhazia 244, 272–3, 274, 280
Abu Dhabi 285, 286, 294
accidents 32–3, 58–9, 207, 209
Achebe, Chinua 117
Addis Ababa 136, 137, 138, 139
Afghan Veterans Association 234
Afghanistan 6, 134, 139, 173, 246, 247, 258, 309, 310, 320
Africa 113–56, 284
    Central 133, 320
    civil wars in 126, 131, 139, 140, 143, 144, 151, 315
    colonisation of 150–3
    corruption in 122, 124, 127–8, 129, 130, 154, 155
    East 135, 292
    economy in 128, 130, 154
    'elite' in 129, 130, 138, 153, 154
    ethnic groups in 118, 119, 130, 138–9
    factories in 127, 130, 131, 133
    Gates Foundation, The 154
    independence 151, 153–6
    investments in 128, 129–30, 134, 139, 141, 153
    land seizures in 145, 146–7, 152–3
    Madagascar 46, 155
    négritude (anti-colonial movement) 131, 151–2
    OAU (Organisation of African Unity) 130
    political systems of 148–56
    Sahel 119, 125–6, 132, 135, 247
    schools in 128, 144, 145
    sub-Saharan 7, 113, 131, 154–5
    Sudan 138, 308
    tobacco business 128–9, 130, 143, 144–7
    West (see French West Africa)
    see also Eritrea; Ethiopia; French West Africa; Mozambique; Nigeria
African(s)
    'black consciousness' 131
    children 124, 137, 144, 152, 154–5
    culture 117, 119, 133, 147, 151, 154
    government 120, 124, 126, 128, 129, 135, 140, 141, 152, 153, 155–6
    history 148–9
    men 125–6, 135, 143, 144, 150
    politics 146, 152, 153
    prejudice about 116–17, 124
    slave trade 121–2, 125–6, 135, 149, 150, 156
    smoking by 128
    society 113–14, 125–6, 135, 147, 152, 156
    tribes 119, 127, 128, 130
    white 146–7
    women 125–6, 135, 140, 145, 150
    see also French West African(s); Nigerian(s)
afterlife 286, 309–10
agriculture 46, 93–4, 153, 155, 249

agronomists 62, 145
aid
　foreign 48, 76, 80, 128, 145, 147, 165, 320
　from Laos 27
　looting of 161
　military 191
　workers 31, 262
alcohol 128, 130, 162, 201, 205, 234, 287
Al-Jazeera (news channel) 295
Al-Qaeda 126
American(s)
　in Cambodia 74–5
　in Laos 23–4, 25, 26, 31, 35
　in Nicaragua 169, 171, 172
　in the Philippines 108
　in Russia 220, 232
　in Vietnam 55, 60, 61, 65, 264
Amman 296, 299
Amnesty International report 166, 167, 176
Angkor Wat 71, 72–3, 85
Animists 118, 138
Arab Spring 299, 309, 311
Arab states 284–95
　government 288
　homosexuality in 293
　oil wealth 285, 290, 294–5
　Oman 149, 290–4, 295, 311–12
　political systems of 294–5
　Saudi Arabia 6, 104, 286, 288–9, 294, 295, 301
　workplace 287, 288–9, 290–2
Arabian Peninsula 149, 283, 285–6, 290, 295
　see also Bahrain; Jordan; Kuwait; Oman; Qatar; Saudi Arabia; UAE (United Arab Emirates)
Arabic (language) 283–4, 285, 290, 295, 297, 307, 309, 311
Arabs 272, 283, 285, 288–9, 294–5
Argentina 160, 180, 192
　Guevara, Che (revolutionary) 192
　Peronism 192
Armenia 244, 247, 266, 268, 269, 271, 272, 274–80
Armenians 272, 275–6, 277–8
army/armies 128, 293
　Chinese 24, 95
　mercenary 173–4, 278
　Pathet Lao 25, 30–2, 35, 37, 38, 47
　Red 248
　Tatmadaw 83, 84, 92–3, 95–6
　Vietnamese 55, 55n1, 65
　White 248
arrests 75, 83, 89, 90–1, 107, 179–80, 181, 193, 232
Artsakh 244, 276, 277–8
　see also Nagorno-Karabakh
ASEAN (Association of Southeast Asian Nations) 89
Asmara 139, 141
assassinations 76, 121, 163, 166–7, 174, 203, 223, 231
Australians 23, 24, 42
Austrians 248, 261, 265
autocracy/autocrats
　in Belarus 254, 255–6
　in Burma 83
　in Cambodia 74, 75
　in Central Asia 279
　in the Middle East 293, 308, 309–10, 311

in Nicaragua 174
in Russia 199–200, 206, 212, 218
in Singapore 97–8
in Tunisia 155n4, 319
Azerbaijan 244, 265–70, 271, 275, 277, 279, 303
　Aliyev, Heydar (President) 279
　Aliyev, Ilham (President) 267
Azeris 257, 266, 269, 274, 275, 276–7, 278, 280

B

Bahrain 286, 290, 295
Baku 164, 257, 267, 268
Bangkok 22, 25, 28, 36–7, 39, 40, 52, 66, 84
Bangladesh 92
bank(s)/banking 29, 266, 320
　bankers 19, 227, 231
　crisis 227–8, 230
　loans 227, 228
　looting of reserves 161
　notes 47, 67, 87, 120, 166, 171
BAT (British American Tobacco) 50, 316
　in Latin America 159, 166, 169, 176, 185
　in Myanmar 84, 86, 88
　in Singapore 39, 100–1, 103, 104
BBC (British Broadcasting Corporation) 107, 152
　Buerk, Michael (journalist) 153
Beijing 60, 81, 103
Beirut 179, 299, 304, 306, 309
Belarus 242, 254–6
　Lukashenko, Alexander (President) 254, 255

Shushkevich, Stanislav (politician) 242
Belli, Giaconda 162–3, 168, 173–4
Benin 114, 121, 124, 149n1
betrayal 200, 219, 233, 278
Bion, Wilfred 6–7
Bishkek 257, 261, 262
Bizot, François 78
Black Sea 217, 251, 252, 272–3
Black Lives Matter 151, 192
black(s) 7n3, 15, 23, 24, 131, 146, 151, 152, 188
Boko Haram 126
Bolivia 191, 192
bombs/bombing 39, 168, 243, 297, 299
bottling plants (Cola) 24, 136, 137–8, 140–1, 159, 221–3, 228, 316
Brazil 160, 191, 192
bribe/bribery 155, 219–20, 221, 269, 320
Bribery Act (2010) 102, 319
Brinkley, Joel 74
Britain 99, 165, 189, 307, 324
　Africans in 149, 152
　Arabs in 288
　Brexit 321, 322–3
　economy 97
　refugees in 232, 266
　removal of the sultan in Oman 292–3
　vagrancy 183
　see also UK/United Kingdom
British, the 25, 106, 267n7
　attitude to former colonies 126–7
　in Burma 87, 108
　in Chile 178, 179
　Consulate 171, 285

Embassy 37, 42
  in Oman 292–3
Brothers Karamazov, The 212
Buddha 71, 86n2
Buddhism/Buddhist(s) 34, 47, 73, 86–7, 89
Burma 27, 43, 49, 82–94, 106, 108
  economy 83, 84
  Indian immigrants in 83, 94
  military rule in 82–4
  name change to Myanmar 82
  Ne Win (President) 83–4
  Tatmadaw army 83, 84, 92–3, 95–6
  see also Myanmar
Burmese/Burmans 82, 89–94
  government 82, 84, 90, 94
  kings 83–4
  society 86–7

C

Cairo 294, 306, 307
Cambodia 27, 51, 68, 71–81, 95, 271, 320
  Angkor Wat 71, 72–3, 85
  Chartres Cathedral 72–3
  Chau Doc 79–80
  economy 74–5
  elections 76, 81
  holocaust 75–6, 77
  Hun, Sen (Prime Minister) 74, 75, 76, 79, 80, 81
  Khmer Rouge (Communist Party of Kampuchea) 27, 71, 75–80
  killing fields/Choeung Ek 76, 77, 78
  Norodom, Sihamoni (King) 75
  Norodom, Sihanouk (King/Prime Minister) 75
  Pol Pot regime 51, 76
  prison 76–8, 105
  religion 73
  Siem Reap 45, 71–2
  temples 71–3
  Tonle Sap 73
  tourists in 71–5, 77–8
  Tuol Sleng Museum of Genocide 76–7, 78
  see also Phnom Penh
Cambodian(s)
  children 72, 77
  government 71, 74, 78–80
  kings 71, 73, 75, 80
  peasants 74, 77, 79
  prisoners 77, 78
  society 74–5, 79, 80–1
Cambodia's Curse: The Modern History of a Troubled Land 74
campesinos (peasant farmers) 167, 174, 191
capitalism 183, 207, 286
  crony 44, 104
  in Kyrgyzstan 264–5
  in Laos 44
  in Nicaragua 160, 161, 174
  in Russia 207
  in the United States 317
  in Vietnam 63–4, 69
Caribbeans 151, 152, 165
Caspian Sea 208, 217, 265, 267–8, 272
Catholicism 159, 284
Caucasus, the 216, 245, 265, 271–80
  ethnicities/ethnic groups 275, 279
  history 271–2
  independence 271–2, 279
  politics 271, 272, 278–80

religion 271, 272, 276
Russia's influence on 244,
    271–3, 275, 277, 279–80
see also Armenia; Azerbaijan;
    Georgia
Central America 159, 160, 164–7,
    191, 192, 193
see also Nicaragua
Central Asia 141, 216, 245, 257–70,
    279, 303
    Communism in 257–8, 260
    ethnicities 257, 258, 259–60
    horsemen 263–4
    Islam in 258–9, 260, 262, 284
    mountains 258, 263–4, 266
    oil wealth 267–8, 269–70
    workers 260, 262, 264–5
    see also Azerbaijan; Kyrgyzstan
Chechnya 206, 242–3
child/children
    African 124, 137, 144, 152, 154–5
    Burmese 94
    Cambodian 72, 77
    Lao 22, 28–9
    Nicaraguan 170
    Singaporean 100
    Vietnamese 52, 55–6, 68, 80
Chile 159, 176–90, 194
    Alessandri, Jorge (President) 187
    Allende, Salvador (President) 176, 178, 179, 180, 181, 183, 184, 186, 187, 315–16
    Aylwin, Patricio (President) 181
    Bachelet, Michelle (President) 188
    Boric, Gabriel (President) 190
    curfew in 185
    democracy in 180–1, 183, 186, 187, 190
    economy in 178, 180, 183–5, 192, 321
    elections 187, 190
    military coup 176, 178–80
    Neruda, Pablo (Communist poet) 186
    Piñera, Sebastiàn (President) 186, 190
    Pinochet, Augusto (President) 176, 177, 178–84, 185–7, 190
    plebiscite 186
    professional stint in 176–7, 185, 189
    Tercera, La (newspaper) 186, 188
    see also Santiago
Chilean(s)
    in Africa 137
    attitudes 188
    Communists 181, 183, 186
    coup victims 178–80
    government 183–4, 186, 190
    men 188–9
    police 179, 185, 187
    politics 185–7, 190
    society 177–8, 180, 181, 183
    women 178, 188–9
China 6, 94, 108, 201, 212, 324
    border sharing with Laos 27, 49
    and Cambodia 76
    Deng, Xiaoping (revolutionary and statesman) 104
    economy 104
    Mao, Zedong (President) 76
    on Myanmar military coup 95
    PLA (People's Liberatio Army) 103–4
    tobacco import into 103–4

and Vietnam 61, 69, 323
Yunnan (province) 48, 69
Chinese, the 24, 27, 240
in Africa 133–4, 145
army 24, 95
Communist Party 76
entrepreneurs 104, 145
government 324
influence in Laos 44, 47, 48
investors 88, 95
rail projects 48, 134
in Singapore 97, 100, 101, 106
in Vietnam 60, 63, 69
Chomsky, Noam 18
Christianity 138, 271, 273
Christians 118, 251, 272, 275–6, 278, 294, 299
churches 141, 165, 206, 213, 232, 234, 251
CIA (Central Intelligence Agency) 171, 172, 173, 186
cigarettes 103, 128, 218, 234, 235, 296, 301
civil rights 151, 266
civil service 20, 37, 126, 274
civil war(s)
in Africa 126, 131, 139, 140, 143, 144, 151, 315
in Burma 83
Chechen 279
in Colombia 191
in Lebanon 304
in Nicaragua 163, 172, 173, 174
in Spain 180, 182
in Tajikistan 260
civilian deaths 83, 95–6, 179, 180, 182, 191, 208
civilisation 6, 152, 257, 258, 322
Clayton Act (1914) 317

Coca-Cola
bottling 136, 137–8, 140–1, 159, 221–3, 228, 316
company (see TCCC (the Coca-Cola Company))
in Eritrea 139, 140–1, 316–17
in Ethiopia 136–8
O'Neill, Michael (manager) 198, 202, 207, 221, 222
in Russia 198, 207, 221–3, 226, 228
in Vietnam 53
Cold War 194, 247
collectivisation 46, 249, 254, 263
Colombia 191, 194, 269
colonialism/colonial rule/
colonisation 60, 64, 108, 139, 150–1, 152–3, 156, 324
Comecon, the 201, 230, 242
Commonwealth, the 126, 322
communal behaviour 6–7
Communism
in Belarus 255
in Cambodia 75, 81
in Central Asia 257–8, 260
collapse of 5, 7, 102, 211, 220
in Laos 31, 37, 38, 42, 46
in Latin America 160, 183
in Russia 213, 231
in Vietnam 51, 65, 68, 69
Communist(s) 25, 37, 254, 260, 310
anti- 323–4
British 179
in Central Asia 257–8
Chilean 181, 183, 186
Chinese 76
flags 46, 68, 95
ideology 46–7
Italian 218

régimes 69, 178
Soviet 201
states 42, 46, 51, 81
in Ukraine 251
Conquest, Robert 199–200
Constable, Pamela 181
consumer goods 20, 144
corruption
    action against 102–3
    in Africa 122, 124, 127–8, 129, 130, 154, 155
    in Cambodia 71, 79–80
    in China 104
    in Japan 20
    in Jordan 301–2
    in Laos 47
    in Latin America 160–1, 165, 176, 187, 193
    in Russia 209–10, 219–20, 232, 240
Cossacks 217, 244, 248, 250
Costa Rica 165, 167, 171, 192
coup 160, 172n3, 185
    in Cambodia 75
    in Chile 176, 178–80
    in Ethiopia 136
    in Liberia 151
    military 95, 127, 130, 135, 176, 178–80
    in Myanmar 95
courts 33, 97, 219, 231
Covid-19 69, 312, 322
CPIB (Corrupt Practices Investigation Bureau) 102–3
Crimea 244, 245, 250, 251, 252, 253, 254
crime(s) 103, 107, 149–50, 193, 232
    in Cambodia 77, 78
    in Chile 181–2, 183
    against humanity 78, 181–2, 183
    in Japan 21
    in Nicaragua 165
culture(s) 6, 97, 148, 315, 325
    African 117, 119, 133, 147, 151, 154
    chasm/difference/gap in 14, 117, 119, 133
    Hispanic 189
    Japanese 12–14, 17–18, 20, 21
    Lao 47–9, 80
    Latin American 176
    Middle Eastern 284, 302–3, 309–10, 311
    Russian 210–11, 246–7
    Singaporean 100, 102, 106
    Vietnamese 63, 66, 69–70
customs (duty) 22–3, 43, 89, 130, 131, 172, 197, 219
Cyprus 41, 305
Czechoslovakia 249

D

Daesh (militant group) 135
Death and the Maiden 180
deference 13, 85, 98, 297
democracy/democracies 202, 226, 311, 324, 325
    dictatorship and 180–1, 183
    genuine 66, 186, 187, 190
    liberal 21, 59, 74, 108, 156, 194, 241, 253, 257
    multi-party 79
    pluralist 192
    protests for 83, 84
    sham 84, 94–5, 177–8, 192
    Western 5, 190, 279
deportations 83, 179, 276
dictatorship(s)/dictators 127, 160, 192, 233, 256, 320
    in Azerbaijan 266, 269

in Burma 82–4
in Chile 180–1
in Egypt 316
in Guinea 129
in Iraq 310
diplomacy 6, 7, 242, 295, 325
dissent 93, 233, 245, 255, 310
Dorfman, Ariel 180
Dostoevsky, Fyodor 212
drug trade 21, 95, 135, 166, 169, 191, 193, 244
see also heroin; opium
Dubai 286, 287, 289, 294, 295, 301
Dutch, the 108, 121–2
Dyer, Geoff 72

E

East Asia 11–109
Mekong (river) 22, 25, 32, 33, 38, 39, 40, 42, 52, 66, 73, 74
political systems of 108–9
see also Cambodia; Japan; Laos; Myanmar; Singapore; Vietnam
economic growth
in Africa 131, 138
in East Asia 21, 84, 97–8, 99
in Latin America 186
populism vs. 321
in Russia 224, 226, 230, 239
economy
bubble 226, 227
cash 29
dirigiste 19, 69, 97, 239
market 51, 94, 209–10, 262
see also economy under individual countries
Ecuador 159, 191

education
in Africa 131, 152
in East Asia 48, 94
in Jordan 297
in Latin America 174, 183
re- 37, 65
in Russia 197, 209, 246
in Saudi Arabia 288
in USSR 211
Egypt 138, 149, 294, 295, 301, 303, 306–9, 312, 316
Morsi, Mohamed (President) 308
mosque 306–7
Mubarak, Hosni (President) 301, 308
Nasser, Gamal Abdel (President) 308
Paşa, Ahmed Fuad (Sultan/King) 307–8
el-Sisi, Abdel Fattah (President) 308
Tulun, Ahmad ibn (Tulunid dynasty founder) 306–7
Egyptians 307, 308, 311
El Salvador 165
election(s)
in Azerbaijan 266
in Cambodia 76, 81
in Costa Rica 167
free 20, 97
in Japan 20
in Latin America 174, 187, 190, 192, 194
in Myanmar 89, 91
in Russia 202, 233
in Singapore 97
in Ukraine 253
electorate 5, 190, 194, 233, 252
elite/élite, the 95, 311

in Africa 129, 130, 138, 153, 154
in Central Asia 260, 270
in Japan 12
in Latin America 165, 174, 183, 187, 191
military 88, 306
in Russia 211, 216, 224, 228, 231, 240
embassies 36, 37, 42, 50, 52, 169, 198, 278
emirs 119, 120, 295, 308
employment 19, 21, 126, 127, 145, 220, 223
England 28, 115, 169, 238, 292
English (language)
in Cambodia 79
in Japan 14, 15, 16, 17, 18
in Laos 33
in the Middle East 291, 296–7
in Nicaragua 165
in Nigeria 116, 122
in Russia 219
in Singapore 104, 106
in Vietnam 56, 58, 60, 64–5
entrepreneur(s)/entrepreneurship
Chinese 104, 145
Latin American 165, 185
Russian 225, 227, 247
Vietnamese 67
equality 70, 194, 223, 310
Eritrea 113, 138–42, 316–17
Afwerki, Isaias (President) 141, 316
Aseb 141–2
Massawa 140, 141–2
Ethiopia 113, 136–42, 153–4
Ahmed, Abiy (Prime Minister) 138–9, 142
Mariam, Mengistu Haile (President) 136

Selassie, Haile (Emperor) 138
ethnicity/ethnicities/ethnic groups
in Africa 118, 119, 130, 138–9
in Burma 93–4 (*see also* Myanmar, Rohingya crisis)
in the Caucasus 275, 279
in Central Asia 257, 258, 259–60
conflicts 242–4, 261, 275
in Laos 45
see also tribes
EU (European Union) 6, 189, 202, 230, 239, 319
Europe 132, 142, 146, 218, 305
bottling lines in 223
Caucasus mountain range 271
Central 230, 248
colonisation in 150, 151
Eastern 230, 243–7, 287
Moldova 243, 244
opposition to the USSR 246
Western 237
Europeans 149, 174, 270, 287
executions 50, 77, 180, 199–200
exile 79, 180, 185, 216, 231, 247
expatriates
in Chile 186
in French West Africa 126, 127, 131–2, 133
in Japan 16–17
in Kyrgyzstan 262
in Laos 37, 42
in the Middle East 286
in Nicaragua 161, 164–5, 167–73
in Nigeria 117, 121
in Russia 224–5, 228

in Singapore 98, 99–100
see also foreigners
exploitation 149, 150, 174, 323
export(s) 123, 144–5, 149, 185, 208, 294
extortion 154, 231, 320

F

factory/factories
 in Africa 127, 130, 131, 133
 in Armenia 275
 in Chile 185
 in Kyrgyzstan 261–2, 264
 in Laos 39–40
 in Nicaragua 173
 in Russia 200, 207, 209, 218, 234, 236
 in Singapore 98, 99, 100, 103
 in Vietnam 54, 61
farmers
 peasant 80, 167, 193 (see also peasant(s)/peasantry)
 subsistence 48, 93–4, 147, 155
 tobacco 145–7
 white 146–7
fascism 233, 245
fatalism 81, 225, 230, 278
FCPA (Foreign Corrupt Practices Act) 102, 319
feudalism 14, 16, 119, 287, 295, 311, 312
Figes, Orlando 211, 212
financial crisis 5, 7
financiers 98, 232, 248, 276
Finland 50, 98
First World War 192, 248, 276, 307
food 37, 85, 137, 164
 lack/shortage 178, 184, 208, 247
 in the Middle East 298–9
 in Nigeria 116–17, 121
 in Singapore 99, 101
 in Vietnam 59, 67
foreigners 5, 20, 238, 316
 in Eritrea 139–41
 in Ethiopia 136–8
 in Japan 14–17, 18, 21
 in Kyrgyzstan 262, 264
 in Laos 22, 23–4, 25, 27, 28, 31–2, 40–1, 49
 in the Middle East 287, 304–5, 307
 in Myanmar 85–7
 in Russia 202, 208, 215, 219, 225, 226, 233
 in Singapore 98
 in Vietnam 51–60
 see also expatriates; tourists
forests 46, 148, 155, 254, 256
France 121, 129, 183, 312
 Bonaparte, Napoleon (Emperor) 217, 307
free-market principles 19, 193, 202, 220, 321
free press 20, 91, 92, 181, 187, 271
free speech 107, 246
freedom 63, 91, 94–5, 109, 197, 244, 252, 271, 272, 279, 288–9
 see also independence
French, Howard W. 150
French, the 108, 150, 212, 237, 324
 attitude to former colonies 126–7
 in Laos 23, 26, 30–1, 34, 39, 40, 45, 47–8
 in Nigeria 121
 in Vietnam 60

French West Africa 125–35, 151–2
  Bloomberg Foundation 128–9
  Burkina Faso 127–9
  cities 125–6, 131, 132
  Côte d'Ivoire 127, 131–2, 315
  Diawara, Lassiné (board president) 127–8, 132, 133, 134
  economy 128, 130
  expatriates 126, 127, 131–3
  Guinea 127, 128, 129–31
  mineral wealth 128, 129–30, 133–4
  professional stint in 125, 130, 131–2, 133
  Senegal 131, 132–3, 152
  Senghor, Léopold Sédar (Senegalese President) 151–2
  tobacco products 128–9, 130
French West African(s)
  government 126, 128, 129, 135
  men 125–6, 135
  society 135
  women 125–6, 135
FSB (Federal Security Bureau) 206, 206n4, 222, 224, 235
Fukuyama, Francis 5, 226

G

gaols *see prisons*
gas 239, 252, 255–6
Georgia 244, 247, 271, 272–5, 278, 279–80
  Gamsakhurdia, Zviad (President) 274
  Saakashvili, Mikheil (President) 273, 274
Germans 244, 249

Germany 221, 234, 247
  Hitler, Adolf (Nazi dictator) 199, 217, 245
Gostandart 200, 213, 221
government(s) 6, 19, 108, 153, 155–6, 310, 311, 318
  Arabian 288
  Azerbaijani 267
  Burmese 82, 84, 90, 94
  coalition 32, 36
  Cambodian 71, 74, 78–80
  Chinese 324
  Egyptian 301
  Eritrean 140, 141
  federal 119, 317
  French West African 126, 128, 129, 135
  Georgian 274
  Kyrgyz 262
  Lao 32, 36, 39, 40, 42, 44, 45, 46–8, 317
  Latin American 167, 183–4, 186, 190, 192, 193, 194
  Lebanese 305
  Mozambiqan 143, 146, 147
  Nigerian 120, 124, 152
  revenue 48, 62, 128, 325
  Russian 200, 203, 221, 227, 231, 252
  Singaporean 97–8, 103, 104, 107
  Transnistrian 243–4
  Ukrainian 252, 253
  US 166, 172, 173–4
  Vietnamese 62, 67, 69, 317
  Western 5, 319
governors 14, 207, 222–3, 243
Great Terror, The: Stalin's Purge of the Thirties 199–200
Greeks 149, 272

Greene, Graham 50, 169
Grossman, Vasily 197, 200, 205
'groups without purpose' 6–7
guerrilla(s) 141, 173, 301
Guinea 127, 128, 129–31
    Condé, Alpha (President) 129–31
gunfire 32, 33, 83, 168, 169
guns 124, 163, 169, 170

H

haram (forbidden) 126, 288, 293, 310
Hastings, Max 60, 69
haves and have-nots 159, 183, 187–8
heroin 24, 43, 265
hierarchy/hierarchies
    in Africa 147
    in Japan 12–15, 18, 20
    in the Middle East 284, 295
    in Russia 212–13, 246
    in Spain 159
    in Vietnam 63, 69
    zonia 93
History of Laos, A 25
Ho Chi Minh City 50, 51–2, 53, 61
    see also Saigon
holocaust 75–6, 276
Hong Kong 27, 103–4, 106, 108
housing 66, 99, 167, 183, 294, 297
human rights 154, 183, 232, 246, 248
humanity 7, 78, 113–14, 181–2

I

illiteracy 38, 136, 153, 187, 212, 301
imams 284, 288, 309
immigrants 17, 83, 192, 290
immigration 89, 93, 155n4, 172, 197–8, 289, 321
Imperial Tobacco 40, 125, 230, 234, 237, 266, 316
imperialism 75, 115, 242, 264, 286, 292, 325
import(s) 27, 103–4, 145, 184, 214, 234, 255, 268, 294, 316
    duties 128, 130, 181
impoverishment 83, 153, 210
imprisonment/prisoners 77, 78, 90, 92, 166–7, 231–2
In Praise of Shadows 19
Inchcape 104, 136, 137, 159, 220
inclusion 18, 43
independence 108, 153, 242
    of the Caucasus 271–2, 279
    Central Asia upon 259, 265
    of Comecon states 242
    of Eritrea 140
    Latin America upon 159, 191
    Myanmar upon 90–1, 95
    Nigeria post- 148
    Singapore at 98
    of Ukraine 251–2
    of Vietnam 50
    see also freedom
India 6, 16, 87, 150, 258, 292, 306
Indian(s) 191, 192
    East Asian 35, 83, 94, 97, 106, 152, 206, 286
Indochina 22, 27, 39, 50, 51, 71, 80–1, 108
    see also Cambodia; Laos; Vietnam
Indonesia 108, 113, 172n3, 284
inflation 183–4, 260, 322
infrastructure 48, 89, 147, 153, 165, 223, 226

invaders 208, 217, 271–2, 276, 277, 310
invasion(s) 108, 217, 256, 310
    of Afghanistan 247
    of Cambodia 51, 76
    of the Caucasus 271–2
    of Iraq 247
    in Laos 30, 38, 48
    of Sicily 323
    of Ukraine 240–1, 245, 246, 247, 251, 322
investment(s) 5, 262, 307, 316
    in Africa 128, 129–30, 134, 139, 141, 153
    army's control of 95–6
    in East Asia 20, 40, 47, 54, 66, 87–8, 98, 99
    foreign 40, 87–8, 129, 140, 227, 255
    inward 66, 130, 203, 305
    in Latin America 183–4
    in Russia 198–9, 203, 218–19, 226, 227
investors 95, 130
    Chinese 133–4
    foreign 86, 129, 202, 232, 262
    Western 88, 133, 207, 218
Iran 266–7, 271, 294, 295, 301, 309
    Pahlavi (Shah) 267, 310
Iraq 6, 247, 294, 301, 302, 306, 320
    Hussein, Saddam (President) 310
Islam
    in Central Asia 258–9, 260, 262, 284
    in French West Africa 126
    fundamentalism/extremism 260, 269, 309–10

Hezbollah (Islamist political party) 304, 305
Islamists 260, 310
    in the Middle East 283–6, 295, 297–8, 309, 311
    radical 286, 301
    see also Muslim(s)
Islamic states 296–312
    Egypt 138, 149, 294, 295, 301, 303, 306–9, 312, 316
    Jordan 288, 295, 296–303, 306, 311, 312
    Lebanon 179, 303–6
    political systems of 309–12
isolationist policies 83–4, 323
Israel 283, 294, 296, 305, 308, 310
Italians 139, 192, 218, 323
Italy 237, 239, 280

J
Jaguar Smile, The: A Nicaraguan Journey 163
Japan 11–21, 98, 108, 216, 235
    burakumin (underclass) 16
    a collectivist society 13, 20
    crimes in 21
    daimyo (feudal system) 14, 16
    economy 19–21
    elections 20
    gaijin (foreigners) 14–17, 18, 21
    hierarchical system 12–15, 18, 20
    Liberal Democratic Party 20
    MacArthur, Douglas (American military governor, Japan) 14
    marriages in 11, 13, 14, 17

misogyny 13–15, 21
MITI (Ministry of International Trade and Industry) 19
social life 11–12, 14–17
ugliness in 18–19
Yakuza gangs 21
zaibatsu (mega-companies) 19
see also Tokyo
Japanese (language) 17–18
Japanese, the
    art and literature 19
    culture 12–14, 17–18, 20, 21
    men 12–16
    society 11–12, 13, 14–16, 20, 21
    'tent' 16, 20, 21
    women 12, 13–16, 21, 216
    youth 13
Jews 138, 233, 247, 248–9, 251, 275–6, 278, 294
jihadism 135, 243, 286
joint ventures 18, 39, 87, 202, 220, 232, 315
Jordan 288, 295, 296–303, 306, 311, 312
journalists 92, 153, 240
Judah, Tim 252
judiciary 47, 181, 233
    independent 20, 91, 187, 271

K

Kalashnikovs (rifles) 35, 43
Kapuściński, Ryszard 242, 257, 259
Kazakhs 257, 259
Kazakhstan 265, 269
    Tretchikoff, Vladimir (artist) 213
Keenan, Brian 179

Kiev 249, 250, 252, 253–4
Kievan Rus 250, 255
king(s)/kingdom(s)
    Belgian 152
    Burmese 83–4
    Cambodian 71, 73, 75, 80
    Lao 42, 45–6, 47–8
    Middle Eastern 285, 286, 295, 308, 312
    Nigerian 121
Koran 284, 285, 309
Kremlin 223, 233, 240, 247, 253
Kurds 7, 301
Kuwait 294, 295
Kyrgyz 257, 259, 262, 264, 265
Kyrgyzstan 260, 261–5, 303

L

labour 65, 94, 220, 321
    camps 199–200
    Chinese 134
    foreign/imported 191, 265
    immigrant 17, 290
    indentured 286
    in Latin America 165, 181, 191, 192
    slave 150
Lagos 113–14, 119, 120, 123
land seizures/land grabbing 145, 146–7, 152–3
Lao
    children 22, 28–9
    culture 47–9, 80
    ethnicities 44, 45
    government 32, 36, 39, 40, 42, 44, 45, 46–8, 317
    royal family 30, 42, 45–6
    trait 43
    values 32–4, 34n3, 48
    women 30, 36, 41, 45

young/youth 25, 30, 33, 41
Laos 22–49, 68, 201, 264
  baci ceremony 36, 38, 43, 45
  bombing 39
  buildings 30–1, 32
  a cash economy 29
  Chinese influence in 44, 47, 48
  Communist control in 31, 37, 38, 42, 46
  foreigners in 22, 23–4, 25, 27, 28, 31–2, 40–1, 49
  forest 46
  French influence in 23, 30–1, 47–8
  Lang Xang kingdom ('a million elephants') 47–8
  liberation and parade 35–6
  living experience 30–4, 37–9
  Luang Prabang (city) 31, 43, 44–6, 47
  oil import 26–7
  Pathet Lao (Lao People's Liberation Army) 25, 30–2, 35, 37, 38, 47
  Phomvihane, Kaysone (President) 25, 47
  religion 34, 48
  revisit to 40–6
  royalist regime 22–3, 24, 33, 35, 37
  Six Click City 25, 37
  social life 27, 33, 34–5
  streets 23, 31, 37
  Talat Sao (morning market) 24, 31, 33, 35, 37
  That Luang (monument) 30, 35, 46
  tobacco business 39–40, 316
  travellers in 22–5, 31
  work in 25–9
  see also Vientiane
Latin America 50, 159–94, 210
  see also Chile; Nicaragua
Lebanese 296, 304, 309
Lebanon 179, 303–6
Lewis, C.S. 6, 107
Lewis, Norman 34n3, 81n10, 95n6
liberation 27, 35, 77
Liberia 151
Libya 6, 308, 310, 319
Life and Fate 205
London 15, 38, 59, 101, 116, 181, 198, 222, 238, 298, 299
loyalty 147, 153, 199, 200, 249, 310

M

McCarthy, John 179
Mackintosh-Smith, Tim 285, 297
Madrid 159, 189
mafia 323–4
Malaysia 22, 97, 105, 108, 269
Mamluks 307, 308
Managua 159, 161, 164, 168, 171, 172, 177
manufacturing 66, 309, 322
market(s)
  black 130, 315, 323
  economy 51, 94, 209–10, 262
  free 19, 47, 59, 193, 202, 220, 224, 321
  open 184
marriage(s)
  arranged 64, 268
  inter- 260
  Islamic 293, 309
  in Japan 11, 13, 14, 17

in Laos 33
in the Middle East 293, 296, 309
in Myanmar 94
in Nicaragua 162
in the West 14
martyrs 176, 286, 309–10
Marxism 69, 197, 199, 286
Marxism-Leninism 44, 63, 286, 320
massacres 217, 249, 260, 276
Mecca 285
men
    African 125–6, 135, 143, 144, 150
    Arabian 288, 289
    Chilean 188–9
    Japanese 12–16
    Nicaraguan 162
    Russian 205–6, 209, 223–4
    Vietnamese 55, 56, 62
Mensheviks 199
mercenaries 135, 307, 308
metro (rail) 12, 67, 201, 210, 211, 225, 236
Mexico 160, 165–6, 191
middle class, the
    educated 266–7
    Latin American 161, 163, 165, 167, 174, 177, 188, 191
    liberals 311
    Russian 225, 228
Middle East, the 149, 265, 283–312
    Arab states 284–95
    autocracy/autocrats in 293, 308, 309–10, 311
    culture 284, 302–3, 309–10, 311
    foreigners in 287, 304–5, 307
    government 288, 301, 305, 310, 311
    Islam in 283–6, 295, 297–8, 309, 311
    Islamic states 296–312
    kings/kingdoms 285, 286, 295, 308, 312
    language 283–4, 285, 290, 295, 297, 307, 309, 311
    marriages in 293, 296, 309
    Muslims 283, 294, 301, 308, 309
    oil wealth 285, 290, 294–5
    politics 283, 284, 308
    religion 283–6, 295, 297–8, 303, 308, 309, 311
    slaves in 292, 306, 307
    work in 287, 288–9, 290–2, 296–303
    see also Arabian Peninsula; Egypt; Iran; Iraq; Türkiye
migrants 142, 319
military 14, 65, 187, 316
    coup 95, 127, 130, 135, 176, 178–80
    dictatorship 82, 83, 129
    French 126
    Lao 35–6, 37
    Myanmar 82–3, 84, 88, 89, 91–2, 93, 95, 96
    Russian 208, 217, 218, 230, 243, 244, 246, 247, 253, 272, 277, 323
    Thai 32
    Ukrainian 245
minorities 90, 93–4, 138, 190, 242, 244, 251, 252, 279
Minsk 217, 256
misogyny 13–15, 21, 146, 176, 224, 285, 287

monarchy 46, 307–8, 311–12
Mongols 203, 272
morality 303, 318, 319, 324
Morocco 303, 308, 311–12
    Mohammed VI (King) 295, 312
Morris, Jan 292
Morrison, Toni 7, 7n3
Moscow 60, 81, 201, 213, 214, 217, 237, 238, 259, 280
    the destitute in 210
    economic growth in 224, 230
    liveability in 225–6
    Music Academy 211
    Nagorno-Karabakh allocation to Azerbaijan 277
    and Ukraine 245–6, 249, 250, 251–3
Mozambique 143–7
Muscat 293
music 32, 36, 37, 136, 153–4, 211
    musicians 138–9, 181
Muslim(s)
    in Azerbaijan 266, 269
    Brotherhood 301, 308
    in Ethiopia 138
    in Georgia 274, 279
    language of 283
    in the Middle East 283, 294, 301, 308, 309
    in Nigeria 118
    in Russia 216–17, 233, 242–3
    Shia 259, 284, 294, 301, 310
    Sunni 259, 284, 294, 301, 310
Myanmar 82–96, 317, 320
    army's control over economy 83, 92, 95–6
    Aung San Suu Kyi (Former State Counsellor) 82, 89, 91–2, 96
    buildings 85, 87, 89
    business investment in 85–8
    coup 95
    economy 94, 95–6
    elections 89, 91
    ethnic minorities 90, 93–4
    Mandalay 90, 92, 95
    military 82–3, 84, 88, 89, 91–2, 93, 95, 96
    a pariah state 82, 87
    prison 90
    professional stint in 84–8
    Rohingya crisis 82, 92, 94–5
    a sham democracy 84, 94–5
    Shwedagon pagoda 86–7, 86n2
    SLORC (State Law and Order Restitution Committee) 84
    tobacco industry 84, 86, 88
    tourists in 86–7, 89–91, 94–5
    see also Burma

N

Nagorno-Karabakh 244, 266, 276–7, 280
nation state 7, 13, 97, 249, 306
nationalism 181, 230, 233, 254, 261, 265
nationalists 216, 248, 250, 252, 260
Nazis 77, 246, 248, 249
Netherlands 27
newspapers 79, 81, 107, 162, 166–7, 186, 188
NGOs 74, 154, 318
Nicaragua 159, 160–75, 177, 315
    capitalism in 160, 161, 174
    Chamorro, Pedro Joaquim Cardenal (journalist) 166–7

Chamorro, Violetta (President) 174
'contras' in 173–4
corruption in 160–1, 165
cricket matches 164–5, 171
earthquake 161
elections 174
expatriates in 161, 164–5, 167–73
neighbouring countries 164–6
Ortega, Daniel (President) 174, 175, 194
Prensa, La (newspaper) 166–7, 174
Sandinistas in 162–4, 168, 172, 173, 174–5, 315
Sandino, Augusto César (revolutionary) 163, 173
Somoza Debayle, Anastasio (President) 160–3, 166–7, 169, 170, 172
an uncongenial country 161–2, 167–8
US involvement in 160–1, 166, 172, 173–4
weekend killings 162
see also Managua
Nicaraguan(s) 162–4
men 162
middle class 161, 163, 165, 167, 174
society 161–2, 174
women 162–3, 168, 173–4
Nigeria 113–24, 134, 148
buildings 114, 120
Dahomey 120–1 (*see also* Benin)
ethnic backgrounds 118, 119, 130
food 116–17, 121

lagoon 114, 116, 121
oil in 123, 124
polity in 119
prejudice, cultural 116–17, 124
riots 123–4
Takoradi 121–2
travels within 116, 119–21
Victoria Island 114, 121, 123–4
witch doctors 118, 121
see also Lagos
Nigerian(s) 114–18, 120, 122–3, 124
the English about 114, 115–17
government 120, 124, 152
NLD (National League for Democracy) 91
Nobel Peace Prize 89, 138, 142
nomads 119, 258, 263–4, 283

O

oil
in Azerbaijan 267–8, 269–70
exports 123, 294
import in Laos 27
in the Middle East 285, 290, 294–5
in Nigeria 123, 124
revenue 268, 269–70, 290
in Venezuela 191–2
oligarchs/oligarchy 207, 224, 227, 231, 236, 237, 239, 247
Oman 149, 290–4, 295, 311–12
Haitham bin Tariq Al Said (Sultan) 295, 312
Qaboos bin Said (Sultan) 293–4
Omanis 290–2
one-party states 46, 64, 66, 69, 76, 141

OPEC (Organization of the Petroleum Exporting Countries) 294–5
opium 24, 103
oppression 66, 162, 310, 312
Oromos, the 138–9
Orthodox Church 206, 213, 232, 234
Ottomans 248, 307

P

Palestinians 278, 283, 289, 296, 310
Panamá 165, 171, 172, 176, 177
pariah 82, 87, 182, 323
Paris 81, 127, 134, 302
parliament 14, 46, 91, 233, 251, 279
paternalism 13, 21, 97, 148, 265
peasant(s)/peasantry 210, 240
　in Africa 136, 138, 155
　in Belarus 256
　in Cambodia 74, 77, 79
　in Europe 150
　farmers 80, 167, 174, 191, 193
　improvement in the lives of 192–3
　in Iran 267
　in Latin America 167, 174, 191, 192–3
　revolutionary 77
　in Ukraine 250
　in Vietnam 64
Persia 258, 310
Persians 217, 259, 272
Peru 191, 192
　García, Alan (President) 193
Philip Morris (tobacco company) 176, 185, 235
Philippines 108, 182
　Marcos, Ferdinand (President) 182
Phnom Penh 22, 73–4, 76, 79, 81
pilots 26, 28, 169, 171, 173
Plokhy, Serhii 240, 248, 252, 255
poets 151–2, 173, 186
pogroms 247, 249
Poles 244, 248
Politburo 259, 277
police
　Azerbaijani 269
　Chilean 179, 185, 187
　Georgian 274
　Lao 33
　Middle Eastern 288, 297
　Nicaraguan 161
　Russian 221
　Singaporean 102
　Thai 22
political orthodoxy 47, 49, 59, 60, 64, 65, 230, 242, 317
political system(s) 260–1, 316
　of Africa 148–56
　of Arabs 294–5
　of East Asia 108–9
　inequalities of 5
　of Islamic states 309–12
politicians 39, 79, 129, 147, 153, 251, 252, 270, 318
politics 11, 63, 148, 256, 266
　African 146, 152, 153
　of the Caucasus 271, 272, 278–80
　global 61
　Islamicist 260
　Latin American 160, 176, 185–7, 190, 192, 193–4
　left-wing 320
　of Middle East 283, 284, 308

Russian 200, 210, 233
trade and 315, 318, 322, 323, 324–5
Western 48
Portugese, the 143, 159
Potemkin Villages 217, 240
poverty 121, 124, 131, 137, 153, 173, 174–5
prejudice 3, 116–17, 124, 316
press 18, 47, 188, 267n1
   in Africa 129
   free 20, 91, 92, 181, 187, 271
   in Japan 20
   in Kyrgyzstan 262
   Russian 221
   Western 92
prisons 76–7, 78, 79, 82, 90, 105, 232
   see also imprisonment/ prisoners
privatisation 182, 206–7, 209, 316
Prophet Mohammed 283–6, 295, 310
protectionism 321
protests 83–4, 89, 161, 185, 190, 246, 263, 297, 299, 310, 318
purges 76, 199–200, 233, 276
purse strings 13, 14, 88
Putin, Vladimir (Russian President) 205, 210, 223, 237, 244–7, 254, 280
   authority over ex-Soviet states 244–6
   contempt for ordinary people 253
   curricular restrictions 211–12
   invasion of Ukraine 240–1, 245, 246, 247, 251, 322
   a KGB officer 240
   oligarchy control 231

   regime 230, 231–4, 242
   'Special Military Operation' 247
   targeting of opposers 231–3
   a tyrant 246
Putin's People: How the KGB took back Russia and then took on the West 231

Q

Qatar 293, 295, 309
Quiet American, The 50–1

R

railways 12, 13, 48, 133–4, 140, 217
   see also metro (rail)
Rangoon 83, 87, 88, 95
Red Cross 59, 173
Red Sea 140, 292
refugees 41, 51, 296, 305, 319
religion(s) 108, 119, 128, 139, 249, 266
   in Africa 118
   in Cambodia 73
   in the Caucasus 271, 272, 276
   in Central Asia 258–9, 260
   in Laos 34, 48
   in the Middle East 283–6, 295, 297–8, 303, 308, 309, 311
   in Russia 212, 232–3, 242–3
   in Ukraine 251
   see also Buddhism; Christianity; Islam
Remnick, David 226
revolution(s) 143, 311, 315
   in Czechoslovakia (Velvet Divorce) 249

in Nicaragua 163, 165, 173–4
(see also Sandinistas, the)
in Russia 205–6, 247, 248
in Myanmar 87
rice 28, 31, 38, 67, 72, 93–4, 101, 116–17, 130, 164
riots 123–4, 139, 188
ritual(s) 37, 48, 86, 143, 264, 298
Romanovs 242, 244
Romans 149, 272
Rushdie, Salman 163
Russia 6, 197–247, 250–6, 269, 296, 300, 310
   art in 213–16
   autocratic rule 199–200, 206, 212, 218
   banking crisis 227–8, 230
   breweries 202, 206–7, 208–9, 220, 223
   capture of Chechnya 242–3
   Catherine the Great (Russian Empress) 217, 248
   and the Caucasus 244, 271–3, 275, 277, 279–80
   Coca-Cola business in 198, 207, 221–3, 226, 228
   control over Georgia 244, 272–3, 279
   corruption in 209–10, 219–20, 232, 240
   creation of Transnistria 243–4
   dacha (summer house) 216, 254
   economy 206–7, 209–10, 224, 226–8, 230–1, 233–4, 239, 240, 247, 318, 323
   education system 211–12
   elections 202, 233
   'elite' in 211, 216, 224, 228, 231, 240
   environmental damage 208–9
   ethnic conflicts and resolution 242–4, 261
   expansionism 216–17
   expatriates in 224–5, 228
   factories in 200, 207, 209, 218, 234, 236
   foreigners in 202, 208, 215, 219, 225, 226, 233
   health care in 209–10, 220
   invaders in 208, 217
   investments in 198–9, 203, 218–19, 226, 227
   Kazan 203, 222
   a kleptocracy 210, 220, 231
   krysha (protection) 225, 237
   the Kyrgyz in 265
   life expectancy 209–10, 234
   the Metro in 201, 210, 211, 225, 236
   the middle class in 225, 228
   Muslims in 216–17, 233, 242–3
   'near abroad policy' of 245, 252
   Nemtsov, Boris (oblast governor; Deputy Prime Minister) 222–3
   Nizhny Novgorod 214, 222
   post-Soviet 197, 209–10, 211
   privatisation coupon programme 206–7, 209
   professional stint in 198–9, 202–7, 220–3, 226, 228, 234–9
   Putin regime in 230, 231–4, 240–1, 242
   religion in 212, 232–3, 242–3

salaries in 225, 228
samogon (hooch) 205
serfdom in 150, 212
Skripal, Sergei (intelligence officer) 231–2
Sterlitamak 203–4
theft/larceny in 204, 218–20
TNK-BP (oil company) 232
tobacco business in 234–9
Trotsky, Leon (revolutionary) 199
Tsarist 205, 212, 213
Ukraine invasion by 240–1, 245, 246, 247, 251, 322
Volga (river) 207, 208–9, 217, 221, 244
Volgograd 207–9, 221, 225, 235
Wagner Group (Russian mercenary group) 127, 135
World Cup, the 239–40
Yekaterinburg 206, 207, 209, 222
Yeltsin, Boris (President) 202, 222–3, 226, 227, 231, 242, 243, 244, 251
see also Moscow
Russian Federation *see* Russia
Russian (language) 198, 203, 249–50, 252–3, 255, 262, 278
Russian Revolution 205–6, 247, 248
Russian(s)
   artists 213, 214–16
   attributes/characteristics 208, 210, 213, 215–16, 218
   babushkas (old women) 210, 230, 256
   citizens 202, 204, 209, 227, 246
   compliant nature 231, 237, 243, 247
   culture 210–11, 246–7
   dissidents 216, 229, 247
   drinking habit 204–6, 209, 223, 227
   entrepreneurs 225, 227, 247
   ethnic 257, 264
   fatalism 225, 230
   in French West Africa 135
   government 200, 203, 221, 227, 231, 252
   history 197, 202, 203, 211, 216, 229, 231
   'Little' 250 (*see also* Ukrainians)
   men 205–6, 209, 223–4
   military 208, 217, 218, 230, 243, 244, 246, 247, 253, 272, 277, 323
   oblasts 203, 207, 221, 222
   oligarchs 207, 224, 227, 231, 236, 237, 239, 247
   passivity 210, 212–13
   politics 200, 210, 233
   Slavic 232, 242, 259
   smoking habit 209, 234
   society 200, 210, 216, 224
   soldiers 206, 208, 277, 278
   in Vietnam 55, 60
   women 223–4
   writers 212–13
Rwanda 113, 156, 319

S

Saigon 22, 51, 57, 58, 61, 65–7, 81, 83, 172
   see also Ho Chi Minh City

Sandinistas, the 162–4, 168, 172, 173, 174–5, 315
Santiago 176, 177, 178, 185, 188
Saudi Arabia 6, 104, 286, 288–9, 294, 295, 301
school(s) 184, 215
 in Africa 128, 144, 145
 converted to prison 76–7, 78
 in Japan 13, 17
 in Singapore 100
 in Vietnam 80
Second World War 14, 83, 206, 207–8, 217, 249, 250, 254, 294, 308, 323–4
servants
 civil 129, 220
 domestic 98, 126, 290, 291, 296
Shell 11, 25–7, 41, 44, 52
Sherman Act (1890) 317
Siberia 216, 235
Silk Road 257, 259
Singapore 39, 50, 51, 59, 65–6, 69, 97–107, 315
 culture 100, 102, 106
 democracy 97, 107, 108
 economy 97–9
 elections 97
 food 99, 101
 gifting 102, 105
 government 97–8, 103, 104, 107
 Lee, Kuan Yew (Prime Minister) 69, 97, 183
 professional stint in 98, 99–103, 105
 social life 101–2, 107
 society 98, 102, 107
 students 98–9, 100
Tay, Choon Hai (BAT export agent) 84, 87–8, 103, 104–6, 317
 tobacco business 98, 100–1, 103–4
 tourism and shopping 99
Singaporeans 39–40, 61, 98–101, 107
slavery/slave(s)
 abolition of 149, 150
 Caribbean 151, 152, 165
 in different parts of the world 138, 149–50, 192, 292
 in the Middle East 292, 306, 307
 trade 121–2, 125–6, 135, 149, 150, 156, 292
 unification of 151–2
slogans 13, 173
slums 114, 147, 183, 191
Smith, Adam 239
smoking 30, 128, 209, 234, 297
smuggling 128, 130, 135, 163, 311
social cohesion 13, 19–20
social life
 in Georgia 273–4
 in Japan 11–12, 14–17
 in Laos 27, 33, 34–5
 in Nicaragua 161
 in Singapore 101–2, 107
 in Vietnam 53, 63
social structure 18, 151
socialism 69, 180, 215
socialist realism 211, 213, 215
society/societies 6, 109, 134, 148, 262, 324, 325
 African 113–14, 125–6, 135, 147, 152, 156
 Belarusian 255
 Burmese 86–7

Cambodian 74–5, 79, 80–1
Chilean 177–8, 180, 181, 183
Georgian 273–4
Japanese 11–12, 13, 14–16, 20, 21
liberal 316
Nicaraguan 161–2, 174
open 69, 251
peasant 74, 77, 79
Russian 200, 210, 216, 224
Singaporean 98, 102, 107
Ukrainian 251
Vietnamese 54, 66–7, 69
white-dominated 7n3
soldiers 176, 182, 248
Lao 31, 35, 36
Russian 206, 208, 277, 278
Tatmadaw 83, 95–6
South America 132, 159, 160, 320
see also Chile
South Korea 98, 108
Rhee, Syngman (President) 69
South Ossetia 244, 272, 273, 280
Soviet Union, the 60, 192, 204, 210, 230, 245, 257, 264
aid deal for the 27
centralised control in 200–1
collapse 199, 201–2, 234, 242, 254, 255, 260, 277, 279
collectivisation of agriculture in 249, 254
economy 201
Gorbachev, Mikhail (Secretary General of Communist Party) 201–2, 205, 242, 251
KGB (State Security Committee) 27, 200, 206, 215, 231, 240
Khrushchev, Nikita (Secretary General of Communist Party) 250
legacy of 242–3
Lenin, Vladimir (revolutionary/politician) 201, 276
Stalin, Joseph (revolutionary/politician) 76, 199, 200, 208, 211–12, 215, 233, 241, 257–8, 259
see also Russia
Spain 159, 189, 306
Franco, Francisco (military general) 181–2
Garzón, Baltasar (procurator general) 181, 182
Spanish, the 108, 159, 174, 180, 181, 189, 237
Stalingrad *see* Russia, Volgograd
starvation 59, 136, 249
Stewart, Rory 258
Stuart-Fox, Martin 25, 35, 38
subsistence agriculture 48, 93–4, 119, 146, 147, 153, 155
Sultan in Oman 292
Swain, John 78
Sweden 217, 247
Swelim, Tarek 306, 308, 309, 312
Syria 6, 206, 246, 301, 305, 310

T

Taiwan 98, 108
Tanizaki, Junchiro 19
tariff(s) 181, 183–4, 185, 255, 321, 322
Tashkent 257, 260
Tatars 203, 208, 217, 244, 248
Tatarstan 202–3

Tajikistan 258, 260, 265
Tajiks 257, 259
Tbilisi 274, 278, 279
TCCC (the Coca-Cola Company) 137, 139, 198, 202, 206, 226
teachers 71, 79, 144, 169, 209, 215, 225
technology 20, 61, 98, 223, 322
Tehran 266, 267
television 105, 144, 186, 244
temporal power 73, 284
terracing 93–4
terrorism 135, 295
Tett, Gillian 258
Thailand 28, 34, 41, 43, 45, 52
    Chiang Mai consulate 22
    Chinese high-speed rail project 48
    a sham democracy 95
    Shell 25, 26, 27
    tourists in 71
    see also Bangkok
Thais 22, 30, 32, 39, 88, 93, 95, 100
theft 118, 124, 204, 220
Theroux, Paul 106–7
Things Fall Apart 117
Thubron, Colin 240, 258–9, 261
Tigrayans 136, 139, 142
tips 72, 79, 90
toadying 200, 233
tobacco/tobacco business 315–16, 325
    in Africa 128–9, 130, 143, 144–7
    in Azerbaijan 266
    in Chile 176–7, 185
    excise duty on 128
    in Laos 39–40, 316
    in Myanmar 84, 86, 88
    in Nicaragua 164
    in Russia 234–9
    in Saudi Arabia 288
    in Singapore 98, 100–1, 103–4
    in Vietnam 54, 61–3
    see also BAT (British American Tobacco); Imperial Tobacco; Philip Morris (tobacco company); Vietnam, Vinataba
Tokyo 12, 14–15, 17, 18
Tolstoy, Leo 200
totalitarianism 199, 310
tourism 73, 79, 126, 132, 167, 285
tourists
    in Cambodia 71–5, 77–8
    in Laos 22–3, 44, 45
    in the Middle East 286, 301, 309
    in Myanmar 86–7, 89–91, 94–5
    in Singapore 99
    in Thailand 71
    in Vietnam 53–9
trade 66, 108, 129, 165, 218, 317–18, 321–5
    barriers 129, 322
    drug 21, 95, 135, 166, 169, 191, 193, 244
    free 321
    grain 322, 323
    land grab 152–3
    maritime 103
    and politics 315, 318, 322, 323, 324–5
    slave 121–2, 125–6, 135, 149, 150, 156, 292
    socialising and 86, 88, 101, 236–8, 290–2

tourist 45 (*see also* tourism; tourists)
trust and 16, 102, 220, 237, 317, 318, 325
trafficking 135, 244
Transnistria 243–4, 276
trauma 42, 50, 79, 180
travellers 12, 22, 23, 297–8
tribes 119, 128, 134, 259
    allegiance among 139, 147, 151–2, 153
    Ashanti 149–50, 151
    Bedouin 283, 285
    Burkinabés 127
    desert 289
    Fulani 118, 130
    hill (*miao*) 44, 45, 93, 94
    hostility among 149, 216–17, 262
    Sauds 288
    Zulu 151
Tsars, the 218, 234, 249, 254
Tunisia 155n4, 295, 311, 319
Turkic (language) 259, 284, 307
Türkiye 6, 247, 271, 275, 276, 277, 303
Turks 134, 149, 217, 221, 222, 262, 272, 276, 306
tyranny 173, 199–200
tyrants 160, 179, 186, 206, 246

U

UAE (United Arab Emirates) 290, 295
Uighurs 7, 257, 259
UK/United Kingdom 121, 152, 188, 231, 318
    Bribery Act (2010) 102, 319
    economy 320, 323
    and expatriates in Nicaragua 168, 169, 171
    Macmillan, Harold (Prime Minister) 153
    Queen Elizabeth II 274–5
    Russians relocating to the 232, 247
    Sandhurst 293, 312
    Stone, Norman (historian) 217–18
    Thatcher, Margaret (Prime Minister) 181
    tobacco business meeting 237–8
    Truss, Liz (Prime Minister) 320–1
    see also Britain
Ukraine 7, 206, 238, 239, 248–54, 256, 277, 279, 318, 323
    anti-kulak programme 199–200
    Dnieper (river) 250, 253
    elections 253
    government 252, 253
    history of 248–51
    independence of 251–2
    invasion of 240–1, 245, 246, 247, 251, 322
    Jews in 248–9
    Kravchuk, Leonid (President) 202, 242, 251, 252
    language in 249–50, 255
    Moscow and 245–6, 249, 250, 251–3
    Odessa 254
    Petlyura, Symon (nationalist leader) 248
    religion in 251
    rulers of 248, 250
    shifting of minorities 244

society 251
territory and borders 250
workplace in 253
Zelensky, Volodymyr (President) 7, 253
see also Kiev
Ukrainians 240, 245, 248, 249–53, 255, 278
ultra-nationalists 13, 274
UN, the/United Nations, the 7, 155, 243, 246, 247, 273, 308, 318
   UNESCO heritage site 44, 73
   UNHCR (UN High Commission for Refugees) 26, 30
untouchables 16, 150
Uruguay 192, 194
US, the/USA, the/United States, the 5–6, 58, 76, 189, 269, 317
   Browder, Bill (financier) 232
   capitalist corruption model 160–1
   Carter, Jimmy (President) 172–3
   and Costa Rica 167
   drug traffic to Oklahoma 166, 169
   FCPA (Foreign Corrupt Practices Act) 102, 319
   foreign policy 6, 320
   government 166, 172, 173–4
   invasion of Sicily 323
   and liberal democracy in Latin America 192–3
   Mexicans in 165
   opposition to the USSR 246
   Trump, Donald (President) 194, 317–18, 323
   Universal Leaf tobacco company 145–6
   USAID (United States Agency for International Development) 25, 209
   'war on drugs' 166, 191
   Washington 60, 81, 172
USSR (Union of Soviet Socialist Republics) *see* Soviet Union, the
Uzbekistan 259, 260, 303
Uzbeks 257, 259

V

Valenzuela, Arturo 181
Venezuela 191–2
   Maduro, Nicholás (President) 194
Vientiane 24, 26, 30–3, 35–6, 37, 41–6, 81
Vietnam 27, 42, 43, 49, 50–70, 84, 94, 140, 201
   Amerasians in 55
   ARVN (Army of the Republic of Vietnam) 55, 55n11, 65
   bicycles 66
   Cambodian border 79–80
   Communist state 51, 65, 68, 69
   Dalat 58
   Do Moi policy 51, 60, 64, 69, 275
   Dong Nai (province) 54, 61, 62
   economy 51, 63–4, 66, 80
   foreigners in 51–60
   Hanoi 69
   independence 50, 58
   Marxist 57–9, 64, 69
   North 60–1, 65

population 64, 66
poverty 59, 60
present-day 66–70
professional stint in 61–3
social life 53, 63
South 55n1, 65
tobacco industry in 54, 61–3
tour 53–60
trade in Chinese goods 323
Vinataba 61, 62, 65, 68
Vuong, Tran Quoc (Professor) 69–70
war 50, 55, 60–1, 68, 264
Vietnamese, the 52, 53, 54, 58–9, 61
   capitalist nature of 63–4
   children 52, 55–6, 68, 80
   culture 63, 66, 69–70
   freeing of Norodom 75
   government 62, 67, 69, 317
   men 55, 56, 62
   society 54, 66–7, 69
   women 55, 56, 63
voters 6, 20, 187

W

War and Peace 200
wars
   Biafra 121
   Chechen 243
   civil (see civil war(s))
   Ethiopia–Eritrea 138, 140, 141
   Great Patriotic 205, 245–6
   Indochina 22, 50, 51, 80–1
   Tigrayan 139, 142
   Ukraine 247 (see also Ukraine, invasion of)
   Vietnam 50, 55, 60–1, 68, 264
   World (*see* First World War; Second World War)
wats 30, 43, 45, 46, 71–3, 85
Westerners 14, 44, 63, 69, 71, 78, 99, 226, 286, 287, 303
women/woman
   African 125–6, 135, 140, 145, 150
   Arabian 288, 289
   Canadian 169
   Chilean 178, 188–9
   Japanese 12, 13–16, 21, 216
   Korean 16–17
   Kyrgyz 265
   Lao 30, 36, 41, 45
   Lebanese 304
   Nicaraguan 162–3, 168, 173–4
   Russian 204, 210, 223–4, 230, 256
   Singaporean 98
   Vietnamese 55, 56, 63
workers 12, 25
   aid 31, 262
   in Central Asia 260, 262, 264–5
   factory 54, 264–5
   industrial 192–3
   sex 287
WTO (World Trade Organization) 128, 317–18

X

xenophobia 246, 265

Y

Year of Living Dangerously, The 172
Yerevan 276, 277, 278
youth/young people 63, 94
   Japanese 13

Kyrgyz 265
Lao 25, 30, 33, 41
Middle Eastern 287
Nicaraguan 161
Singaporean 98–9
Spanish 189

Z
Zimbabwe 143, 144–5
    Mnangagwa, Emmerson (President) 154
    Mugabe, Robert (President) 146, 154

Non-fiction from Envelopebooks
www.envelopebooks.co.uk

A Road to Extinction
JONATHAN LAWLEY

When Britain colonised the Andamans in 1857, the welfare of its African pygmy inhabitants was of no concern. Nine tribes died out. Dr Lawley now assesses survival prospects for the three remaining tribes and weighs up the legacy of his grandfather, who ran the colony in the early 1900s. EB2

Artist Spy Prisoner
GEORGE TOMAZIU

Artist George Tomaziu half-expected to be imprisoned and tortured for monitoring Nazi troop movements through Bucharest during the Second World War but thought that his heroism would be recognised when Socialism came to Romania in 1950. He was terribly mistaken. EB10

Postmark Africa
MICHAEL HOLMAN

Made an Amnesty Prisoner of Conscience while he was under house arrest as a student in Southern Rhodesia, the author went on to document Africa's emergence from colonialism as Africa Editor of the *Financial Times*. EB1

Why My Wife Had To Die
BRIAN VERITY

There is no known cure for Huntington's disease, a wasting condition that sufferers acquire from a parent. In this painful account, the author vents his rage at society, lawmakers, health services and the church for not grasping the need, as he sees it, to legalise compulsory sterilisation and assisted dying. EB9

Other titles from EnvelopeBooks
www.envelopebooks.co.uk

Princess Brainy
STEPHEN GAMES

She couldn't help being clever and couldn't help being hated for it but it didn't help that her mother was modern and that her father had banned the fairies. But what was she meant to do when disaster came to Rainland and the rivers dried up? Accept her deadly fate or get sacrificed to the revolution? EB16

From Bedales to the Boche
ROBERT BEST

Bedales, the progressive boarding school founded by J.H. Badley in 1893, instilled values that sustained many of its pupils through the rest of their lives. Robert Best recalls its influence on him as an enthusiastic army recruit in 1914 and, from 1916, in the Royal Flying Corps. EB3

My Modern Movement
ROBERT BEST

London's Festival of Britain in 1951 marked the belief that Modern design was visually, morally and commercially superior. Robert Best, the UK's leading lighting manufacturer, thinks the dice were loaded. This is his memoir. EB8

The Hopeful Traveller
JANINA DAVID

A collection of short stories about—and told by—single women who have put the past behind them but are still looking for their anchor in the present. It includes bitter-sweet accounts of the freedoms of postwar life, of foreign travel, of the rekindling of old friendships and of the search for new ones. EB4

Fiction from Envelopebooks
www.envelopebooks.co.uk

Frances Creighton: Found and Lost
KIRBY PORTER

Love demands trust, but trust is a lot to ask for victims of abuse. Having been bullied by two teachers in Belfast as a boy, Michael Roberts suppresses his childhood pains until the death of a girlfriend years later forces him to revisit lost memories and come to terms with his adolescent self. EB7

Belle Nash and the Bath Soufflé
WILLIAM KEELING ESQ.

In the first volume of The Gay Street Chronicles, bachelor Belle Nash attempts to navigate bigotry and corruption in Regency Bath without compromising the nephew of Immanual Kant or the legal talents of Gaia Champion. EB9

Lagos, Life and Sexual Distraction
TUNDE OSOSANYA

Twelve short stories, mostly focused on the struggle to survive in Lagos, Nigeria's commercial capital, illustrating the tensions that exist between the generations, between the sexes and between the country's different social classes and ethnicities. EB13

The Attraction of Cuba
CHRIS HILTON

Chris Hilton went to Cuba to escape the boredom of everyday life and to make money, only to be entranced by the beauty of the country and of Yamilia, a street girl who brought meaning to his life but who could not help him from falling into an inevitable downward spiral. EB14

More fiction from Envelopebooks
www.envelopebooks.co.uk

Belle Nash and the Bath Circus
WILLIAM KEELING ESQ.
In Volume Two of *The Gay Street Chronicles*, bachelor Belle Nash returns to Regency Bath from Grenada, inspired by a new love that leads him into various pretences that may compromise the ambitions of black circus impresario Pablo Fanque. EB16

The Train House on Lobengula Street
FATIMA KARA
An anguished but life-affirming novel, set within the Indian community in Bulawayo in Rhodesia of the 1950s and 1960s, about the capacity of women to gain the same advantages as men in the modern world while remaining faithful to traditional Muslim values. Affectionate and passionate. EB12

A Sin of Omission
MARGUERITE POLAND
An emotionally intense novel, set in 1870s South Africa at a time of rising anti-colonial resistance. The book examines the tragedy of a promising black preacher, hand-picked for training in England as a missionary, only to be neglected by the Church he loves. Winner of the 2021 *Sunday Times* CNA 'Book of the Year' Award in South Africa. EB6

Mustard Seed Itinerary
ROBERT MULLEN
When Po Cheng falls into a dream, he finds himself on the road to the imperial Chinese capital. Once there he rises to the heights of the civil service before discovering that there are snakes as well as ladders. Carrollian satire at its best. EB5

Printed in Dunstable, United Kingdom